FRENCH-ENGLISH ENGLISH-FRENCH

Dictionary & Phrasebook

DICTIONARY AND PHRASEBOOKS

Albanian
Arabic (Eastern)
Australian
Azerbaijani
Basque
Bosnian
Breton
British English
Chechen
Croatian
Esperanto
Georgian
German
Greek
Hebrew *Romanized*
Igbo
Ilocano
Irish
Italian
Japanese *Romanized*
Lao *Romanized*
Lingala
Malagasy
Maltese
Maya (Yucatec)
Pilipino (Tagalog)
Polish
Romansch
Russian
Shona
Slovak
Somali
Spanish (Latin American)
Tajik
Thai *Romanized*
Ukrainian

FRENCH-ENGLISH
ENGLISH-FRENCH
Dictionary & Phrasebook

HIPPOCRENE BOOKS, INC.
New York

Phrasebook originally published in Scotland by Geddes & Grosset, an imprint of Children's Leisure Products Ltd.

ISBN 0-7818-0856-1

Cataloging-In-Publication Data available from the Library of Congress

For information, address:
Hippocrene Books, Inc.
171 Madison Ave.
New York, NY 10016
www.hippocrenebooks.com

Printed in the United States of America

CONTENTS

INTRODUCTION

From Europe, North and South America, to Asia and Africa, nearly 100 million people throughout the world speak French. For practical reasons, this dictionary and phrasebook focuses on France, but it will be of help to you whether your destination is the mainland or one of its former colonies. The phrasebook will give you the means for basic communication in most situations that you will encounter while traveling. It is complemented by a 6,000-word two-way dictionary. A brief grammar section will teach you the essentials you need to form a sentence.

Your efforts to speak their language will be most appreciated by French people, and will make your stay all the more enjoyable. Remember to use your hands, as gestures will easily replace words unknown to you. Don't ever be shy to start a conversation (in French!) with a native, for it will give you a unique insight into the country.

Bon voyage!

THE FRENCH ALPHABET

A	ah
B	bay
C	say
D	day
E	er
F	ef
G	jay
H	ash
I	ee
J	jee
K	ka
L	el
M	em
N	en
O	oh
P	pay
Q	kew
R	ayr
S	ays
T	tay
U	ew
V	vay
W	doo-bler-vay
X	eeks
Y	eeh-grayk
Z	zayd

PRONUNCIATION GUIDE

Guide to French Pronunciation Scheme

ah	as in b**a**d, f**a**r, f**a**ther
ai	as in m**e**t, **e**xcuse, w**e**ll, m**e**rcy
ay	as in ob**ey**, d**ay**
aw	as in f**ou**ght
ee	as in m**ea**l, f**ee**l, souven**i**r
er	as in th**e**, t**u**ck, speak**er**
ew	as in b**eau**tiful*
oo	as in tr**ue**, bl**ue**, gl**ue**
oh	as in n**o**te, b**oa**t

*There is no exact equivalent in English for the French "closed" **oo** sound. Try with your lips to make the oo shape, while saying the ee sound through them.

The other area of French pronunciation without exact equivalents in English is the **ng** sounds, reduced here for simplicity to two:

an	as in French *comprend* (sounds like ong, as in s**ong**)
ern	as in French *bien* (sounds like ang, as in b**ang**)

French consonants are pronounced much as in English. In the majority of cases, the final letter of a word is mute.

ABBREVIATIONS

adj.	adjective
adv.	adverb
art.	article
conj.	conjunction
f.	feminine
inter.	interjection
m.	masculine
m/f.	masculine and feminine
n.	noun
num.	numeral
pl.	plural
prep.	preposition
pron.	pronoun
sing.	singular
v.	verb

A BRIEF GRAMMAR

Articles

All nouns in French are either masculine or feminine. Their articles are the only indications of gender. *The* is **le** (*lerh*) before masculine nouns, **la** (*lah*) before feminine nouns, and **l'** (*leh*) before nouns beginning with a vowel. **Les** (*layh*) is the word used for both genders in the plural form. **Au** (*oh*) is used instead of **à le**, and **aux** (*oh*) is used instead of **à les**.

Masc.	*Fem.*
le soleil *the sun*	la plage *the beach*
l'arbre *the tree*	l'orange *the orange*
les enfants *the children*	les filles *the girls*

The indefinite article *a* is **un** (*ernh*) before masculine nouns and **une** (*ewn*) before feminine nouns.

Masc.	*Fem.*
un enfant *a child*	une église *a church*

To say *some* or *any*, **du** (*dew*) is used before masculine nouns, **de la** (*derh lah*) before feminine nouns, **de l'** (*derh leh*) before nouns beginning with a vowel, and **des** (*dayh*) before plural nouns. **Du** is used instead of **de le**, and **des** is used instead of **de les**.

Masc.	*Fem.*
du chocolat *some chocolate*	de la farine *some flour*
des bonbons *some candies*	des fleurs *some flowers*

Nouns

Most French nouns have a different form for singular and for plural. The genders attributed to objects never change. *Une table* (a table) will always be feminine, and *un lit* (a bed) always masculine.

Many of the words referring to people and animals have a masculine and a feminine form. To form the feminine form of these nouns, you simply add *–e* at the end. When the masculine noun ends in *–e*, its feminine is the same. The plural is formed by adding

–*s*, which is not pronounced. When the singular noun ends in –*s*, –*x*, or –*z*, the plural is the same.

Masc.	*Fem.*
un ami *a (male) friend*	un**e** ami**e** *a (female) friend*
des ami**s** *some (male) friends*	des ami**es** *some (female) friends*

Some masculine words require more modifications than the simple addition of –*e* in the feminine. Following is a list of these different endings:

Masc.	*Fem.*
un pays**an** *a (male) farmer*	une pays**anne** *a (female) farmer*
un chi**en** *a (male) dog*	une chi**enne** *a (female) dog*
un bouch**er** *a (male) butcher*	une bouch**ère** *a (female) butcher*
un chant**eur** *a (male) singer*	une chant**euse** *a (female) singer*
un li**on** *a lion*	une li**onne** *a lioness*

The word for *actor* is an exception: un act**eur**, une act**rice.**

Most nouns ending in –*al* in the singular change their endings to –*aux* in the plural. Most nouns ending in –*au*, –*eu*, –*eau*, and –*œu* in the singular take –*x* in the plural. Nouns ending in –*ail* in the singular usually take –*s* in the plural.

Adjectives

French adjectives are usually placed after a noun. Some, such as *bon* (good), *petit* (small, short), and *grand* (big, large) are placed before the noun. The adjectives change to agree in number and gender with the nouns that they modify. You usually add –*e* to the masculine form to make it a feminine adjective. If the adjective already ends in –*e*, it stays the same. In the dictionary, only the masculine form is given.

le chapeau bleu *the blue hat*
la robe bleu**e** *the blue dress*

When the masculine form ends in –*l* or –*n*, you usually double that vowel and add –*e* to form the feminine. When the masculine ends in *–eux* or *–eur*, the feminine usually becomes *–euse*. The masculine forms *–er* and *–if* usually become *–ère* and *–ive* in the feminine.

The plural is generally formed by adding *–s* to the adjective.

les chapeaux bleu**s** *the blue hats*
les robes bleue**s** *the blue dresses*

Like the nouns, adjectives that end in *–s* or in *–x* in the singular have the same ending in the plural, adjectives that end in *–al* in the singular change into *–aux* in the plural, and adjectives ending in *–eau* add *–x* in the plural to become *–eaux*.

The comparatives are formed by adding *plus* (more), *moins* (less), or *aussi* (as) before the adjectives.

Mon frère est **plus jeune que** moi. *My brother is younger than I.*
Cette église est **moins récente**. *This church is less recent.*
Il est **aussi grand que** toi. *He is as tall as you.*

The superlatives are formed by adding **le** ou **la** in front of the comparative.

Cette montagne est **la plus haute** d'Europe. *This mountain is the highest one in Europe.*
Ce restaurant est **le moins cher** de Paris. *This restaurant is the least expensive one in Paris.*

As in English, *bon* (good) and *mauvais* (bad) have irregular comparatives and superlatives:

bon *good*	meilleur *better*	le, la, les meilleur/e/s *best*
mauvais *bad*	pire *worse*	le, la, les pire/s *worst*

Pronouns

Direct and indirect pronouns

Both the direct and the indirect pronoun usually are placed before the verb. If they both appear in the same sentence, the indirect object will be placed first.

Subject (who)	D. O. (whom)	I. O. (to whom)	I.O. after a preposition
je	me	me	moi
tu	te	te	toi
il/elle/on	le/la	lui	lui/elle/son
nous	nous	nous	nous
vous	vous	vous	vous
ils/elles	les	leur	eux/elles

Possessive pronouns

English	*Masc. Singular*	*Feminine Singular*	*Masc. and Feminine Plural*
my	mon	ma	mes
your	ton	ta	tes
his/her	son	sa	ses
our	notre	notre	nos
your	votre	votre	vos
their	leur	leur	leurs

C'est **ma** valise. *This is my suitcase.*
Son vélo est tout neuf. *His bike is brand new.*
Leur chat est gris. *Their cat is gray.*

Ce sont **tes** livres. *These are your books.*
Voilà **nos** enfants. *Here are our children.*
Leurs maris sont à la maison. *Their husbands are at home.*

However, when a feminine noun begins with a vowel, the masculine possessive pronoun is used, to avoid breaking the fluidity of a sentence.

Jessica est **mon** amie. *Jessica is my friend.*

Reflexive pronouns

Many verbs that are not reflexive in English are reflexive in French. They use the following reflexive pronouns, which must agree with the subject of the sentence:

Subject	*Reflexive Pronoun*
je	me
tu	te
il/elle/on	se
nous	nous
vous	vous
ils/elles	se

Je **me** couche de bonne heure. *I go to bed early.*
Elle **s'**appelle Eva. *Her name is Eva* (lit. *She is called Eva*).
Nous **nous** levons tard le dimanche. *We get up late on Sundays.*
Ils **se** sont rasés la tête. *They shaved their heads.*

Y and *En*

Y is the equivalent of *there*, and it replaces a noun that was introduced by a preposition of location. *En* is the equivalent of *of.* It takes the place of a noun introduced by *de, d', de l', du, de la,* and *des.*

Nous **y** allons demain (Nous allons **en France** demain). *We are going there (to France) tomorrow.*
Ils **en** ont peu (Ils ont peu **de chevaux**). *They have few of them (horses).*

Verbs

Unlike English, French verbs have a different conjugation for each person. *On* is the indefinite pronoun that corresponds to *one, you, or we* in English. It is conjugated in French like the third person singular.

English	*French*
I	je
you	tu
he/she	il/elle
we	nous
you	vous
they	ils/elles

In French, one distinguishes between a formal you, *vous*, and an informal one, *tu*. *Tu* is used to address family, people whom you know well, children, or informally among young people. *Vous* is used in all other situations. You should wait until someone invites you to use *tu* (*tutoyer* is the verb) with them before doing so. As a rule of thumb, always use *vous* (*vouvoyer* is the verb) when you first meet somebody. Relations are more formal in Europe, and the French will appreciate that mark of respect. It is not rare that people who have known each other for a long time, but who mostly interact in a formal setting (i.e. work, large age difference) address each other by their first names but still use *vous* as a sign of respect.

French verbs can be divided in four categories: three regular ones and one irregular. Verbs that belong to the latter group have to be learned, since their conjugations don't follow any specific model. Verbs are put in their distinctive categories according to their infinitive endings, which can be either *–er*, *–ir*, or *–re*. The *–er* category is the largest. Many irregular verbs have a *–re* ending, yet they do not belong to that category.

–er Verbs

Infinitive	mang**er** *to eat*
Past participle	mang**é**
Je	mang**e**
Tu	mang**es**
Il/elle/on	mang**e**
Nous	mange**ons**
Vous	mang**ez**
Ils/elles	mang**ent**

–ir Verbs

Infinitive	fin**ir** *to finish*	dorm**ir** *to sleep*
Past participle	fin**i**	dorm**i**
Je	fin**is**	dor**s**
Tu	fin**is**	dor**s**
Il/elle/on	fin**it**	dor**t**
Nous	fin**issons**	dorm**ons**
Vous	fin**issez**	dorm**ez**
Ils/elles	fin**issent**	dorm**ent**

Only the following verbs follow the model of dormir: *partir* (to leave), *sentir* (to smell), *servir* (to serve), and *sortir* (to go out).

–re Verbs

Infinitive	descend**re** *to go down*
Past participle	descend**u**
Je	descend**s**
Tu	descend**s**
Il/elle/on	descend
Nous	descend**ons**
Vous	descend**ez**
Ils/elles	descend**ent**

Some Irregular Verbs

Infinitive	être *to be*
Past participle	été
Je	suis
Tu	es
Il/elle/on	est
Nous	sommes
Vous	êtes
Ils/elles	sont

Infinitive	avoir *to have*
Past participle	eu
J'	ai
Tu	as
Il/elle/on	a
Nous	avons
Vous	avez
Ils/elles	ont

Infinitive	aller *to go*
Past participle	allé
Je	vais
Tu	vas
Il/elle/on	va
Nous	allons
Vous	allez
Ils/elles	vont

Infinitive	devoir *must*
Past participle	dû
Je	dois
Tu	dois
Il/elle/on	doit
Nous	devons
Vous	devez
Ils/elles	doivent

Infinitive	faire *to do*
Past participle	fait
Je	fais
Tu	fais
Il/elle/on	fait
Nous	faisons
Vous	faîtes
Ils/elles	font

Infinitive	pouvoir *can, to be able to*
Past participle	pu
Je	peux
Tu	peux
Il/elle/on	peut
Nous	pouvons
Vous	pouvez
Ils/elles	peuvent

Infinitive	venir *to come*
Past participle	venu
Je	viens
Tu	viens
Il/elle/on	vient
Nous	venons
Vous	venez
Ils/elles	viennent

Infinitive	vouloir *to want*
Past participle	voulu
Je	veux
Tu	veux
Il/elle/on	veut
Nous	voulons
Vous	voulez
Ils/elles	veulent

As in English, *aller* can be used to express the future.

Nous **allons** visiter ce musée demain. *We are going to visit this museum tomorrow.*

The past tense of most verbs is constructed by using the appropriate form of the auxiliary verb *avoir* and the past participle of the verb.

Nous **avons mangé** dans un petit restaurant. *We ate in a small restaurant.*
Il **a dû** partir. *He had to leave.*

Some verbs, including all the reflexives, use the auxiliary verb *être* instead of *avoir*. Following are some examples:

aller	*to go*
descendre	*to go down*
entrer	*to enter*
laver (se)	*to wash*
sortir	*to go out*
monter	*to go up*
mourir	*to die*
naître	*to be born*

Questions

The simplest way to formulate a question in French is to raise your voice at the end of a declarative sentence, as you would do in English (1).
Est-ce que is also used, placed before a declarative sentence (2).
The third possible way is to inverse the pronoun and the verb (3).

1. Tu as bien dormi ? *You slept well?*
2. Est-ce que tu as bien dormi ? *Did you sleep well?*
3. As-tu bien dormi ? *Have you slept well?*

Interrogative words

1. combien	*how much* (non-quantifiable amount); *how many* (quantifiable amount)
2. comment	*how*
3. où	*where*
4. pourquoi	*why*

5. quand *when*
6. que *what*
7. qui *who*

1. **Combien** est-ce que ça coûte ? *How much does it cost?*
   Combien sont-ils ? *How many are they?*
2. **Comment** allez-vous ? *How are you doing?*
3. **Où** est-il ? *Where is he?*
4. **Pourquoi** pleures-tu ? *Why are you crying?*
5. **Quand** est-elle partie ? *When did she leave?*
6. **Que** fais-tu ? *What are you doing?*
7. **Qui** est avec eux ? *Who is with them?*

Negation

Ne ... pas is used most frequently in French to express the negation. It is the equivalent of the *do/does not* English.

Je **n'**aime **pas** l'hiver. *I do not like winter.*
Elle **ne** va **pas** se baigner toute seule. *She does not go and swim by herself.*

Other negations are as follow:

ne ... aucun/e *not any*
ne ... jamais *never*
ne ... pas encore *not yet*
ne ... personne *no one*
ne ... plus *no longer*
ne ... rien *nothing*

Tu **n'**as **aucune** chance. *You do not have any luck.*
Il **ne** va **jamais** à l'étranger. *He never goes abroad.*
Vous ne pouvez **pas encore** comprendre. *You cannot understand yet.*
Je **ne** connais **personne**. *I do not know anybody.*
Nous **ne** faisons **plus** de ski. *We do not ski anymore.*
Ils **ne** savent **rien**. *They do not know anything.*

Neither ... nor is expressed by *ne ... ni ... ni.*

Il **ne** sait **ni** lire **ni** écrire. *He can neither read nor write.*

Conjunctions

Conjunctions join similar words, sentences, or clauses. The most common ones in French are:

car	because, for
donc	so
ensuite	next
et	and
mais	but
ni	neither, nor
or	well
ou	or
puis	then

J'aime le chocolat **et** la vanille. *I like chocolate and vanilla.*
Elle va souvent au cinéma, **mais** jamais au musée. *She often goes to the movies, but never to the museum.*
Nous sommes allées en France, **puis** en Suisse. *We went to France, then to Switzerland.*

Adverbs

In most cases, adverbs are formed by adding *–ment* to the feminine form of the adjective. If the masculine ending of the adjective is *–e*, simply add *–ment* to it.

Masc.	*Feminine*	*Adverb*
grand *big*	grande	grandement *largely*
doux *soft*	douce	doucement *softly*
simple *simple*	simple	simplement *simply*

Adverbs form their comparatives and superlatives on the same model as the adjectives. Some exceptions include:

Adverb	*Comparative*	*Superlative*
beaucoup *a lot*	plus	le plus
bien *well*	mieux	le mieux
mal *badly*	pire	le pire
peu *not much; few*	moins	le moins

Prepositions

Prepositions link the noun they precede to either another noun, an adjective or a verb. That noun is an indirect object.

à	at, in, to
à côté de	beside, next to
après	after
à travers	across, through
autour de	around
avant	before
avec	with
chez	at (somebody's)
contre	against
dans	in
de	about, from, of
depuis	for, since
derrière	behind
devant	in front of
durant	during
en	in, on, to
en face de	across from, opposite
entre	between
environ	approximately
hors de	outside of
jusqu'à	until
loin de	far from
par	by
pendant	during, while
pour	for
près de	close to
sans	without
sauf	except
sous	under
sur	on
vers	toward

FRENCH-ENGLISH DICTIONARY

A

à *prep.* at; to
abbaye *n.f.* abbey
abcès *n.m.* abscess
abeille *n.f.* bee
abîmer *v.* to damage; to spoil
à bord *adv.* aboard
abréviation *n.f.* abbreviation
abri *n.m.* shelter
accélérateur *n.m.* accelerator
accélérer *v.* to accelerate
accent *n.m.* accent; stress
accepter *v.* to accept
accès *n.m.* access
accident *n.m.* accident; crash
accord *n.m.* agreement
accorder *v.* to grant
accrocher *v.* to hang; to hook
accueil *n.m.* welcome
accueillir *v.* to greet, to welcome
accuser *v.* to accuse
achat *n.m.* purchase
acheter *v.* to buy, to purchase
acier inoxydable *n.m.* stainless steel
acné *n.f.* acne
à côté de *prep.; adv.* beside
acte *n.m.* act
acteur/actrice *n.m/f.* actor
activité *n.f.* activity
adapter *v.* to adapt
addition *n.f.* addition; check (*restaurant*)
additionner *v.* to add; to total
adjectif *n.m.* adjective
administration *n.f.* administration
adolescence *n.f.* adolescence
adolescent/adolescente *n.m/f.* teenager
adopter *v.* to adopt
adresse *n.f.* address
adulte *n.m/f.* adult, grown-up
adversaire *n.m.* opponent
aéroport *n.m.* airport
affaire/affaires *n.f.* business; deal
affamé *adj.* hungry
affamer *v.* to starve
affreux *adj.* awful
Africain/Africaine *n.m/f.; adj.* African
Afrique *n.f.* Africa
âge *n.m.* age
agence *n.f.* agency
agent de police *n.m.* police officer
agent *n.m.* agent
agression *n.f.* aggression
à haute voix *adv.* aloud
aide *n.f.* help
aider *v.* to assist; to help
aigre *adj.* sour
aiguille *n.f.* needle; hand (*clock*)
ail *n.m.* garlic
aile *n.f.* wing
aimable *adj.* friendly; kind
aimant *n.m.* magnet
aimer *v.* to love; to enjoy; to like
aimer bien *v.* to like
air *n.m.* air
aisselle *n.f.* armpit
ajouter *v.* to add
alarme *n.f.* alarm
à l'avance *adv.* ahead; in advance
alcool *n.m.* alcohol; liquor
algue *n.f.* seaweed
à l'envers *adj.* upside-down
à l'étranger *adv.* abroad
Allemagne *n.f.* Germany
Allemand/Allemande *n.m/f.; adj.* German
aller *v.* to go; to fit (*clothes*)
allergie *n.f.* allergy
allergique *adj.* allergic
alliance *n.f.* wedding ring
allumage *n.m.* ignition
allumé *adj.* on (*TV*)
allumer *v.* to light; to switch on
allumette *n.f.* match

alors *adv.* then
alphabet *n.m.* alphabet
altitude *n.f.* height (*plane*); altitude
ambassade *n.f.* embassy
ambassadeur/ambassadrice *n.m/f.* ambassador
ambulance *n.f.* ambulance
amende *n.f.* fine
amener *v.* to bring
amer *adj.* bitter
Américain/Américaine *n.m/f.; adj.* American
Amérique *n.f.* America
ami/amie *n.m/f.* friend
amical *adj.* friendly
à mi-temps *adj.; adv.* part-time
amitié *n.f.* friendship
à moins que *conj.* unless
amour *n.m.* love
ampoule *n.f.* light bulb; blister
amuse-gueule *n.m.* appetizer
amygdales *n.f.pl.* tonsils
an *n.m.* year
ancêtre *n.m.* ancestor
ancien *adj.* former; old; ancient
ancre *n.f.* anchor
âne *n.m.* donkey
anémie *n.f.* anemia
anesthésie *n.f.* anesthesia
Anglais/Anglaise *n.m/f.; adj.* English
Angleterre *n.f.* England
animal *n.m.* animal
animal domestique *n.m.* pet
année *n.f.* year
année bissextile *n.f.* leap year
anniversaire *n.m.* birthday
annonce *n.f.* announcement
annuaire *n.m.* telephone book
annuel *adj.* annual
annulation *n.f.* cancellation
annuler *v.* to cancel
antenne *n.f.* antenna
antiquité *n.f.* antiquity
août *n.m.* August
à part *adv.* apart (*to one side*)
à partir de *prep.* from
à peu près *adv.* about
à plein temps *adj.; adv.* full time
appareil *n.m.* appliance
appareil photo *n.m.* camera
appareil photo numérique *n.m.* digital camera
apparence *n.f.* appearance; look
appartement *n.m.* apartment
appartenir *v.* to belong
appât *n.m.* bait
appel en PCV *n.m.* collect call
appeler *v.* to call
appendicite *n.f.* appendicitis
appétit *n.m.* appetite
applaudir *v.* to applaud
applaudissement *n.m.* applause
apporter *v.* to bring (*thing*)
apprendre *v.* to learn
approcher *v.* to approach
approprié *adj.* appropriate
approuver *v.* to approve
après *adv.; prep.* after
après-midi *n.m.* afternoon
à propos de *prep.* about
Arabe *n.m/f.; adj.* Arab; Arabic
araignée *n.f.* spider
arbitre *n.m.* referee
arbre *n.m.* tree
arc *n.m.* bow (*weapon*)
arc-en-ciel *n.m.* rainbow
arche *n.f.* arch
architecture *n.f.* architecture
archive *n.f.* archive
arête *n.f.* bone (*fish*)
argent *n.m.* cash; money; silver
argot *n.m.* slang
arme *n.f.* weapon
armée *n.f.* army
armer *v.* to arm
armoire *n.f.* cupboard
arrestation *n.f.* arrest
arrêt *n.m.* stop
arrêter *v.* to stop; to arrest
arrhes *n.f.pl.* deposit
arrière *n.m.* rear; back (*of vehicle*)
arrière-grand-mère *n.f.* great-grandmother
arrière-grand-père *n.m.* great-grandfather

arrivée *n.f.* arrival
arriver *v.* to arrive; to come; to happen
arroser *v.* to water
art *n.m.* art
article *n.m.* article; item
articulation *n.f.* joint (*bones*)
artificiel *adj.* artificial
artisan *n.m.* craftsman
artiste *n.m/f.* artist
ascenseur *n.m.* elevator
Asiatique *n.m/f.; adj.* Asian
Asie *n.f.* Asia
asile *n.m.* asylum
aspirateur *n.m.* vacuum cleaner
aspirine *n.f.* aspirin
assaisonner *v.* to season
(s') asseoir *v.* to sit
assez *adv.* enough; quite
assiette *n.f.* plate
assoiffé *adj.* thirsty
assortir *v.* to match
assurance *n.f.* insurance
assurer *v.* to assure; to insure
athlète *n.m.* athlete
à travers *prep.; adv.* across (*cross-wise*); through
attacher *v.* to fasten; to tie
attaque *n.f.* stroke (*medical*)
attendre *v.* to wait; to expect
attente *n.f.* wait; expectation
attention *n.f.* attention; caution
atterrir *v.* to land
attirer *v.* to attract
attitude *n.f.* attitude
attraper *v.* to catch; to grab
auberge *n.f.* inn
auberge de jeunesse *n.f.* youth hostel
aucun/e *pron.* none
augmentation *n.f.* raise (*salary*); increase
augmenter *v.* to increase
aujourd'hui *adv.* today
au lieu de *adv.* instead of
Au revoir ! *inter.* Bye!, Good-bye!
Au secours ! *inter.* Help!
aussi *adv.* too; also
auteur *n.m.* author
authentique *adj.* authentic
autochtone *n.m.* native
automatique *adj.* automatic
automne *n.m.* fall (*season*)
autorisation *n.f.* authorization
autoriser *v.* to authorize
autour *adv.* around
autre *adj.; pron.* another; other
avaler *v.* to swallow
avancer *v.* to move forward; to advance
avant *n.m.* front (*vehicle*)
avant *prep.; adv.* before
avant-bras *n.m.* forearm
avec *prep.* with
avenir *n.m.* future
avenue *n.f.* avenue
averse *n.f.* shower (*rain*)
averti *adj.* aware
avertir *v.* to caution; to warn
avertissement *n.m.* warning
aveugle *adj.* blind
avion *n.m.* airplane
avis *n.m.* opinion
avocat *n.m.* attorney, lawyer
avoir *v.* to have
avoir besoin de *v.* to need
avoir confiance *v.* to trust
avoir les moyens (de) *v.* to afford
avoir mal au cœur *adj.* to feel sick
avortement *n.m.* abortion
avril *n.m.* April

B

baby-sitter *n.f.* baby-sitter
bactérie *n.f.* bacteria
bagage *n.m.* baggage
bague *n.f.* ring
baguette *n.f.* rod
baie *n.f.* bay; berry
baignoire *n.f.* bathtub
bail *n.m.* lease
bâiller *v.* to yawn
bain *n.m.* bath
baiser *n.m.* kiss

bal *n.m.* ball (*dance*)
balai *n.m.* broom
balai à franges *n.m.* mop
balance *n.f.* scales
balançoire *n.f.* swing
balayer *v.* to sweep
balcon *n.m.* balcony
balle *n.f.* ball (*tennis; golf*); bullet
ballon *n.m.* ball (*soccer*)
banc *n.m.* bench
banlieue *n.f.* suburbs
banque *n.f.* bank
banquet *n.m.* banquet
banquier *n.m.* banker
baptême *n.m.* baptism
barbe *n.f.* beard
barrière *n.f.* fence
bas *n.m.* bottom (*page*); stocking; *adj.* low
bateau *n.m.* boat; ship
bâtiment *n.m.* building
batterie *n.f.* battery (*car*)
(se) battre *v.* to fight; to beat
bavoir *n.m.* bib
beau *adj.* beautiful
beaucoup *adv.* much; many
beau-fils *n.m.* son-in-law; stepson
beau-frère *n.m.* brother-in-law; stepbrother
beau-père *n.m.* father-in-law; stepfather
beauté *n.f.* beauty
beaux-parents *n.m.pl.* in-laws
bébé *n.m.* baby
Belge *n.m/f.; adj.* Belgian
Belgique *n.f.* Belgium
belle-fille *n.f.* daughter-in-law; stepdaughter
belle-mère *n.f.* mother-in-law; stepmother
belle-sœur *n.f.* sister-in-law; stepsister
béquille *n.f.* crutch
berceau *n.m.* cradle
béret *n.m.* beret
besoin *n.m.* need
bête *n.* animal ; *adj.* dumb; silly
béton *n.m.* concrete
Bible *n.f.* Bible
bibliothèque *n.f.* bookcase; library
bicyclette *n.f.* bicycle
bien *adv.* well; good
bien sûr *adv.* of course
bientôt *adv.* soon
Bienvenue ! *inter.* Welcome!
bière *n.f.* beer
bifurcation *n.f.* fork (*roads*)
bijoutier *n.m.* jeweler
bijoux *n.m.pl.* jewelry
bilingue *adj.* bilingual
billard *n.m.* pool (*game*)
billet *n.m.* ticket
billet de banque *n.m.* bill (*cash*)
bizarre *adj.* odd; weird
blanc *adj.* white; blank
blanchir *v.* to bleach
blanchisserie *n.f.* laundry (*place*)
blé *n.m.* wheat
blesser *v.* to injure; to offend
blessure *n.f.* wound; injury
bleu *n.m.* bruise; *adj.* blue
bloc *n.m.* block
blond *adj.* blond
bloquer *v.* to block
bocal *n.m.* jar
boire *v.* to drink
bois *n.m.* wood
boisson *n.f.* drink; beverage
boîte *n.f.* box
boîte aux lettres *n.f.* mailbox
boîte de conserve *n.f.* can
boîte de nuit *n.f.* dance club
boiter *v.* to limp
bol *n.m.* bowl
bombe *n.f.* bomb
bon *adj.* good
bon marché *adj.* cheap
bonbon *n.m.* candy
bonheur *n.m.* happiness
Bonjour ! *inter.* Hello!
bonne *n.f.* maid
bord *n.m.* side; edge; border
borne *n.f.* milestone
botte *n.f.* boot
bouche *n.f.* mouth
bouchée *n.f.* bite (*food*)
boucher *n.m.* butcher; *v.* to plug

bouchon *n.m.* cap; cork (*bottle*); plug
boucle *n.f.* curl
boucle d'oreille *n.f.* earring
boucler *v.* to curl (*hair*)
boue *n.* mud
bouée *n.f.* buoy
bouger *v.* to move
bougie *n.f.* candle
bouillir *v.* to boil
bouilloire *n.f.* kettle
boulanger *n.m.* baker
boulangerie *n.f.* bakery
boulevard *n.m.* boulevard
bouquet *n.m.* bunch
bourse *n.f.* scholarship
boussole *n.f.* compass
bout *n.m.* tip (*top*)
bouteille *n.f.* bottle
bouton *n.m.* button; knob
bracelet *n.m.* bracelet
brancher *v.* to connect (*install*); to plug
bras *n.m.* arm
bretelle d'accès *n.f.* ramp (*highway*)
brillant *adj.* bright
briller *v.* to shine
briquet *n.m.* lighter
brise *n.f.* breeze
bronchite *n.f.* bronchitis
bronzage *n.m.* tan
bronzer *v.* to tan
brosse *n.f.* brush
brosse à dents *n.f.* toothbrush
brosser *v.* to brush
brouillard *n.m.* fog
bruit *n.m.* noise
brûler *v.* to burn
brûlure *n.f.* burn
brun *adj.* brown
brushing *n.m.* blow-dry
bruyant *adj.* loud; noisy
bûche *n.f.* log
budget *n.m.* budget
bureau *n.m.* office; desk
bus *n.m.* bus
but *n.m.* goal

C

cable *n.m.* cable
câbles de démarrage *n.m.pl.* jumper cables
cacher *v.* to hide
cadeau *n.m.* present; gift
cadre *n.m.* frame
café *n.m.* coffee; coffee shop
cage *n.f.* cage
caillou *n.m.* small rock; pebble
caissier/caissière *n.m/f.* cashier
calculatrice *n.f.* calculator
calculer *v.* to calculate
calendrier *n.m.* calendar
calme *adj.* quiet
cambrioler *v.* to burglarize
cambrioleur *n.m.* burglar
camelote *n.f.* junk (*objects*)
caméscope *n.m.* camcorder
camion *n.m.* truck
camionnette *n.f.* van
camp *n.m.* camp
campagne *n.f.* countryside
camper *v.* to camp
Canada *n.m.* Canada
Canadien/Canadienne *n.m/f.; adj.* Canadian
canapé *n.m.* couch, sofa
canapé-lit *n.m.* sofa bed
cancer *n.m.* cancer
canif *n.m.* pocketknife
canne *n.f.* cane
canne à pêche *n.f.* fishing rod
canoë *n.m.* canoe
capable *adj.* able; capable
capitaine *n.m.* captain
capitale *n.f.* capital
capot *n.m.* hood
caractère *n.m.* temper
caravane *n.f.* trailer; camper
carburant *n.m.* fuel
carême *n.m.* Lent
carnet *n.m.* notebook
carré *n.m.* square
carte *n.f.* card; menu; map
carte d'abonnement *n.f.* pass (*season ticket*)
carte de crédit *n.f.* credit card

carte d'embarquement *n.f.* boarding pass
carte de téléphone *n.f.* calling card
carte d'identité *n.f.* identity card
carte postale *n.f.* postcard
carton *n.m.* cardboard
cartouche *n.f.* carton (*cigarettes*)
casier *n.m.* locker
casino *n.m.* casino
casque *n.m.* helmet
casquette *n.f.* cap
casse-croûte *n.m.* snack
casserole *n.f.* pan
cathédrale *n.f.* cathedral
catholicisme *n.m.* Catholicism
catholique *n.m/f.; adj.* Catholic
cauchemar *n.m.* nightmare
causette *n.f.* chat
caution *n.f.* deposit; bail
cave *n.f.* cellar
CD *n.m.* CD
CD-ROM *n.m.* CD-ROM
ce *pron.* this
céder la priorité *v.* to yield (*car*)
ceinture *n.f.* belt
ceinture de sécurité *n.f.* seat belt
célibataire *adj.* single; not married
cendre *n.f.* ash
cendrier *n.m.* ashtray
cent *num.* hundred
centimètre *n.m.* centimeter
centre *n.m.* center
centre commercial *n.m.* mall
centre médical *n.m.* clinic
cercle *n.m.* circle
cercueil *n.m.* coffin
cérémonie *n.f.* ceremony
cérémonieux *adj.* formal
certain *adj.* sure
cette nuit *n.f.; adv.* tonight
chaîne *n.f.* range (*mountain*); chain
chaise *n.f.* chair
chaleur *n.f.* heat
chambre (à coucher) *n.f.* bedroom
chambre libre *n.f.* vacancy
champ *n.m.* field
champignon *n.m.* mushroom
chance *n.f.* chance; likelihood; luck
changement *n.m.* change
changer *v.* to change; to exchange (*currency*)
chanson *n.f.* song
chanter *v.* to sing
chanteur/chanteuse *n.m/f.* singer
chapeau *n.m.* hat
chasse *n.f.* hunt
chasser *v.* to hunt
chasseur *n.m.* hunter
chat *n.m.* cat
château *n.m.* castle
chatouiller *v.* to tickle
chaud *adj.* hot; warm
chaudière *n.f.* boiler
chauffer *v.* to heat
chaussette *n.f.* sock
chaussure *n.f.* shoe
chauve *adj.* bald
chef *n.m.* chief; leader; chef
chef d'orchestre *n.m.* conductor
chemin *n.m.* path; way
cheminée *n.f.* fireplace
chemise *n.f.* shirt
chemisier *n.m.* blouse; shirt (*woman*)
chèque *n.m.* check
chèque de voyage *n.m.* traveler's check
cher *adj.* expensive; dear
cheval *n.m.* horse
cheveux *n.m.pl.* hair
cheville *n.f.* ankle
chèvre *n.f.* goat
chic *adj.* stylish
chien/chienne *n.m/f.* dog
chirurgie *n.f.* surgery
chirurgien *n.m.* surgeon
choc *n.m.* shock
choisir *v.* to choose; to select
choix *n.m.* option; choice
chope *n.f.* mug (*beer*)
chose *n.f.* thing
choses *n.f.pl.* stuff

chrétien *adj.* Christian
christianisme *n.m.* Christianity
chute *n.f.* fall
cible *n.f.* target
cicatrice *n.f.* scar
ciel *n.m.* sky
cigare *n.m.* cigar
cigarette *n.f.* cigarette
cil *n.m.* eyelash
cimetière *n.m.* cemetery; graveyard
cinéma *n.m.* movie theater
cinq *num.* five
cintre *n.m.* hanger
cirage *n.m.* shoe polish
circulation *n.f.* flow (*blood*); traffic
cire *n.f.* wax
cirque *n.m.* circus
ciseaux *n.m.pl.* scissors
citoyen/citoyenne *n.m/f.* citizen
citron *n.m.* lemon
clair *adj.* fair (*hair; skin*); clear; light (*color*)
classique *adj.* classic
clavier *n.m.* keyboard
clé *n.f.* key
clerc *n.m.* clerk
client/cliente *n.m/f.* client; customer
clignoter *v.* to flash (*light*); to blink
climat *n.m.* climate
climatisation *n.f.* air-conditioning
cloche *n.f.* bell
cloque *n.f.* blister
clou *n.m.* nail (*metal*)
code postal *n.m.* zip code
cœur *n.m.* heart
coffre *n.m.* chest (*box*); trunk
coffre-fort *n.m.* safe
coiffeur *n.m.* hairdresser; barber
coin *n.m.* corner
col *n.m.* collar; pass (*mountain*)
colère *n.f.* anger
colle *n.f.* glue
collection *n.f.* collection
collège *n.m.* junior high school
coller *v.* to glue; to stick
collier *n.m.* necklace
colline *n.f.* hill
collision *n.f.* collision
co-locataire *n.m.* roommate
colonne *n.f.* column
colonne vertébrale *n.f.* backbone; spine
comité *n.m.* committee
commande *n.f.* order
commander *v.* to order
comme *conj. prep.* as; like
commencer *v.* to start, to begin
comment *adv.* how
commerce *n.m.* trade
commissariat de police *n.m.* police station
commission *n.f.* commission
commun *adj.* common
communication *n.f.* call (*phone*); communication
communiquer *v.* to communicate
compagnie *n.f.* company
compagnie aérienne *n.f.* airline
comparer *v.* to compare
compartiment *n.m.* compartment
complet *adj.* complete; full (*hotel*)
compliment *n.m.* compliment
comportement *n.m.* behavior
(se) comporter *v.* to behave
composer *v.* to compose; to dial
composter *v.* to validate (*train ticket*)
comprendre *v.* to understand
comptable *n.m/f.* accountant
compte *n.m.* account (*bank*)
compter *v.* to count; to calculate
comptoir *n.m.* counter
concert *n.m.* concert
concierge *n.m.* janitor
concours *n.m.* competition
condamner *v.* to condemn
condition *n.f.* condition
condoléances *n.f.pl.* condolences
conducteur/conductrice *n.m/f.* driver
conduire *v.* to drive (*car*)
conférence *n.f.* lecture
confesser *v.* to confess

confession *n.f.* confession
confiance *n.f.* confidence; trust
confirmer *v.* to confirm
confiture *n.f.* jam
confortable *adj.* comfortable
congélateur *n.m.* freezer
connaissance *n.f.* acquaintance; knowledge
connaître *v.* to know (*person*)
conscient *adj.* conscious
conseil *n.m.* advice
consigne *n.f.* checkroom
consonne *n.f.* consonant
constipation *n.f.* constipation
construire *v.* to build
consul *n.m.* consul
consulat *n.m.* consulate
contact *n.m.* contact
contacter *v.* to contact
contagieux *adj.* contagious
contaminer *v.* to contaminate; to infect
content *adj.* glad
contenu *n.m.* content
continent *n.m.* continent
continuer *v.* to continue
contraceptif *n.m.; adj.* contraceptive
contraire *n.m.; adj.* opposite; contrary
contrarier *v.* to upset (*someone*)
contrat *n.m.* contract
contre *prep.* against; versus
contrôle *n.m.* control
contrôler *v.* to check (*passport*); to control
contrôleur *n.m.* conductor (*train*)
convaincre *v.* to convince
convenir de *v.* to agree on (*price; date*)
conversation *n.f.* conversation
copie *n.f.* copy
copier *v.* to copy
coquillage *n.m.* sea shell
coquille *n.f.* shell
corbeille *n.f.* basket
corde *n.f.* cord; rope
cordonnier *n.m.* shoemaker; cobbler
corne *n.f.* horn
corps *n.m.* body
correspondance *n.f.* connection (*flight*); correspondence
corriger *v.* to correct
costume *n.m.* suit
côte *n.f.* coast; side; rib
coton *n.m.* cotton
couche *n.f.* diaper (*baby*); layer
coucher de soleil *n.m.* sunset
coude *n.m.* elbow
coudre *v.* to sew
couler *v.* to sink; to flow
couleur *n.f.* color
coup *n.m.* shot; hit
coup de téléphone *n.m.* call
coupable *adj.* guilty
coupe de cheveux *n.f.* haircut
couper *v.* to cut
couple *n.m.* couple
coupon *n.m.* voucher
coupure *n.f.* cut
cour *n.f.* courtyard; court
couramment *adv.* fluently
courant *n.* power (*electricity*); current (*power*); flow; *adj.* current (*present*)
courant d'air *n.m.* draft
courir *v.* to run
courrier *n.m.* mail
courrier électronique *n.m.* E-mail
cours *n.m.* lecture (*school*)
course *n.f.* race (*competition*)
courses *n.f.pl.* shopping; horse racing
court *adj.* short
cousin/cousine *n.m/f.* cousin
coussin *n.m.* cushion
coût *n.m.* cost
couteau *n.m.* knife
coûter *v.* to cost
coutume *n.f.* custom
couture *n.f.* seam
couvent *n.m.* convent
couvercle *n.m.* cover (*jar*); lid
couverture *n.f.* cover; blanket
couvrir *v.* to cover
cracher *v.* to spit

craindre *v.* to fear
cravate *n.f.* tie
crayon *n.m.* pencil
crème *n.f.* cream
crème à raser *n.f.* shaving cream
crème solaire *n.f.* sunscreen
crémerie *n.f.* dairy
crever *v.* to burst (*tire; balloon*)
cri *n.m.* shout, yell, scream
cric *n.m.* jack
crier *v.* to cry, to yell, to scream
crime *n.m.* crime
critique *n.f.* criticism; review (*movie*)
critiquer *v.* to criticize
crochet *n.m.* hook
croire *v.* to believe
croisement *n.m.* intersection
croisière *n.f.* cruise
croissance *n.f.* growth
croix *n.f.* cross
croûte *n.f.* crust
croyance *n.f.* belief
cru *adj.* raw
crustacés *n.m.pl.* shellfish
cuillère *n.f.* spoon
cuillère à café *n.f.* teaspoon
cuillère à soupe *n.f.* tablespoon
cuir *n.m.* leather
cuire *v.* to cook
cuire au four *v.* to bake
cuisine *n.f.* kitchen
cuisiner *v.* to cook
cuisinier *n.m.* cook
cuisinière *n.f.* stove; cook (*person*)
cuisse *n.f.* thigh
culture *n.f.* culture
cure-dents *n.m.* toothpick
curieux *adj.* curious; nosy
cuvette *n.f.* basin

D

dame *n.f.* lady
danger *n.m.* danger
dangereux *adj.* unsafe; dangerous
dans *prep.* in; into
danse *n.f.* dance
danser *v.* to dance
date *n.f.* date
de *prep.* from; of
début *n.m.* beginning; start
débutant/débutante *n.m/f.* beginner
décaféiné *adj.* decaffeinated
décapotable *adj.* convertible
décembre *n.m.* December
décharger *v.* to unload
déchirer *v.* to tear
déchirure *n.f.* tear (*fabric*)
décision *n.f.* decision
déclarer *v.* to declare
décoller *v.* to take off
décoration *n.f.* decoration
décorer *v.* to decorate
découvrir *v.* to discover
décrire *v.* to describe
dédommager *v.* to compensate
défaire *v.* to undo; to unpack
défaut *n.m.* defect; fault
défendre *v.* to defend
défense *n.f.* defense
définition *n.f.* definition
dégâts *n.m.pl.* damage
dégeler *v.* to thaw
dégonfler *v.* to deflate
dégoût *n.m.* disgust
dégoûtant *adj.* filthy, disgusting
degré *n.m.* degree
dehors *adv.* out
déjà *adv.* already
déjeuner *n.m.* lunch
délicieux *adj.* delicious
demain *adv.* tomorrow
demande en mariage *n.f.* proposal (*marriage*)
demander *v.* to ask; to inquire
démangeaison *n.f.* itch
déménagement *n.m.* move (*home*)
demi *adj* half
demi-frère *n.m.* stepbrother
demi-pension *n.f.* half-board
demi-sœur *n.f.* stepsister
demi-tour *n.* U-turn
démocratie *n.f.* democracy
démodé *adj.* old-fashioned

de nos jours *adv.* nowadays
de nouveau *adv.* again
dent *n.f.* tooth
dentelle *n.f.* lace
dentifrice *n.m.* toothpaste
dentiste *n.m.* dentist
déodorant *n.m.* deodorant
dépanneuse *n.f.* tow truck
départ *n.m.* departure; start
dépasser *v.* to exceed
(se) dépêcher *v.* to rush; to hurry
dépense *n.f.* expense
dépenser *v.* to spend
déplacé *adj.* uncalled-for
déplier *v.* to unfold
dépression *n.f.* nervous breakdown
depuis *prep.* for; since
député *n.m.* representative (*Congress*)
de retour *adv.* back; returned
dernier *adj.* last
derrière *adj.* rear; behind
descendre *v.* to descend
descente *n.f.* descent
désert *n.m.* desert
(se) déshabiller *v.* to undress
déshydratation *n.f.* dehydration
désir *n.m.* desire
désirer *v.* to desire; to long for
désobéir *v.* to disobey
de soirée *adj.* formal
désolé *adj.* sorry
désordre *n.m.* mess
dessert *n.m.* dessert
dessin *n.m.* drawing
dessiner *v.* to draw (*picture*)
détective *n.m.* detective
(se) détendre *v.* to relax
détour *n.m.* detour
détritus *n.m.* litter
détruire *v.* to destroy
dette *n.f.* debt
deux *num.* two
deux fois *adv.* twice
devant *adv.* ahead; in advance; *prep.* before; in front
devis *n.m.* estimate
devoir *n.m.* duty; *v.* must; to owe
devoirs *n.m.pl.* homework
d'habitude *adv.* usually
diabète *n.m.* diabetes
diable *n.m.* devil
diagnostic *n.m.* diagnosis
dialecte *n.m.* dialect
dialogue *n.m.* dialogue
diamant *n.m.* diamond
diapositive *n.f.* slide (*photo*)
dictionnaire *n.m.* dictionary
Dieu *n.m.* God
différence *n.* difference
différent *adj.* different
difficile *adj.* difficult
difficulté *n.f.* difficulty
digérer *v.* to digest
digestion *n.f.* digestion
digital *adj.* digital
dimanche *n.m.* Sunday
dîner *n.m.* dinner; supper
diplôme *n.m.* degree; diploma
diplômé *n.m.* graduate
dire *v.* to tell; to say
direct *adj.* direct
directeur/directrice *n.m/f.* manager; director
direction *n.f.* direction; leadership
discours *n.m.* speech; talk
discret *adj.* discreet
discussion *n.f.* discussion; talk
discuter *v.* to discuss
disparaître *v.* to disappear
disponible *adj.* available
dispute *n.f.* argument; quarrel
disque *n.m.* record (*music*); disk
disquette *n.f.* floppy disk
dissolvant *n.m.* nail polish remover
distance *n.f.* distance
distraire *v.* to distract
distribuer *v.* to distribute
distributeur automatique *n.m.* ATM
divan *n.m.* couch
divorce *n.m.* divorce
divorcer *v.* to divorce
dix *num.* ten
d'occasion *adj.* used

docteur/doctoresse *n.m/f.* doctor
doigt *n.m.* finger
dollar *n.m.* dollar
donner *v.* to give
dormir *v.* to sleep
dortoir *n.m.* dormitory
dos *n.m.* back
dossier *n.m.* file
douane *n.f.* customs
double *n.m.; adj.; adv.* double
douche *n.f.* shower
(se) doucher *v.* to shower
douleur *n.f.* ache; pain
douloureux *adj.* painful; sore
doute *n.m.* doubt
douter de *v.* to doubt
doux *adj.* mild; sweet; soft
douzaine *n.f.* dozen
doyen/doyenne *n.m/f.* dean
drame *n.m.* tragedy (*event*)
drap *n.m.* sheet
drapeau *n.m.* flag
drogue *n.f.* drug
droit *n.m.* law (*study*); *adj.* straight
droite *n.f.* right (*direction*)
drôle *adj.* funny
dû *n.m.; adj.* due
du dessus *adj.* upper
dur *adj.* hard; tough
durée *n.f.* length (*time*)
durer *v.* to last

E

eau *n.f.* water
eau de Javel *n.f.* bleach
eau du robinet *n.f.* tap water
écaille *n.f.pl.* scale (*fish*)
échanger *v.* to exchange
échantillon *n.m.* sample
écharpe *n.f.* scarf
échec *n.m.* failure
échecs *n.m.pl.* chess
échelle *n.f.* ladder; scale
éclair *n.m.* flash; lightning
éclairer *v.* to light (*a room*)
école *n.f.* school
économie *n.f.* economy
écouter *v.* to listen
écran *n.m.* screen
écran total *n.m.* sunblock
(s') écraser *v.* to crash (*plane*)
écrire *v.* write
écrivain *n.m.* writer
édition *n.f.* edition
édredon *n.m.* comforter; quilt
éducation *n.f.* education
effacer *v.* to erase
effet *n.m.* effect
effort *n.m.* effort
effrayé *adj.* afraid
effrayer *v.* to frighten
égal *adj.* equal
égalité *n.f.* tie (*sports*)
église *n.f.* church
égratignure *n.f.* scratch
élastique *n.m.; adj.* rubber band; elastic
électricien *n.m.* electrician
électricité *n.f.* electricity
électrique *adj.* electric
élégant *adj.* elegant
élevé *adj.* high (*price*)
élever *v.* to raise
elle *pron.* she
elles *pron.* they
emballer *v.* to pack; to wrap
embarrasser *v.* to embarrass
embrasser *v.* to kiss
émigrer *v.* to emigrate
emmener *v.* to take (*someone*)
empêcher *v.* to prevent; to keep somebody from
emploi *n.m.* employment
employé/employée *n.m/f.* employee
employeur *n.m.* employer
empreinte digitale *n.f.* fingerprint
emprisonner *v.* to put in jail
emprunter *v.* to borrow
ému *adj.* touched
en *prep.* in
en arrière *adv.* backwards; back
en avant *adj.; adv.* forward
en bas de *prep.* down

en bonne santé *adj.* healthy
encaisser *v.* to cash
enceinte *adj.* pregnant
encore *adv.* again; more
endormi *adj.* asleep
endroit *n.m.* place
énergie *n.f.* energy
en face *adj.* opposite (*across*)
enfance *n.f.* childhood
enfant *n.m.* child
enfer *n.m.* hell
enfler *v.* to swell (*medical*)
en forme *adj.* fit
engager *v.* to hire
en haut *adv.* up; upstairs
enlever *v.* to remove
ennemi/ennemie *n.m/f.* enemy
ennuyer *v.* to bother
énorme *adj.* enormous
en outre *adv.* besides
en plein air *adj.* outdoor
en plus *prep.* besides
en public *adj.* live (*performance*)
en recommandé *adj.* certified mail
enregistrer *v.* to register; to record
en retard *adj.* late
enseigner *v.* to teach
ensemble *adv.* together
ensoleillé *adj.* sunny
entendre *v.* to hear
enterrement *n.m.* funeral
enterrer *v.* to bury
entier *adj.* whole; entire
entraîner *v.* to train (*sports*)
entre *prep.* among; between
entrée *n.f.* entrance
entrer *v.* to enter
entrer en collision *v.* to collide
enveloppe *n.f.* envelope
envers *n.m.* reverse (*fabric*)
environ *adv.* about
environnement *n.m.* environment
environs *n.m.pl.* surroundings
envoyer *v.* to send; to mail
épais *adj.* thick
épaule *n.f.* shoulder
épeler *v.* to spell
épicerie *n.f.* grocery store
épicier *n.m.* grocer
épidémie *n.f.* epidemic
épingle *n.f.* pin
épingle de nourrice *n.f.* safety pin
éponge *n.f.* sponge
éponger *v.* to mop
épouser *v.* to marry
épuiser *v.* to exhaust
équipage *n.m.* crew
équipe *n.f.* team
équivalent *n.m.; adj.* equivalent
erreur *n.f.* error
éruption *n.f.* rash (*skin*)
escalade *n.f.* climb
escalader *v.* to climb (*mountain*)
escalator *n.m.* escalator
escalier *n.m.* stairs
escalier roulant *n.m.* escalator
escorte *n.f.* escort
escorter *v.* to escort; to accompany
espace *n.m.* space
Espagne *n.f.* Spain
Espagnol/Espagnole *n.m/f.; adj.* Spanish
espérer *v.* to hope
espoir *n.m.* hope
esprit *n.m.* mind
essayer *v.* to try
essence *n.f.* gas
essuyer *v.* wipe
est *n.m.* east
estimation *n.f.* estimate
estomac *n.m.* stomach
et *conj.* and
étage *n.m.* floor
étagère *n.f.* shelf
étang *n.m.* pond
état *n.m.* state
États-Unis *n.pl.* United States
été *n.m.* summer
(s') étendre *v.* to lie down
éternuer *v.* to sneeze
étiquette *n.f.* label (*clothes*)
étoile *n.f.* star
étonner *v.* to amaze
étrange *adj.* unfamiliar; strange

étranger/étrangère *n.m./f.* foreigner; alien; *adj.* foreign
être *v.* to be
être d'accord *v.* to agree
étreinte *n.f.* hug
étroit *adj.* narrow
étudiant/étudiante *n.m/f.* student
étudier *v.* to study
étui *n.m.* case (*glasses*)
euro *n.m.* euro
Europe *n.f.* Europe
Européen/Européenne *n.m/f.; adj.* European
évacuer *v.* to evacuate
(s') évanouir *v.* to faint
évanouissement *n.m.* faint
événement *n.m.* occasion; event
évident *adj.* obvious
évier *n.m.* sink
éviter *v.* to avoid
exact *adj.* accurate; correct; exact
exagérer *v.* to exaggerate
examen *n.m.* examination
examiner *v.* to examine
excellent *adj.* excellent
exception *n.f.* exception
exciter *v.* to excite
exclure *v.* to exclude
excursion *n.f.* excursion
excuse *n.f.* excuse
(s') excuser *v.* to apologize; to excuse
exemple *n.m.* example
exercice *n.m.* exercise
expéditeur *n.m.* sender
expérience *n.f.* experience
expert *n.m.; adj.* expert
expirer *v.* to expire
explication *n.f.* explanation
expliquer *v.* to explain
exposition *n.f.* show; art exhibit
exprès *adj.* express
expression *n.f.* phrase
expulser *v.* to expel
extérieur *n.m.; adj.* outside
externe *adj.* external
extincteur *n.m.* extinguisher

F

fâché *adj.* angry
fâcher (se) *v.* to be angry
facile *adj.* easy
facilement *adv.* easily
facture *n.f.* bill; invoice
faible *adj.* faint; weak
faim *n.f.* hunger
faire *v.* to do; to make
faire des achats *v.* to shop
faire du jogging *v.* to jog
faire la course *v.* to race
faire la cuisine *v.* to cook
faire les bagages *v.* to pack (*suitcase*)
faire mal *v.* to hurt
faire payer *v.* to charge (*price*)
faire peur *v.* to frighten; to scare
faire un somme *v.* to nap
falaise *n.f.* cliff
fameux *adj.* famous
famille *n.f.* family
farine *n.f.* flour
fatigué *adj.* tired
faute *n.f.* mistake
fauteuil *n.m.* armchair
faux *adj.* false; wrong
favori/favorite *n.m/f.; adj.* favorite
félicitations *n.f.pl.* congratulations
féliciter *v.* to congratulate
femelle *n.f.; adj.* female (*animal*)
féminin *adj.* feminine; female (*human*)
femme *n.f.* wife; woman
fenêtre *n.f.* window
fer *n.m.* iron (*metal*)
fer à repasser *n.m.* iron (*for clothes*)
ferme *adj.* firm; steady
fermé *adj.* closed
ferme *n.f.* farm
fermer *v.* to close; to shut
fermer à clé *v.* to lock
fermeture éclair *n.f.* zipper
fermier *n.m.* farmer
ferry *n.m.* ferry
fête *n.f.* party

fêter *v.* to celebrate
feu *n.m.* fire
feu d'artifice *n.m.* fireworks
feuille *n.f.* sheet (*paper*); leaf (*tree*)
février *n.m.* February
fiable *adj.* reliable
fiançailles *n.f.* engagement
ficelle *n.f.* string
fidèle *adj.* faithful
fier *adj.* proud
fierté *n.f.* pride
fièvre *n.f.* fever
filet *n.m.* net
fille *n.f.* daughter; girl
filleul *n.m.* godson
filleule *n.f.* goddaughter
film *n.m.* film; movie
fils *n.m.* son
filtre *n.m.* filter
fin *n.f.* end
final *adj.* final
financier *adj.* financial
finir *v.* to finish
fixe *adj.* flat (*rate*)
flamme *n.f.* flame
flash *n.m.* flash (*camera*)
flèche *n.f.* arrow
fleur *n.f.* flower
fleuriste *n.m/f.* florist
flocon de neige *n.m.* snowflake
flotter *v.* to float
foi *n.f.* faith
foie *n.m.* liver
foire *n.f.* fair
folklorique *adj.* folk (*music; dance*)
fondation *n.f.* foundation
fondre *v.* to melt
fontaine *n.f.* fountain
football *n.m.* soccer
football américain *n.m.* football
force *n.f.* force; strength
forcer *v.* to force
forêt *n.f.* forest
forme *n.f.* shape
formidable *adj.* great
formulaire *n.m.* form
fort *adj.* strong; loud (*voice*)
fossé *n.m.* ditch
fou *adj.* crazy; mad
fouiller *v.* to search
foulard *n.m.* scarf (*light*)
foule *n.f.* crowd
four *n.m.* oven
fourchette *n.f.* fork
fournir *v.* to provide
fourrure *n.f.* fur
fragile *adj.* fragile
frais *n.m.pl.* charges; *adj.* cool; fresh
frais de scolarité *n.m.pl.* tuition
Français/Française *n.m/f.; adj.* French
France *n.f.* France
frapper *v.* to hit; to knock
frelon *n.m.* hornet
fréquent *adj.* frequent
frère *n.m.* brother
frire *v.* to fry
friser *v.* to curl (*hair*)
froid *n.m.; adj.* cold
fromage *n.m.* cheese
front *n.m.* forehead
frontière *n.f.* border (*country*)
fruit *n.m.* fruit
fuite *n.f.* leak
fumée *n.f.* smoke
fumer *v.* to smoke
fusible *n.m.* fuse
fusil *n.m.* rifle; gun
futur *n.m.; adj.* future

G

gagnant/gagnante *n.m/f.* winner
gagner *v.* to earn; to win
galerie *n.f.* gallery
gallon *n.m.* gallon
gamin/gamine *n.m/f.* kid
gant *n.m.* glove
garage *n.m.* garage
garantie *n.f.* guarantee
garantir *v.* to guarantee
garde *n.f.* guard
garder *v.* to guard; to keep
garder les enfants *v.* to baby-sit
garderie *n.f.* daycare
gare *n.f.* (train) station

gâteau *n.m.* cake
gauche *n.f.* left
gay *adj.* gay, homosexual
gaz *n.m.* gas
geler *v.* to freeze
gencive *n.f.* gum
genou *n.m.* knee
gens *n.m.pl.* people; folk
gentil *adj.* nice; kind
gentillesse *n.f.* kindness
géographie *n.f.* geography
geste *n.m.* wave (*hand*); gesture
gibier *n.m.* game (*hunting*)
gilet de sauvetage *n.m.* life jacket
glacé *adj.* icy
glace *n.f.* ice; ice cream
glaçon *n.m.* ice cube
glisser *v.* to slide
gorge *n.f.* throat
gorgée *n.f.* sip
goût *n.m.* flavor; taste
goûter *v.* to taste; to sample
goutte *n.f.* drop
gouvernement *n.m.* government
graisse *n.f.* fat; grease
grammaire *n.f.* grammar
gramme *n.m.* gram
grand *adj.* great; large; tall (*person*); big
grande tasse *n.f.* mug
Grande-Bretagne *n.f.* Great Britain
grandir *v.* to grow up
grand-mère *n.f.* grandmother
grand-père *n.m.* grandfather
grands-parents *n.m.pl.* grandparents
grange *n.f.* barn
gras *adj.* fat
gratuit *adj.* free
grave *adj.* serious
graver *v.* to engrave
gravure *n.f.* engraving
grêle *n.f.* hail
grenier *n.m.* attic
griffer *v.* to scratch
gril *n.m.* grill
grimper *v.* to climb
grippe *n.f.* flu
gris *adj.* gray
gros *adj.* big; fat
grossier *adj.* rude
grotte *n.f.* cave
groupe *n.m.* group
grouper *v.* to group
guêpe *n.f.* wasp
guérir *v.* to cure; to heal
guerre *n.f.* war
gueule de bois *n.f.* hangover
guichet *n.m.* counter; window (*bank*)
guide *n.m.* guide
gynécologue *n.m/f.* gynecologist

H

(s') habiller *v.* to dress
habitant/habitante *n.m/f.; adj.* inhabitant
habiter *v.* to live
habits *n.pl.* clothes
habituel *adj.* usual
haine *n.f.* hate
haleine *n.f.* breath
hall *n.m.* hall; entrance; lobby (*hotel*)
hameçon *n.m.* hook (*fishing*)
hanche *n.f.* hip
handicap *n.m.* handicap
handicaper *v.* to handicap
haut *adj.* tall; high
hauteur *n.f.* height (*object*)
haut-parleur *n.m.* loudspeaker
hélicoptère *n.m* helicopter
herbe *n.f.* grass
hésiter *v.* to hesitate
heure *n.f.* hour
heures supplémentaires *adv.* overtime
heureux *adj.* happy
hier *adv.* yesterday
histoire *n.f.* history; story
historique *adj.* historical
hiver *n.m.* winter
hockey sur glace *n.m.* ice hockey
hommage *n.m.* tribute
homme *n.m.* man

honoraires *n.m.pl.* fee (*physician*)
honte *n.f.* shame
hôpital *n.m.* hospital
horaire *n.m.* schedule (*train*)
horloge *n.f.* clock (*large*)
hospitalité *n.f.* hospitality
hôte *n.m.* host
hôtel *n.m.* hotel
hôtesse *n.f.* hostess
hôtesse de l'air *n.f.* flight attendant (*female*)
huile *n.f.* oil
huileux *adj.* oily
huit *num.* eight
humain *adj.* human
humeur *n.f.* mood
humide *adj.* damp; humid; moist
humidité *n.f.* moisture
humour *n.m.* humor
hurler *v.* to yell
hygiène *n.f.* hygiene

I

ici *adv.* here
idée *n.f.* idea
identifier *v.* to identify
identique *adj.* identical
identité *n.f.* identity
idiot *n.m.* fool
ignorer *v.* to ignore
il *pron.* he
île *n.f.* island
illégal *adj.* illegal
illimité *adj.* unlimited
illustration *n.f.* illustration
ils *pron.* they
il y a *adv.* ago; there is, there are
image *n.f.* image; picture
immangeable *adj.* inedible
immédiatement *adv.* immediately
immobile *adj.* still
imperméable *n.m.* raincoat; *adj.* waterproof
important *adj.* important
importation *n.f.* import
importer *v.* to import
impossible *adj.* impossible
impôts *n.m.pl.* taxes
incapable *adj.* unable
inconfortable *adj.* uncomfortable
inconnu/inconnue *n.m/f.* stranger; *adj.* strange (*not known*); unfamiliar
inconscient *adj.* unconscious
incroyable *adj.* unbelievable
inculper *v.* to charge (*law*)
index *n.m.* index; forefinger
indigestion *n.f.* indigestion
indiquer *v.* to point; to indicate
industrie *n.f.* industry
infecter *v.* to infect
infection *n.f.* infection
infirmier/infirmière *n.m/f.* nurse
information *n.f.* information
informations *n.f.pl.* news (*TV; radio*)
ingénieur *n.m.* engineer
initiale *n.f.* initial
injecter *v.* to inject
injection *n.f.* injection
innocent *adj.* innocent
inondation *n.f.* flood
inonder *v.* to flood
inoubliable *adj.* unforgettable
(s') inquiéter *v.* to worry
insecte *n.m.* insect
insectifuge *n.m.* repellent
insister *v.* to insist
insolation *n.f.* sunstroke
insolite *adj.* unusual
insomnie *n.f.* insomnia
inspecter *v.* to inspect
inspecteur *n.m.* inspector
installation *n.f.* installation
instant *n.m.* moment
instituteur/institutrice *n.m/f.* teacher (*elementary*)
instrument *n.m.* instrument
insulte *n.f.* insult
insulter *v.* to insult
intelligence *n.f.* intelligence
intelligent *adj.* clever; smart
interdiction *n.f.* ban
interdire *v.* to forbid; to prohibit
interdit *adj.* forbidden
intéressant *adj.* interesting
intérêt *n.m.* interest

intérieur *n.m.; adj.* inside
international *adj.* international
Internet *n.m.* Internet
interpréter *v.* to interpret
interroger *v.* to ask; to question
interrupteur *n.m.* switch
interview *n.f.* interview
intestin *n.m.* intestine
intimité *n.f.* privacy
inventer *v.* to invent
invention *n.f.* invention
invitation *n.f.* invitation
invité/invitée *n.m/f.* guest
inviter *v.* to invite
Islam *n.m.* Islam
isolation *n.f.* insulation
isoler *v.* to insulate; to isolate
Italie *n.f.* Italy
Italien/Italienne *n.m/f.; adj.* Italian
itinéraire *n.m.* route
ivre *adj.* drunk, intoxicated

J

jamais *adv.* ever; never
jambe *n.f.* leg
jambon *n.m.* ham
janvier *n.m.* January
jardin *n.m.* yard; garden
jardin d'enfants *n.m.* kindergarten
jardinier *n.m.* gardener
jaune *adj.* yellow
je *pron.* I
jetable *adj.* disposable
jeter *v.* to throw; to discard; to toss
jeton *n.m.* token
jeu *n.m.* game
jeu de carte *n.m.* deck of cards
jeudi *n.m.* Thursday
jeune *adj.* young; juvenile
jeunesse *n.f.* youth
joindre *v.* to join
joli *adj.* nice; pretty
joue *n.f.* cheek
jouer *v.* to act (*theater*); to play; to gamble
jouet *n.m.* toy
jour *n.m.* day
jour de semaine *n.m.* weekday
jour férié *n.m.* holiday
journal *n.m.* newspaper; journal
journal intime *n.m.* diary
journaliste *n.m/f.* journalist
Joyeux Noël ! *inter.* Merry Christmas!
juge *n.m.* judge
Juif/Juive *n.m/f.* Jew; *adj.* Jewish
juillet *n.m.* July
juin *n.m.* June
jumeau/jumelle *n.m/f.; adj.* twin
jupe *n.f.* skirt
jus *n.m.* juice
jusqu'à *prep.* until
juste *adj.* fair; just; right
justice *n.f.* justice
juteux *adj.* juicy
juvénile *adj.* juvenile

K

kascher *adj.* kosher
kilo *n.m.* kilo
kilomètre *n.m.* kilometer
kiosque à journaux *n.m.* newsstand

L

là *adv.* there
lac *n.m.* lake
lacet *n.m.* shoe lace
laid *adj.* ugly
laine *n.f.* wool
laisser *v.* to leave; to let
laissez-passer *n.m.* pass; permit
lait *n.m.* milk
laiterie *n.f.* dairy
lame *n.f.* blade
lame de rasoir *n.f.* razor blade
lampe *n.f.* lamp
lampe de poche *n.f.* flashlight
lancer *v.* to throw
langage des signes *n.m.* sign language

langue *n.f.* language; tongue
lapin *n.m.* rabbit
laque *n.f.* hairspray
large *adj.* wide
larme *n.f.* tear (*cry*)
lavande *n.f.* lavender
(se) laver *v.* wash
laverie automatique *n.f.* Laundromat
laxatif *n.m.* laxative
le; la; l'; les *art.* the
leçon *n.f.* lesson
lecteur de CD *n.m.* CD player
lecteur/lectrice *n.m/f.* reader
légal *adj.* legal; lawful
léger *adj.* light (*weight*)
légitime *adj.* legitimate
légume *n.m.* vegetable
lent *adj.* slow
lentille *n.f.* lens
les deux *adj.* both
lettre *n.f.* letter
(se) lever *v.* to rise; to get up
lever de soleil *n.m.* sunrise
lèvre *n.f.* lip
liberté *n.f.* freedom; liberty
librairie *n.f.* bookstore
libre *adj.* free; vacant
lien *n.m.* link
lieu *n.m.* place; location
ligne *n.f.* line
ligue *n.f.* league
limite *n.f.* limit
limiter *v.* to limit
lin *n.m.* linen (*fabric*)
linge *n.m.* linen (*clothes*); laundry
liquide *n.m.; adj.* liquid
lire *v.* to read
liste *n.f.* list
lit *n.m.* bed
lit d'enfant *n.m.* crib
lit de camp *n.m.* cot
litre *n.m.* liter
littérature *n.f.* literature
livraison *n.f.* delivery
livre *n.f.* pound; *n.m.* book
livrer *v.* to deliver
local *adj.* local
locataire *n.m/f.* tenant
location *n.f.* rental
logement *n.m.* accommodations
loger *v.* to house; to stay
loi *n.f.* law
loin *adv.* away; far
loisir *n.m.* leisure
long *adj.* long
longtemps *adv.* long time
longueur *n.f.* length
louer *v.* to lease; to rent
lourd *adj.* heavy
loyer *n.m.* rent
lumière *n.f.* light
lundi *n.m.* Monday
lune *n.f.* moon
lunettes *n.f.pl.* glasses
lunettes de soleil *n.f.pl.* sunglasses
luxe *n.m.* luxury
luxueux *adj.* luxurious
lycée *n.m.* high school

M

machine à laver *n.f.* washing machine
mâchoire *n.f.* jaw
madame *n.f.* (*pl.* **mesdames**) Mrs.; madam
mademoiselle *n.f.* (*pl.* **mesdemoiselles**) Ms.; miss
magasin *n.m.* shop, store
magazine *n.m.* magazine
magnétoscope *n.m.* VCR
mai *n.m.* May
maigre *adj.* lean
maillot de bain *n.m.* swimsuit
main *n.f.* hand
maintenant *adv.* now
mais *conj.* but
maison *n.f.* house; home
maître *n.m.* master
majorité *n.f.* majority
mal *n.m.* ache; harm
mal à l'aise *adj.* uneasy
malade *adj.* ill; sick
maladie *n.f.* disease; illness

maladie vénérienne *n.f.* venereal disease
mal de dent *n.m.* toothache
mal de mer *n.m.* seasickness
mal de tête *n.m.* headache
mal du pays *n.m.* homesickness
mâle *n.m.; adj.* male
malentendu *n.m.* misunderstanding
malheureux *adj.* unhappy
manche *n.f.* sleeve
manger *v.* to eat
manière *n.f.* fashion; way; manner
manifestation *n.f.* rally; demonstration
mannequin *n.m.* model (*fashion*)
manquer *v.* to miss
manteau *n.m.* coat
maquillage *n.m.* makeup
marais *n.m.* swamp
marchand/marchande *n.m/f.* merchant; trader
marchander *v.* to bargain
marchandise *n.f.* merchandise
marche *n.f.* step (*stairs*)
marché *n.m.* deal; market
marche arrière *n.f.* reverse (*car*)
marché aux puces *n.m.* flea market
marcher *v.* to walk
mardi *n.m.* Tuesday
marée *n.f.* tide
marge *n.f.* margin
mari *n.m.* husband
mariage *n.m.* marriage; wedding
(se) marier *v.* to marry; to get married
mariée *n.f.* bride
marin *n.m.* sailor
marine *n.f.* navy
marque *n.f.* mark
marraine *n.f.* godmother
mars *n.m.* March
marteau *n.m.* hammer
masculin *adj.* male; masculine
masque *n.m.* mask
masse *n.f.* mass
match *n.m.* game (*sports*)
match nul *n.m.* tie (*sports*)
matelas *n.m.* mattress
maternité *n.f.* maternity
matin *n.m.* morning
mauvais *adj.* bad
maximum *n.m.; adj.* maximum
mécanicien *n.m.* mechanic
mécanique *adj.* mechanical
méchant *adj.* mean
médaille *n.f.* medal
médecin *n.m.* physician
médical *adj.* medical
médicament *n.m.* prescription drug; medication
Méditerranée *n.f.* Mediterranean Sea
méduse *n.f.* jelly fish
meilleur *adj.* best; better
mélange *n.m.* blend
mélanger *v.* to blend; to mix
membre *n.m.* limb; member
même *adv.* even; *adj.* same
mémoire *n.f.* memory
mémoire vive *n.f.* RAM
menace *n.f.* threat
mendier *v.* to beg
mener *v.* to lead
mensonge *n.m.* lie
menteur/menteuse *n.m/f.* liar
menthe *n.f.* mint
mentir *v.* to lie
menton *n.m.* chin
menu *n.m.* menu
mépris *n.m.* contempt
mer *n.f.* sea
Merci ! *inter.* Thank you!
mercredi *n.m.* Wednesday
mère *n.f.* mother
message *n.m.* message
messe *n.f.* mass (*church*)
mesure *n.f.* measure
mesurer *v.* to measure
métal *n.m.* metal
météo *n.f.* weather forecast
métier *n.m.* job; occupation
métier artisanal *n.m.* craft
mètre *n.m.* meter
métro *n.m.* subway
mettre *v.* to put; to place

mettre en colère (se) *v.* to get angry
mettre son clignotant *v.* to signal (*vehicle*)
meuble *n.m.* furniture
meurtre *n.m.* murder
meurtrier *n.m.* murderer
miche *n.f.* loaf (*bread*)
microbe *n.m.* germ
midi *n.m.* noon
miel *n.m.* honey
miette *n.f.* crumb
milieu *n.m.* middle
militaire *adj.* military
mille *num.* thousand
milliard *num.* billion
million *num.* million
mince *adj.* thin
mineur/mineure *n.m/f.* minor
minimum *adj.* minimum
minorité *n.f.* minority
minuit *n.m.* midnight
minute *n.f.* minute
miroir *n.m.* mirror
mode *n.f.* fashion
modem *n.m.* modem
moderne *adj.* modern; up-to-date
moine *n.m.* monk
moins *adv.; pron.; prep.* less; *prep.* minus
mois *n.m.* month
moisissure *n.f.* mold
moisson *n.m.* harvest
moitié *n.f.* half
moment *n.m.* moment
monastère *n.m.* monastery
monde *n.m.* world
monnaie *n.f.* change (*coins*); currency
monsieur *n.m.* (*pl.* **messieurs**) Mr.; sir
mont *n.m.* mount
montagne *n.f.* mountain
montant de tente *n.m.* tent pole
monter *v.* to rise
monter à bord *v.* to board (*ship; plane*)
monter dans *v.* to board (*train*)
montre *n.f.* watch
montrer *v.* to show
monture *n.f.* frame (*glasses*)
monument *n.m.* monument
morceau *n.m.* piece; bit
mordre *v.* to bite
morsure *n.f.* bite
mort *n.f.* death; *adj.* dead
mortel *adj.* deadly
mosquée *n.f.* mosque
mot *n.m.* word
moteur *n.m.* engine
moto *n.f.* motorbike
mots croisés *n.m.pl.* crossword
mouche *n.f.* fly
mouchoir *n.m.* tissue
moudre *v.* to grind
mouillé *adj.* wet
moulin *n.m.* mill
moulu *adj.* ground (*coffee*)
mourir *v.* to die
moustache *n.f.* mustache
moustiquaire *n.f.* mosquito net
moustique *n.m.* mosquito
moutarde *n.f.* mustard
mouvement *n.m.* move; motion
moyen *adj.* average
muet *adj.* mute
multiplier *v.* to multiply
mûr *adj.* ripe; mature
mur *n.m.* wall
muscle *n.m.* muscle
musée *n.m.* museum
musicien/musicienne *n.m/f.* musician
musique *n.f.* music

N

nager *v.* to swim
nain *n.m.* dwarf
naissance *n.f.* birth
nappe *n.* tablecloth
narine *n.f.* nostril
natal *adj.* native (*country*)
nation *n.f.* nation
nationalité *n.f.* nationality
nature *n.f.; adj.* nature; plain (*no flavor*)

naturel *adj.* natural
nausée *n.f.* nausea
navette *n.f.* shuttle
naviguer *v.* navigate
né *adj.* born
nécessaire *adj.* necessary
négatif *adj.* negative
neige *n.f.* snow
neiger *v.* to snow
ne pas être d'accord *v.* to disagree
nerf *n.m.* nerve
nerveux *adj.* nervous
nettoyer *v.* to clean
neuf *num.* nine; *adj.* new
neutre *adj.* neutral
neveu *n.m.* nephew
nez *n.m.* nose
nid *n.m.* nest
nièce *n.f.* niece
noblesse *n.f.* nobility
Noël *n.m.* Christmas
nœud *n.m.* bow; knot
noir *adj.* black
nom *n.m.* name; noun
nombre *n.m.* number
nombreux *adj.* numerous
nombril *n.m.* navel
nom de jeune fille *n.m.* maiden name
nommer *v.* to name
non *adv.* no
non autorisé *adj.* unauthorized
non comestible *adj.* toxic
nord *n.m.* north
normal *adj.* normal
note *n.f.* note
noter *v.* to write down
nouer *v.* to tie a knot
nourrir *v.* to feed
nourrissant *adj.* nourishing
nourriture *n.f.* food
nous *pron.* we
nouveau *adj.* new
Nouvel An *n.m.* New Year
nouvelles *n.f.pl.* news
novembre *n.m.* November
noyau *n.m.* core
noyer *v.* to drown
nu *adj.* bare; naked; in the nude
nuage *n.m.* cloud
nuit *n.f.* night
nul *adj.* void
numéro *n.m.* number; issue (*magazine*)
numéro de téléphone *n.m.* telephone number
nu-pieds *adj.* barefoot
nuque *n.f.* neck

O

obèse *adj.* obese
objectif *n.m.* lens (*camera*)
objection *n.f.* objection
objet *n.m.* object
objet de valeur *n.m.* valuables
obligatoire adj. mandatory
obscène *adj.* obscene
obscurité *n.f.* darkness
observer *v.* to observe
obstacle *n.m.* obstacle
obtenir *v.* to get; to obtain
occasion *n.f.* opportunity; occasion; bargain
occupation *n.f.* occupation
occupé *adj.* busy
occuper *v.* to occupy
océan *n.m.* ocean
octobre *n.m.* October
odeur *n.f.* scent; smell; odor
œil *n.m.* (*pl.* **yeux**) eye
œuf *n.m.* egg
officiel *adj.* official
officier *n.m.* officer (*military*)
offre *n.f.* offer
oignon *n.m.* onion
oiseau *n.m.* bird
ombre *n.f.* shade
on *pron.* one, we, you (*indefinite pron.*)
once *n.f.* ounce
oncle *n.* uncle
ongle *n.m.* nail (*finger*)
onze *num.* eleven
opération *n.f.* operation
opinion *n.f.* opinion

opposé *adj.* opposite
opticien *n.m.* optician
option *n.f.* option
or *n.m.* gold
orage *n.m.* thunderstorm; storm
oral *adj.* oral
orange *n.f.; adj.* orange (*fruit; color*)
orchestre *n.m.* orchestra
ordinaire *adj.* ordinary
ordinateur *n.m.* computer
ordonnance *n.f.* prescription
ordre *n.m.* order
ordures *n.f.pl.* trash; garbage
oreille *n.f.* ear
oreiller *n.m.* pillow
organisation *n.f.* organization
organiser *v.* to organize
origine *n.f.* origin
orteil *n.m.* toe
os *n.m.* bone
ou *conj.* or
où *adv.* where
oublier *v.* to forget
ouest *n.m.* west
oui *adv.* yes
ouragan *n.m.* hurricane
ourlet *n.m.* hem
outil *n.m.* tool
ouvert *adj.* open
ouvrir *v.* to open
oxygène *n.m.* oxygen

P

page *n.f.* page
paie *n.f.* pay; wage
paiement *n.m.* payment
paille *n.f.* straw
pain *n.m.* bread
paix *n.f.* peace
palais *n.m.* palate
pâle *adj.* pale
panier *n.m.* basket
panne *n.f.* breakdown
panneau *n.m.* sign (*road*)
pansement *n.m.* bandage
pantalon *n.m.* pants
pantoufle *n.f.* slipper
papa *n.m.* dad
pape *n.m.* pope
papier *n.m.* paper
papier hygiénique *n.m.* toilet paper
Pâques *n.f.* Easter
paradis *n.m.* heaven
paralyser *v.* to paralyze
parapluie *n.* umbrella (*rain*)
parasol *n.m.* umbrella (*sun*)
par avion *n.m.* airmail
parc *n.m.* park
pare-brise *n.m.* windshield
pareil *adj.* alike; same
parent/parente *n.m/f.* relative
parents *n.m.pl.* parents
paresseux *adj.* lazy
parfait *adj.* perfect
parfum *n.m.* flavor, perfume; scent
parking *n.m.* parking lot
parler *v.* to talk, to speak
parole *n.f.* speech
parrain *n.m.* godfather
part *n.f.* share
partager *v.* to share
partenaire *n.m.* partner
parti *n.m.* party (*politics*)
partir *v.* to go, to leave
(ne ...) pas *adv.* not
passager/passagère *n.m/f.* passenger
passé *n.m.* past
passeport *n.m.* passport
passer *v.* to pass (*move*); to spend (*time*); to connect (*call*)
pasteur *n.m.* minister
pâte *n.f.* dough
pâté de maisons *n.m.* block (*buildings*)
patient/patiente *n.m/f.; adj.* patient
patin à glace *n.m.* ice skate
patiner *v.* to skate
pâtisserie *n.f.* pastry
patrie *n.f.* homeland
patron *n.m.* boss
patte *n.f.* paw
paupière *n.f.* eyelid
pause *n.f.* break, pause

pauvre *adj.* poor
payé d'avance *adj.* prepaid
payer *v.* to pay
pays *n.m.* country; land
paysage *n.m.* landscape; scenery
pays natal *n.m.* home country
péage *n.m.* toll
peau *n.f.* skin
pêcher *v.* to fish
pêcheur *n.m.* fisherman
pédale *n.f.* pedal
peigne *n.m.* comb
peignoir *n.m.* (bath)robe
peindre *v.* to paint
peinture *n.f.* paint; painting
pelouse *n.f.* lawn
pendre *v.* to hang
pendule *n.f.* clock
penser *v.* to think
pension complète *n.f.* full board
pension de famille *n.f.* guesthouse
pensionnat *n.m.* boarding school
pente *n.f.* incline; slope
perdre *v.* to lose
perdu *adj.* lost
père *n.m.* father
père Noël *n.m.* Santa Claus
perle *n.f.* pearl
permettre *v.* to allow
permis *n.m.* license; permit
permis de conduire *n.m.* driver's license
perruque *n.f.* wig
personne *n.f.* person; *pron.* nobody, no one
personne âgée *n.f.* senior citizen
perte *n.f.* loss
peser *v.* weigh
petit *adj.* short, small; little
petit déjeuner *n.m.* breakfast
petite-fille *n.f.* granddaughter
petit-fils *n.m.* grandson
petits-enfants *n.m.pl.* grandchildren
peu *adv.* a bit; a little
peuple *n.m.* people (*of a country*)
peu profond *adj.* shallow (*water*)
peur *n.f.* fear
peu sûr *adj.* unsafe
peut-être *adv.* maybe; perhaps
phare *n.m.* headlight
pharmacie *n.f.* pharmacy, drugstore
photocopie *n.f.* photocopy
photo(graphie) *n.f.* photo, picture
photographier *v.* to photograph
phrase *n.f.* sentence
pièce *n.f.* coin; room; part (*machine*); play (*theater*)
pièce de monnaie *n.f.* coin
pièce de rechange *n.f.* spare part
pièce de théâtre *n.f.* drama
pied *n.m.* foot
pierre *n.f.* rock; stone
pierre tombale *n.f.* gravestone; tombstone
piéton *n.m.* pedestrian
pile *n.f.* battery (*remote control*)
pilote *n.m.* pilot
piloter *v.* to pilot
pilule *n.f.* birth control pill
pince à épiler *n.f.* tweezers
pinte *n.f.* pint
pipe *n.f.* pipe (*smoking*)
pique-nique *n.m.* picnic
piquer *v.* to sting
piquet de tente *n.m.* tent peg
piqûre *n.f.* injection; sting; bite (*insect*)
pire *n.m.; adj.* worse
piscine *n.f.* swimming pool
piste *n.f.* track; trail
pistolet *n.m.* gun
placard *n.m.* closet
place *n.f.* seat; town square; space; room
placer *v.* to place, to position
plafond *n.m.* ceiling
plage *n.f.* beach
(se) plaindre *v.* to complain
plainte *n.f.* complaint
plaisanter *v.* to joke
plaisanterie *n.f.* joke
plaisir *n.m.* enjoyment; pleasure
plan *n.m.* street map; plan
planche *n.f.* board

planche à repasser *n.f.* ironing board
plante *n.f.* plant
plaque minéralogique *n.f.* license plate
plastique *n.m.* plastic
plat *n.m.* dish; *adj.* flat
plein *adj.* full
pleurer *v.* to cry, to weep
pleuvoir *v.* to rain
pli *n.m.* wrinkle, pleat (*fabric*); fold
plombier *n.m.* plumber
plongeon *n.m.* dive
plonger *v.* to dive
plongeur/plongeuse *n.m/f.* diver
pluie *n.f.* rain
plume *n.f.* feather
pluriel *n.m.; adj.* plural
plus *prep.* plus
plus de *adv.* more
plus tard *adv.* later
pluvieux *adj.* rainy
pneu *n.m.* tire
poche *n.f.* pocket
poêle *n.f.* frying pan, skillet
poésie *n.f.* poetry
poids *n.m.* weight
poignée *n.f.* handle; handful
poignée de main *n.f.* handshake
poignet *n.m.* wrist
poils *n.m.pl.* hair (*body*)
point de suture *n.m.* stitch (*medical*)
pointe *n.f.* tip
pointure *n.f.* shoe size
poison *n.m.* poison
poisson *n.m.* fish
poitrine *n.f.* chest
poivre *n.m.* pepper
poli *adj.* polite
police *n.f.* police
police d'assurance *n.f.* insurance policy
politique *n.f.* politics; *adj.* political
pomme *n.f.* apple
pompe *n.f.* pump
pompier *n.m.* fireman
pont *n.m.* deck; bridge
porcelaine *n.f.* china
port *n.m.* harbor
(ordinateur) portable *n.m.* laptop
portail *n.m.* gate
porte *n.f.* door; gate (*airport*)
portefeuille *n.m.* wallet
porter *v.* to carry; to wear
poser *v.* to put, to set; to lay
positif *adj.* positive
possessions *n.f.pl.* belongings
possible *adj.* possible
poste *n.f.* post office
poste de police *n.m.* police station
poste de secours *n.m.* first-aid post
postuler *v.* to apply (*job*)
pot *n.m.* jar
pot d'échappement *n.m.* exhaust
poteau *n.m.* pole
poubelle *n.f.* trash can
pouce *n.m.* inch; thumb
poudre *n.f.* powder
poumon *n.m.* lung
poupée *n.f.* doll
pour *prep.* for
pour cent *n.; adj.; adv.* percent
pourboire *n.m.* tip, gratuity
pourquoi *conj.* why
pourri *adj.* rotten
poursuivre en justice *v.* to sue
pousser *v.* to push; to grow (*plant*)
poussière *n.f.* dust
pouvoir *n.m.* power; *v.* can, to be able to
pratique *adj.* useful, handy; practical
précis *adj.* accurate; precise; sharp (*time*)
préférer *v.* to prefer
premier *adj.* first
premier ministre *n.m.* prime minister
prendre *v.* to take
prendre garde *v.* to beware
prendre sa retraite *v.* to retire
prendre un bain *v.* to bathe
près *adj.* close; near
présent *n.m.* present (*time*)
préservatif *n.m.* condom

président/présidente *n.m/f.* president
pression *n.f.* pressure
prêt *n.m.* loan; *adj.* ready
prêter *v.* to lend, to loan
prêtre *n.m.* priest
preuve *n.f.* proof; evidence
prier *v.* to pray
prière *n.f.* prayer
principal *adj.* main; principal
printemps *n.m.* spring (*season*)
prise (de courant) *n.f.* plug; socket; jack
prison *n.f.* jail; prison
prisonnier/prisonnière *n.m/f.* prisoner
privé *adj.* private
prix *n.m.* price; fee
problème *n.m.* problem; trouble
procès *n.m.* trial; lawsuit
prochain *adj.* next (*time*)
proche *adj.* near, close
produit *n.m.* product
produit à lessive *n.m.* laundry detergent
professeur *n.m.* teacher; professor
profession *n.f.* profession
profil *n.m.* profile
profit *n.m.* benefit; profit
profond *adj.* deep
profondeur *n.f.* depth
programme *n.m.* program; schedule
progrès *n.m.* progress
projet *n.m.* project
projeter *v.* to project
promenade *n.f.* walk
promesse *n.f.* promise
proposer *v.* to suggest
proposition *n.f.* proposal
propre *adj.* clean; own
propriétaire *n.m/f.* owner; landlord
propriété *n.f.* property
protection *n.f.* protection
protestant *n.m.; adj.* Protestant
province *n.f.* province
provisions *n.f.pl.* groceries
prudence *n.f.* caution
pub *n.m.* pub
public *n.m.* audience; public
publicité *n.f.* advertisement; commercial
publier *v.* to publish
pull *n.m.* sweater
pur *adj.* pure
pyjama *n.m.* pajamas

Q

qualité *n.f.* quality
quand *adv.; conj.* when
quantité *n.f.* amount; quantity
quarantaine *n.f.* quarantine
quart *n.m.* quarter
quartier *n.m.* neighborhood
quatre *num.* four
que *conj.* that; than
quelqu'un *pron.* somebody
quelque chose *pron.* something
quelquefois *adv.* sometimes
question *n.f.* question; issue
queue *n.f.* line (*of people*)
qui *pron.* who
quitter *v.* to leave
quotidien *adj.* daily

R

rabais *n.m.* reduction (*price*); discount
rabbin *n.m.* rabbi
racisme *n.m.* racism
raconter *v.* to tell (*story*)
radiateur *n.m.* heater
radio *n.f.* radio
radiographie *n.f.* X ray
rafraîchissement *n.m.* refreshment
raide *adj.* straight (*hair*)
rampe *n.f.* ramp
ramper *v.* to crawl
randonnée *n.f.* hike
rang *n.m.* row
rapide *adj.* fast; quick
raquette *n.f.* racquet
rare *adj.* rare

(se) **raser** *v.* to shave
rasoir *n.m.* razor
rassembler *v.* to gather
rayon *n.m.* department (*in store*)
récent *adj.* up-to-date; recent
récepteur *n.m.* receiver
réception *n.f.* reception
recette *n.f.* recipe
recevoir *v.* to receive; to get; to entertain
recherche *n.f.* research; search
récipient *n.m.* container
récolte *n.f.* harvest
recommander *v.* to recommend
récompense *n.f.* reward
récompenser *v.* to reward
reconnaissant *adj.* thankful
reconnaître *v.* to recognize
record *n.m.* record
récréation *n.f.* break (*at school*)
reçu *n.m.* receipt
reculer *v.* to reverse, to back up (*car*); to move back
réduction *n.f.* reduction
réduire *v.* to reduce
réfrigérateur *n.m.* refrigerator
regarder *v.* to look at; to watch
régime *n.m.* diet
région *n.f.* area; region
règlement *n.m.* regulation
régler *v.* to settle (*matter*)
règles *n.f.pl.* menstruation
regret *n.m.* regret
regretter *v.* to regret
régulier *adj.* even; regular; steady
rein *n.m.* kidney
reine *n.f.* queen
relation *n.f.* connection; relationship
relier *v.* to connect
religieuse *n.f.* nun
religieux *adj.* religious
religion *n.f.* religion
remarquer *v.* to notice; to remark
remboursement *n.m.* refund
rembourser *v.* to refund
remercier *v.* to thank
remettre *v.* to put back
remorquer *v.* to tow
remplir *v.* to fill
rencontre *n.f.* encounter; meeting
rencontrer *v.* to encounter; to meet
rendez-vous *n.m.* appointment; date (*romantic*)
rendre visite à *v.* to visit (*someone*)
renommé *adj.* renown
renouveler *v.* to renew
renseignement *n.m.* information
réparation *n.f.* repair
réparer *v.* to repair; to fix
repas *n.m.* meal
repasser *v.* to iron
répéter *v.* to repeat
répondre *v.* to answer; to respond
réponse *n.f.* answer; reply; response
repos *n.m.* rest
(se) **reposer** *v.* to rest
représentant *n.m.* representative
reprise *n.f.* repeat
république *n.f.* republic
réputation *n.f.* reputation
requête *n.f.* request
requin *n.m.* shark
réseau *n.m.* network
réservation *n.f.* reservation
réserver *v.* to book; to reserve
respect *n.m.* respect; regard
respecter *v.* to respect
respirer *v.* to breathe
responsable *adj.* liable; responsible
restaurant *n.m.* restaurant
rester *v.* to stay; to remain
résultat *n.m.* result
résumé *n.m.* summary
retard *n.m.* delay
retarder *v.* to delay
retirer *v.* withdraw
retour *n.m.* return
retourner *v.* to return; to go back
rétrécir *v.* to narrow (*road*); to shrink (*fabric*)
réunion *n.f.* meeting
réussir *v.* to pass (*test*)
rêve *n.m.* dream
réveil *n.m.* alarm clock
(se) **réveiller** *v.* wake (up)

rêver *v.* to dream
revue *n.f.* magazine; review
rhume *n.m.* cold (*sick*)
rhume des foins *n.m.* hay fever
riche *adj.* rich
ride *n.f.* wrinkle (*skin*)
rideau *n.m.* curtain
rien *pron.* nothing
rincer *v.* to rinse
rire *n.m.* laugh; *v.* to laugh
risque *n.m.* risk; hazard
risquer *v.* to risk
rivage *n.m.* shore
rive *n.f.* bank
rivière *n.f.* river
riz *n.m.* rice
robe *n.f.* dress; gown
robinet *n.m.* faucet
roi *n.m.* king
roman *n.m.* novel
rond *adj.* round
ronfler *v.* to snore
rose *n.f.* rose; *adj.* pink
rosée *n.f.* dew
roue *n.f.* wheel
rouge *adj.* red
rouge à lèvres *n.m.* lipstick
rouille *n.f.* rust
rouler *v.* to drive; to roll
route *n.f.* road
route nationale *n.f.* highway
roux *adj.* red (*hair*)
royal *adj.* royal
ruche *n.f.* hive
rue *n.f.* street
ruelle *n.f.* alley
ruine *n.f.* ruin
ruisseau *n.m.* stream

S

sabbat *n.m.* Sabbath
sable *n.m.* sand
sac *n.m.* bag
sac à dos *n.m.* backpack
sac à main *n.m.* purse
sac de couchage *n.m.* sleeping bag
saigner *v.* to bleed
sain *adj.* healthy
Saint-Sylvestre *n.f.* New Year's Eve
saison *n.f.* season
salade *n.f.* salad; lettuce
salaire *n.m.* pay; salary; earnings
sale *adj.* dirty
salé *adj.* savory
saler *v.* to salt
saleté *n.f.* dirt
salive *n.f.* saliva
salle à manger *n.f.* dining room
salle d'attente *n.f.* waiting room
salle de bains *n.f.* bathroom
salle de séjour *n.f.* living room
salon *n.m.* lounge
saluer *v.* to greet
Salut ! *inter.* Hi!
samedi *n.m.* Saturday
sandale *n.f.* sandal
sang *n.m.* blood
sans *prep.* without
Santé ! *inter.* Cheers!
santé *n.f.* health
sauf *prep.* except
saut *n.m.* hop; jump
sauter *v.* to hop; to jump
sauvage *adj.* wild
sauver *v.* to rescue
sauvetage *n.m.* rescue
savoir *v.* to know
savon *n.m.* soap
savoureux *adj.* tasty
science *n.f.* science
scientifique *adj.* scientific
sculpter *v.* to sculpt
sculpture *n.f.* sculpture
sec *adj.* dry
sécher *v.* to dry
séchoir *n.m.* dryer
second *n.m.; adj.* second
seconde *n.f.* second (*time*)
secret *n.m.; adj.* secret
secrétaire *n.f.* secretary
sécurité *n.f.* safety; security
séduisant *adj.* attractive
sein *n.m.* breast
séjour *n.m.* stay
sel *n.m.* salt
sélection *n.f.* selection

self-service *n.m.; adj.* self-service
selle *n.f.* saddle
semaine *n.f.* week
semblable *adj.* similar
semestre *n.m.* semester
sensation *n.f.* feeling (*physical*); feel
sentiment *n.m.* feeling
sentir *v.* to feel; to smell
sentir mauvais *v.* to stink
séparer *v.* to separate
sept *num.* seven
septembre *n.m.* September
sérieux *adj.* serious
seringue *n.f.* syringe
serpent *n.m.* snake
serrer dans ses bras *v.* to hug
serrure *n.f.* lock
serrurier *n.m.* locksmith
serveur *n.m.* waiter
serveuse *n.f.* waitress
serviette *n.f.* napkin; towel
serviette hygiénique *n.f.* sanitary pad
(se) souvenir *v.* to remember
seul *adj.* only; lonely; alone
seulement *adv.* only
sexe *n.m.* sex
shampooing *n.m.* shampoo
short *n.m.* shorts
siècle *n.m.* century
siège *n.m.* seat; headquarters (*business*)
signature *n.f.* signature
signe *n.m.* sign
signer *v.* to sign
signification *n.f.* meaning
signifier *v.* to mean
silence *n.m.* silence
silencieux *adj.* silent
s'il te/vous plaît *inter.* please
simple *adj.* plain; simple
sincèrement *adv.* sincerely
site *n.m.* site
site Web *n.m.* website
six *num.* six
ski *n.m.* ski
ski nautique *n.m.* water-skiing
skier *v.* to ski
sœur *n.f.* sister
soie *n.f.* silk
soif *n.f.* thirst
soigné *adj.* neat
soigner *v.* to treat (*medical*); to nurse; to take care of
soin *n.m.* care
soir *n.m.* evening; night
soirée *n.f.* evening
soja *n.m.* soy
sol *n.m.* ground; soil
solde *n.m.* balance (*bank*)
soldes *n.f.pl.* sale (*reduced price*)
soleil *n.m.* sun
solide *adj.* solid
sombre *adj.* dark
somme *n.m* nap; *n.f.* sum
sommeil *n.m.* sleep
sommet *n.m.* peak; top
somnifère *n.m.* sleeping pill
son *n.m.* sound
sonner *v.* to ring
sonnette *n.f.* bell
sortie *n.f.* exit
sortir *v.* to exit; to come out
souci *n.m.* care; worry; concern
souffrir *v.* to suffer
souhait *n.m.* wish
souhaiter *v.* to wish
soulager *v.* to relieve
soulever *v.* to lift
soupe *n.f.* soup
souper *n.m.* supper
sourcil *n.m.* eyebrow
sourd *adj.* deaf
sourire *n.m.; v.* smile
souris *n.f.* mouse
sous *prep.* under; below
sous la main *adj.* handy (*close*)
sous-sol *n.m.* basement
sous-titre *n.m.* subtitle
sous-vêtements *n.* underwear
souvenir *n.m.* memory; memento; souvenir
souvent *adv.* often
spécial *adj.* special
spécialité *n.f.* specialty
spectacle *n.m.* show

spectateur/spectatrice *n.m/f.* spectator
sport *n.m.* sport; *adj.* casual (*clothes*)
stade *n.m.* stadium
standardiste *n.m/f.* operator (*phone*)
station *n.f.* resort
station thermale *n.f.* spa
statue *n.f.* statue
steward *n.m.* flight attendant (*male*)
stimulateur cardiaque *n.m.* pacemaker
stress *n.m.* stress; tension
stupide *adj.* silly; stupid
stylo *n.m.* pen
succès *n.m.* success
sucer *v.* to suck
sucré *adj.* sweet (*food*)
sucre *n.m.* sugar
sud *n.m.* south
suer *v.* to sweat
sueur *n.f.* sweat
suicide *n.m.* suicide
Suisse *n.f.* Switzerland; *n.m/f.; adj.* Swiss
suivre *v.* to follow
sujet *n.m.* subject
superficiel *adj.* shallow (*person*)
supermarché *n.m.* supermarket
supplémentaire *adj.* additional
sûr *adj.* positive; sure; safe
sur *prep.* on; over
surf des neiges *n.m.* snowboard
surnom *n.m.* nickname
suspect *n.m.; adj.* suspect
symptôme *n.m.* symptom
synagogue *n.f.* synagogue
syndicat d'initiative *n.m.* tourist office

T

tabac *n.m.* tobacco
table *n.f.* table
tableau *n.m.* painting (*art*); board (*notice*)
tablette de chocolat *n.f.* chocolate bar
tache *n.f.* stain
taie d'oreiller *n.f.* pillowcase
taille *n.f.* height; size; waist
tailleur *n.m.* tailor; suit (*women*)
talon *n.m.* heel
tampon *n.m.* tampon
tante *n.f.* aunt
tapis *n.m.* carpet; rug
taquiner *v.* to tease
tard *adj.* late
tarif *n.m.* rate; price
tarte *n.f.* pie
tasse *n.f.* cup
tatouage *n.m.* tattoo
taux *n.m.* rate
taux de change *n.m.* exchange rate
taxe *n.f.* tax
taxer *v.* to tax
taxi *n.m.* cab, taxi
teinture *n.f.* dye
télécommande *n.f.* remote control
téléconférence *n.f.* teleconferencing
téléphone *n.m.* telephone
téléphoner *v.* to call (*phone*)
télévision *n.f.* television
témoin *n.m.* witness
température *n.f.* temperature
tempête *n.f.* storm
temple *n.m.* temple
temporaire *adj.* temporary
temps *n.m.* time; weather
temps libre *n.m.* leisure time, free time
tenir *v.* to keep (*promise*); to hold; to run (*store*)
tennis *n.m.* tennis
tente *n.f.* tent
terminé *adj.* over
terminer *v.* to end; to finish
terrasse *n.f.* terrace
terre *n.f.* earth; land; dirt
tête *n.f.* head
texte *n.m.* text
thé *n.m.* tea

théâtre *n.m.* theater
thermomètre *n.m.* thermometer
ticket *n.m.* ticket (*train*)
tiède *adj.* tepid, lukewarm
timbre *n.m.* stamp
tirer *v.* to draw; to fire; to pull; to shoot
tissu *n.m.* fabric; cloth
titre *n.m.* headline; title
toboggan *n.m.* slide (*playground*)
toilettes *n.f.pl.* rest room
toit *n.m.* roof
tombe *n.f.* grave
tomber *v.* to fall
tonnerre *n.m.* thunder
tort *n.m.* harm; wrong
tôt *adv.* early; soon
total *n.m.* total
toucher *n.m.* touch; *v.* to touch
toujours *adv.* always; at all times
tour *n.m.* ride; turn; tour; tower
tourisme *n.m.* tourism; sight-seeing
touriste *n.m* tourist
tournant *n.m.* turn (*road*)
tourner *v.* to turn
tournevis *n.m.* screwdriver
tournoi *n.m.* tournament
tousser *v.* to cough
tout *adj.* everything; all
toux *n.f.* cough
toxique *adj.* poisonous, toxic
tradition *n.f.* tradition
traducteur/traductrice *n.m/f.* translator
traduction *n.f.* translation
traduire *v.* to translate
trafic *n.m.* traffic
train *n.m.* train
trait d'union *n.m.* hyphen
trajet *n.m.* journey; distance
tranche *n.f.* slice
trancher *v.* to slice
tranquille *adj.* quiet
transfert *n.m.* transfer
transpirer *v.* to perspire
transporter *v.* to carry; to transport
transports en commun *n.m.pl.* public transportation
travail *n.m.* job; work; labor
travailler *v.* to work
traverser *v.* to cross
tremper *v.* to soak
très *adv.* very
tribunal *n.m.* court (*law*)
trimestre *n.m.* quarter
triste *adj.* sad
trois *num.* three
trop *adv.* too
trottoir *n.m.* sidewalk
trou *n.m.* gap; hole
trou de la serrure *n.m.* keyhole
trouver *v.* to find
tu *pron.* you (*informal*)
tuer *v.* to kill
tumeur *n.f.* tumor
tunnel *n.m.* tunnel
typique *adj.* typical

U

ulcère *n.m.* ulcer
un *num.* one
un/une *art.* a
une fois *adv.* once
uni *adj.* solid (*color*)
Union européenne *n.f.* European Union
unique *adj.* only; unique
unité *n.f.* unit
universel *adj.* universal
université *n.f.* college; university
urgence *n.f.* emergency
urgent *adj.* urgent
urine *n.f.* urine
urinoir *n.m.* urinal
urne *n.f.* urn
usage *n.m.* use
usine *n.f.* factory
ustensile *n.m.* utensil
utiliser *v.* to use

V

vacances *n.f.pl.* vacation
vaccin *n.m.* vaccine
vacciner *v.* to vaccinate
vache *n.f.* cow
vague *n.f.* wave
valable *adj.* valid
valeur *n.f.* value
valider *v.* to validate
validité *n.f.* validity
valise *n.f.* suitcase
vallée *n.f.* valley
vanille *n.f.* vanilla
vapeur *n.f.* steam
végétarien *adj.* vegetarian
veille de la Toussaint *n.f.* Halloween
veine *n.f.* vein
vélo *n.m.* bicyle, bike
vendange *n.f.* grape harvest
vendre *v.* to sell
vendredi *n.m.* Friday
vénéneux *adj.* poisonous (*mushroom*)
venimeux *adj.* poisonous (*snake*)
venin *n.m.* venom
venir *v.* to come
vent *n.m.* wind
vente *n.f.* sale
vente aux enchères *n.f.* auction
ventilateur *n.m.* fan
ventre *n.m.* belly
ver *n.m.* worm
verbe *n.m.* verb
verdict *n.m.* verdict
verglacé *adj.* icy (*road*)
verglas *n.m.* black ice (*road*)
vérifier *v.* to check; to verify
véritable *adj.* real; true
vérité *n.f.* truth
vernis à ongles *n.m.* nail polish
verre *n.m.* drink; glass
verre de contact *n.m.* contact lens
verrou *n.m.* bolt
verrouiller *v.* to lock
vert *adj.* green
vertèbre *n.f.* vertebra
vessie *n.f.* bladder
veste *n.f.* jacket
vêtements *n.m.pl.* clothes
vétérinaire *n.m.* veterinarian
veuf *n.m.* widower
veuve *n.f.* widow
viande *n.f.* meat
victime *n.f.* victim
vide *adj.* empty
vie *n.f.* life
vieillir *v.* to age
vierge *n.f.; adj.* virgin
vieux *adj.* old
vif *adj.* sharp (*pain*)
vigne *n.f.* vine
vignoble *n.m.* vineyard
villa *n.f.* villa
village *n.m.* village
ville *n.f.* city; town
vin *n.m.* wine
vinaigre *n.m.* vinegar
viol *n.m.* rape
violent *adj.* violent
violer *v.* to rape
violet *adj.* purple
virgule *n.f.* comma
vis *n.f.* screw
visa *n.m.* visa
visage *n.m.* face
visibilité *n.f.* visibility
visite *n.f.* visit
visiter *v.* to visit (*place*)
visiteur *n.m.* visitor
vite *adv.* fast; quickly
vitesse *n.f.* speed
vitrine *n.f.* window (*store*)
vivre *v.* to live
vocabulaire *n.m.* vocabulary
vœu *n.m.* vow
voie *n.f.* track (*train*); lane
voie ferrée *n.f.* railroad
voile *n.f.* sail
voilier *n.m.* sailboat
voir *v.* to see
voisin *n.m.* neighbor; *adj.* next (*seat*)
voiture *n.f.* car

voix *n.f.* voice
vol *n.m.* flight; robbery; theft;
volaille *n.f.* poultry
volant *n.m.* steering wheel
voler *v.* to fly; to steal; to rob
volet *n.m.* shutter
voleur/voleuse *n.m/f.* thief
voltage *n.m.* voltage
vomi *n.m.* vomit
vomir *v.* to be sick; to vomit
vouloir *v.* to want
vouloir dire *v.* to mean
vous *pron.* you (*formal*)
voyage *n.m.* travel; journey
voyager *v.* to travel
voyageur/voyageuse *n.m/f.* traveler
voyelle *n.f.* vowel
vrai *adj.* true
vue *n.f.* view; sight

W

wagon *n.m.* car (*passenger train*); freight car
wagon-lit *n.m.* sleeper, sleeping car
watt *n.m.* watt
W.C. *n.m.pl.* restrooms
week-end *n.m.* weekend

XYZ

xénophobie *n.f.* xenophobia
yacht *n.m.* yacht
yaourt *n.m.* yogurt
zéro *num.* zero
zone piétonne *n.f.* pedestrian zone
zoo *n.m.* zoo
zoom *n.m.* zoom

ENGLISH-FRENCH DICTIONARY

A

a *art.* un *m.*, une *f.*
abbey *n.* abbaye *f.*
abbreviation *n.* abréviation *f.*
able *adj.* capable
aboard *adv.* à bord
abortion *n.* avortement *m.*
about *prep.* au sujet de, à propos de; *adv.* environ, à peu près
above *prep.* au-dessus de; *adv.* au-dessus
abroad *adv.* à l'étranger
abscess *n.* abcès *m.*
absorb *v.* absorber
abuse *n.* abus *m.*; *v.* abuser de
accelerate *v.* accélérer
accelerator *n.* accélérateur *m.*
accent *n.* accent *m.*
accept *v.* accepter
access *n.* accès *m.*
accessory *n.; adj.* accessoire *m.*
accident *n.* accident *m.*
accommodations *n.pl.* logement *m.*
account *n.* compte *m.* (*bank*)
accountant *n.* comptable *m/f.*
accurate *adj.* exact, précis
accuse *v.* accuser
accustom *v.* accoutumer
ace *n.* as *m.*
ache *n.* mal *m.*, douleur *f.*
achieve *v.* accomplir
acknowledgement *n.* reconnaissance *f.*
acne *n.* acné *m.*
acquaintance *n.* connaissance *f.*
across *prep.; adv.* à travers (*crosswise*); de l'autre côté (*on other side*); d'un côté à l'autre (*side to side*)
act *n.* acte *m.*; *v.* agir; jouer (*theater*)
action *n.* action *f.*
active *adj.* actif
activity *n.* activité *f.*
actor *n.* acteur *m.*
adapt *v.* adapter
add *v.* ajouter
addition *n.* addition *f.*
additional *adj.* supplémentaire
address *n.* addresse *f.*
adjective *n.* adjectif *m.*
adjust *v.* ajuster
administration *n.* administration *f.*
admire *v.* admirer
adolescence *n.* adolescence *f.*
adopt *v.* adopter
adult *n.* adulte *m/f.*
adultery *n.* adultère *m.*
advance *n.* avance *f.*; *v.* avancer
advantage *n.* avantage *m.*
adventure *n.* aventure *f.*
advertise *v.* faire de la publicité (pour)
advertisement *n.* publicité *f.*; annonce *f.* (*classifieds*)
advice *n.* conseil *m.*
affect *v.* affecter
afford *v.* avoir les moyens (de)
afraid *adj.* effrayé
Africa *n.* Afrique *f.*
African *n.; adj.* Africain *m.*, Africaine *f.*
after *adv.; prep.* après
afternoon *n.* après-midi *m/f.*
again *adv.* de nouveau, encore
against *prep.* contre
age *n.* âge *m.*; *v.* vieillir
agency *n.* agence *f.*
agent *n.* agent *m.*
aggression *n.* agression *f.*
aggressive *adj.* agressif
ago *adv.* il y a
agree *v.* être d'accord; convenir de (*price, date*)
agreement *n.* accord *m.*
ahead *adv.* devant; à l'avance (*in advance*)
air *n.* air *m.*; *v.* aérer
air-conditioning *n.* climatisation *f.*

airline *n.* compagnie d'aviation *f.*
airmail *n.* par avion
airplane *n.* avion *m.*
airport *n.* aéroport *m.*
alarm *n.* alarme *f.*; *v.* alarmer
alarm clock *n.* réveil *m.*
alcohol *n.* alcool *m.*
alien *n.; adj.* étranger *m.*, étrangère *f.*
alike *adj.* semblable, pareil; *adv.* de même
alive *adj.* vivant
all *adj.; pron.* tout (*sing*), tous (*m.pl.*), toutes (*f.pl.*); *adv.* tout *m.*, toute *f.*
allergic *adj.* allergique
allergy *n.* allergie *f.*
alley *n.* ruelle *f.*
allow *v.* permettre
almost *adv.* presque
alone *adj.; adv.* seul
aloud *adv.* à haute voix
alphabet *n.* alphabet *m.*
already *adv.* déjà
also *adv.* aussi
altitude *n.* altitude *f.*
always *adv.* toujours
amaze *v.* étonner
ambassador *n.* ambassadeur *m.*
ambiguous *adj.* ambigu
ambition *n.* ambition *f.*
ambulance *n.* ambulance *f.*
America *n.* Amérique *f.*
American *n.; adj.* Américain *m.*, Américaine *f.*
among *prep.* parmi, entre
amount *n.* quantité
ancestor *n.* ancêtre *m.*
anchor *n.* ancre *f.*
ancient *adj.* ancien
and *conj.* et
anemia *n.* anémie *f.*
anesthesia *n.* anesthésie *f.*
angel *n.* ange *m.*
anger *n.* colère *f.*; *v.* fâcher, mettre en colère
angle *n.* angle *m.*
angry *adj.* fâché
animal *n.* animal *m.*
ankle *n.* cheville *f.*
anniversary *n.* anniversaire *m.*
announcement *n.* annonce *f.*
annual *adj.* annuel
another *adj.; pron.* un(e) autre
answer *n.* réponse *f.*; *v.* répondre
antenna *n.* antenne *f.*
antiquity *n.* antiquité
anxiety *n.* anxiété *f.*
any *adj.* du, de l', de la, des
anybody *pron.* n'importe qui
apart *adv.* à part (*to one side*); séparé (*separated*)
apartment *n.* appartement *m.*
apologize *v.* s'excuser
appearance *n.* apparition *f.*; apparence *f.* (*look*)
appendicitis *n.* appendicite *f.*
appetite *n.* appétit *m.*
appetizer *n.* amuse-gueule *m.*
applaud *v.* applaudir
applause *n.* applaudissement *m.*
apple *n.* pomme *f.*
appliance *n.* appareil *m.*
application *n.* application *f.*
apply *v.* appliquer; postuler (*job*)
appointment *n.* rendez-vous *m.* (*meeting*)
apprentice *n.* apprenti *m.*
apprenticeship *n.* apprentissage *m.*
approach *v.* approcher
appropriate *adj.* approprié
approve *v.* approuver
April *n.* avril *m.*
Arab *n.; adj.* Arabe *m/f.*
arch *n.* arche *f.*
architecture *n.* architecture *f.*
archive *n.* archive *f.*
area *n.* région *f.* (*region*); superficie *f.* (*surface*)
argument *n.* dispute *f.* (*quarrel*); argument (*reason*)
arm *n.* bras *m.*; *v.* armer
armchair *n.* fauteuil *m.*
armpit *n.* aisselle *f.*
army *n.* armée *f.*
around *adv.* autour; *prep.* autour de

arrest *n.* arrestation *f.*; *v.* arrêter
arrival *n.* arrivée *f.*
arrive *v.* arriver
arrow *n.* flèche *f.*
art *n.* art *m.*
article *n.* article *m.*
artificial *adj.* artificiel
artist *n.* artiste *m/f.*
as *adv.; conj.* comme; *prep.* comme, en tant que
ash *n.* cendre *f.*
ashtray *n.* cendrier *m.*
Asia *n.* Asie *f.*
Asian *n.; adj.* Asiatique *m/f.*
aside *adv.* de côté
ask *v.* demander
asleep *adj.* endormi
aspirin *n.* aspirine *f.*
assemble *v.* assembler
assign *v.* assigner
assist *v.* aider
assistant *n.* aide *m/f.*
association *n.* association *f.*
assure *v.* assurer
asylum *n.* asile *m.*
at *prep.* à
athlete *n.* athlète *m/f.*
ATM *n.* distributeur automatique *m.*
attempt *n.* tentative *f.*; *v.* tenter
attention *n.* attention *f.*
attentive *adj.* attentif; attentionné (*kind*)
attic *n.* grenier *m.*
attitude *n.* attitude *f.*
attorney *n.* avocat *m.*, avocate *f.*
attract *v.* attirer
attractive *adj.* attrayant, séduisant
auction *n.* vente aux enchères *f.*
August *n.* août *m.*
aunt *n.* tante *f.*
authentic *adj.* authentique
author *n.* auteur *m.*
authority *n.* autorité *f.*
authorization *n.* autorisation *f.*
authorize *v.* autoriser
automatic *adj.* automatique
available *adj.* disponible
avenue *n.* avenue *f.*
average *n.* moyenne *f.*
avoid *v.* éviter
aware *adj.* averti
away *adv.* loin
awful *adj.* affreux

B

baby *n.* bébé *n.*
baby-sit *v.* garder les enfants
baby-sitter *n.* baby-sitter *m/f.*
bachelor *n.* célibataire *m.*
back *n.* dos *m.*; arrière *m.* (*of vehicle*); *adv.* en arrière; de retour (*returned*); *v.* reculer (*person, vehicle*)
backbone *n.* colonne vértébrale *f.*
backpack *n.* sac à dos *m.*
backpacker *n.* randonneur *m.*, randonneuse *f.*
backwards *adv.* en arrière
bacteria *n.* bactérie *f.*
bad *adj.* mauvais
bag *n.* sac *m.*
baggage *n.* bagages *m.pl.*
bait *n.* appât *m.*; *v.* appâter
bake *v.* (faire) cuire au four
baker *n.* boulanger *m.*
bakery *n.* boulangerie *f.*
balance *n.* solde *m.* (*bank*); balance *f.* (*scales*)
balcony *n.* balcon *m.*
bald *adj.* chauve
ball *n.* boule *f.;* balle *f.* (*tennis, golf*); ballon *m.* (*soccer*); bal *m.* (*dance*)
ballet *n.* ballet *m.*
ballpoint pen *n.* stylo à bille *m.*
ballroom *n.* salle de bal *f.*
ban *n.* interdiction *f.*; *v.* interdire
band *n.* bande *f.;* orchestre *m.* (*music*)
bandage *n.* pansement *m.*
bank *n.* banque *f.*; rive *f.* (*river*)
banker *n.* banquier *m.*
banquet *n.* banquet *m.*

baptism *n.* baptême *m.*
baptize *v.* baptiser
bar *n.* bar *m.* (*pub*); barre *f.* (*metal*); tablette *f.* (*chocolate*)
barber *n.* coiffeur (pour hommes) *m.*
bare *adj.* nu
barefoot *adj.* nu-pieds
bargain *n.* occasion *f.* (*good buy*); *v.* marchander (*haggle*)
barn *n.* grange *f.*
basement *n.* sous-sol *m.*
basin *n.* cuvette *f.*; basin *m.*
basis *n.* base *f.*
basket *n.* corbeille *f.*; panier *m.* (*with handle*)
bath *n.* bain *m.*; *v.* donner un bain
bathe *v.* prendre un bain
bathrobe *n.* robe de chambre *f.*
bathroom *n.* salle de bains *f.*
bathtub *n.* baignoire *f.*
battery *n.* batterie *f.* (*car*); pile *f.* (*remote control*)
bay *n.* baie *f.*
be *v.* être
beach *n.* plage *f.*
beard *n.* barbe *f.*
beat *n.* battement *m.*; mesure *f.* (*music*); *v.* battre
beautiful *adj.* beau
beauty *n.* beauté *f.*
because *conj.* parce que
become *v.* devenir
bed *n.* lit *m.*
bedding *n.* literie *f.*
bedroom *n.* chambre (à coucher) *f.*
bee *n.* abeille *f.*
beer *n.* bière *f.*
before *prep.* avant; devant (*space*); *adv.* avant; devant
beg *v.* supplier; mendier (*food*)
begin *v.* commencer
beginner *n.* débutant *m.*, débutante *f.*
beginning *n.* début *m.*
behave *v.* se conduire, se comporter
behavior *n.* conduite *f.*, comportement *m.*
behind *prep.* derrière; en retard sur (*time*); *adv.* derrière; en retard (*late*)
Belgian *n.; adj.* Belge *m/f.*
Belgium *n.* Belgique *f.*
belief *n.* croyance *f.*
believe *v.* croire
bell *n.* cloche *m.*; sonnette *f.* (*door*)
belly *n.* ventre *m.*
belong *v.* appartenir
belongings *n.* possessions *f.pl.*
below *prep.* sous, au-dessous de; *adv.* en dessous
belt *n.* ceinture *f.*
bench *n.* banc *m.*
benefit *n.* profit *m.*; *v.* profiter à
beret *n.* béret *m.*
berry *n.* baie *f.*
beside *prep.* à côté de
besides *prep.* en plus; excepté (*except*); *adv.* en outre, de plus
best *adj.* meilleur
bet *n.* pari *m.*; *v.* parier
better *adj.* meilleur; *adv.* mieux
between *prep.* entre; *adv.* au milieu
beverage *n.* boisson *f.*
beware *v.* prendre garde
beyond *prep.* au-delà de; *adv.* au-delà
bib *n.* bavoir *m.*
Bible *n.* Bible *f.*
bicycle *n.* bicyclette *f.*, vélo *m.*
big *adj.* grand; gros
bilingual *adj.* bilingue
bill *n.* facture *f.*; billet de banque *m.* (*cash*)
billion *n.* milliard *m.*
bird *n.* oiseau *m.*
birth *n.* naissance *f.*
birth control pill *n.* pilule *f.*
birthday *n.* anniversaire *m.*
bit *n.* morceau *m.*; **a bit** un peu
bite *n.* morsure *f.*; bouchée *f.* (*food*); piqûre *f.* (*insect*); *v.* mordre
bitter *adj.* amer
black *adj.* noir
bladder *n.* vessie *f.*
blade *n.* lame *f.*
blank *adj.* blanc; en blanc (*check*)
blanket *n.* couverture *f.*

bleach *n.* eau de Javel *f.*; *v.* blanchir; décolorer (*hair*)
bleed *v.* saigner
blend *n.* mélange *m.*; *v.* mélanger
bless *v.* bénir
blind *adj.* aveugle; *v.* aveugler
blindness *n.* cécité *f.*
blink *v.* cligner des yeux; clignoter (*light*)
blister *n.* cloque *f.*, ampoule *f.*
block *n.* bloc *m.*; pâté de maisons *m.* (*buildings*); *v.* bloquer
blond *adj.* blond
blood *n.* sang *m.*
blouse *n.* blouse *f.*
blow-dry *n.* brushing *m.*
blue *adj.* bleu
board *n.* planche *f.*; panneau *m.* (*wall*); tableau *m.* (*notices*); pension *f.* (*food*); *v.* monter à bord (*ship, plane*); monter dans (*train*)
boarding pass *n.* carte d'embarquement *f.*
boarding school *n.* pensionnat *m.*
boat *n.* bateau *m.*
body *n.* corps *m*
boil *v.* bouillir
boiler *n.* chaudière *f.*
bolt *n.* verrou *m.*; boulon *m.* (*for nut*); *v.* verrouiller
bomb *n.* bombe *f.*; *v.* bombarder
bone *n.* os *m.*; arête *f.* (*fish*)
book *n.* livre *m.*; *v.* réserver
bookcase *n.* bibliothèque *f.*
bookstore *n.* librairie *f.*
boot *n.* botte *f.*
border *n.* bord *m.*; frontière *f.* (*country*); *v.* border
born *adj.* né
boss *n.* patron *m.*
both *adj.* les deux, l'un(e) et l'autre
bother *v.* ennuyer; déranger (*disturb*)
bottle *n.* bouteille *f.*
boulevard *n.* boulevard *m.*
bow *n.* noeud *m.* (*knot*); arc *m.* (*weapon*); révérence *f.* (*body*); *v.* s'incliner
bowl *n.* bol *m.*; boule *f.* (*ball*)
box *n.* boîte *f.*; *v.* mettre en boîte; boxer (*sport*)
boxing *n.* boxe *f.*
bracelet *n.* bracelet *m.*
bread *n.* pain *m.*
break *n.* cassure *f.*; récréation *f.* (*school*); pause (*short*); *v.* (se) casser
breakdown *n.* panne *f.*; dépression *f.* (*nervous*)
breakfast *n.* petit déjeuner *m.*
breast *n.* sein *m.*
breath *n.* haleine *f.*; souffle *m.*
breathe *v.* respirer
breeze *n.* brise *f.*
bride *n.* mariée *f.*
bridge *n.* pont *m.*
brief *adj.* bref
bright *adj.* brillant
bring *v.* amener; apporter (*thing*)
broom *n.* balai *m.*
brother *n.* frère *m.*
brother-in-law *n.* beau-frère *m.*
brown *adj.* brun
bruise *n.* bleu *m.*, contusion *f.*; *v.* contusionner
brush *n.* brosse; *v.* brosser
bubble *n.* bulle *f.*
bucket *n.* seau *m.*
budget *n.* budget *m.*
build *v.* construire, bâtir
building *n.* bâtiment *m.*
bulb *n.* ampoule *f.* (*light*); bulbe *f.* (*flower*)
bullet *n.* balle *f.*
bunch *n.* bouquet *m.* (*flower*); trousseau *m.* (*keys*)
buoy *n.* bouée *f.*
burglar *n.* cambrioleur *m.*
burglarize *v.* cambrioler
burn *n.* brûlure *f.*; *v.* brûler
burst *v.* éclater, crever
bury *v.* enterrer
bus *n.* bus *m.*
business *n.* affaire *f.*; affaires *f.pl.*
busy *adj.* occupé
but *conj.* mais; *prep.* sauf
butcher *n.* boucher *m.*

button *n.* bouton *n.*
buy *v.* acheter
by *prep.* par, de; à côté de (*close*)
Bye-bye! *inter.* Au revoir !

C

cab *n.* taxi *m.*
cable *n.* cable *m.*
cage *n.* cage *f.*
cake *n.* gâteau *m.*
calculate *v.* calculer
calculator *n.* calculatrice *f.*
calendar *n.* calendrier *m.*
call *n.* coup de téléphone *m.*; cri *m.* (*shout*); *v.* appeler
calling card *n.* carte de téléphone *f.*
camera *n.* appareil photo *m.*
camp *n.* camp *m.*; *v.* camper
can *n.* boîte de conserve; bidon *m.* (*oil*); *v.* pouvoir
Canada *n.* Canada *m.*
Canadian *n.; adj.* Canadien *m.*, Canadienne *f.*
cancel *v.* annuler
cancellation *n.* annulation *f.*
cancer *n.* cancer *m.*
candle *n.* bougie *f.*
candy *n.* bonbon *m.*
cane *n.* canne *f.*
canoe *n.* canoë *m.*
cap *n.* casquette *f.*; bouchon *m.* (*tube*); capuchon *m.* (*pen*)
capable *adj.* capable
capital *n.* capitale *f.* (*city*)
captain *n.* capitaine *m.*
car *n.* voiture *f.*
card *n.* carte *f.*
cardboard *n.* carton *m.*
care *n.* soin *m.*; souci *m.* (*worry*); *v.* s'intéresser
careful *adj.* prudent
carpet *n.* tapis *m.*
carry *v.* porter; transporter (*vehicle*)
carton *n.* cartouche *f.* (*cigarettes*)
case *n.* cas *m.*; étui *m.* (*camera*)
cash *n.* argent *m.*; argent liquide *m.* (*pay*); *v.* encaisser
cashier *n.* caissier *m.*, caissière *f.*
casino *n.* casino *m.*
castle *n.* château *m.*
casual *adj.* sport (*clothes*)
cat *n.* chat *m.*
catalog *n.* catalogue *m.*
catch *n.* prise *f.*; *v.* attraper
cathedral *n.* cathédrale *f.*
Catholic *n.*; *adj.* catholique *m/f.*
Catholicism *n.* catholicisme
caution *n.* prudence *f.*; avertissement *m.* (*warning*)
cautious *adj.* prudent
cave *n.* grotte *f.*
CD *n.* CD *m.*, compact disc *m.*, disque compact *m.*
CD player *n.* platine laser *f.*, lecteur de CD *m.*
CD-ROM *n.* CD-ROM *m.*
ceiling *n.* plafond *m.*
celebrate *v.* fêter
cell *n.* cellule *f.*
cellar *n.* cave *f.*
cemetery *n.* cimetière *m.*
center *n.* centre *m.*; *v.* centrer
centimeter *n.* centimètre *m.*
central *adj.* central
century *n.* siècle *m.*
ceremony *n.* cérémonie *f.*
chain *n.* chaîne *f.*
chair *n.* chaise *f.*; chaire *f.* (*university*)
chance *n.* opportunité *f.* (*occasion*); hasard *m.* (*luck*); chance *f.* (*likelihood*)
change *n.* changement *m.*; monnaie *f.* (*money*); *v.* changer
chapter *n.* chapitre *m.*
character *n.* caractère *m.*; personnage *m.* (*movie*)
charge *n.* prix *m.*; inculpation *f.* (*law*); *v.* faire payer; inculper
charges *n.pl.* frais *m.pl.*
chat *n.* causette *f.*; *v.* bavarder
cheap *adj.* bon marché

cheat *v.* tricher
check *n.* chèque *m.*; addition *f.* (*restaurant*); vérification *f.* (*control*); *v.* vérifier; contrôler (*passport*)
checkroom *n.* consigne *f.*
cheek *n.* joue *f.*
Cheers! *inter.* Santé !
cheese *n.* fromage *m.*
chemical *n.* produit chimique *m.*; *adj.* chimique
chess *n.* échecs *m.pl.*
chest *n.* poitrine *f.*; coffre *m.*, caisse *f.* (*box*)
chew *v.* mâcher
child *n.* enfant *m.*
childhood *n.* enfance *f.*
chin *n.* menton *m.*
china *n.* porcelaine *f.*
choice *n.* choix *m.*
choke *v.* étouffer; étrangler
choose *v.* choisir
Christian *adj.* chrétien
Christianity *n.* christianisme *m.*
Christmas *n.* Noël *m.*
church *n.* église *f.*
cigar *n.* cigare *m.*
cigarette *n.* cigarette *f.*
circle *n.* cercle *m.*
circumstance *n.* circonstance *f.*
circus *n.* cirque *m.*
citizen *n.* citoyen *m.*, citoyenne *f.*
city *n.* ville *f.*
civilization *n.* civilisation *f.*
classic *adj.* classique
clean *adj.* propre; *v.* nettoyer
clear *adj.* clair
clever *adj.* intelligent
client *n.* client *m.*, cliente *f.*
cliff *n.* falaise *f.*
climate *n.* climat *m.*
climb *n.* escalade *f.*; *v.* grimper; escalader (*montain*);
clinic *n.* centre médical *m.*
clock *n.* horloge *f.* (*large*); pendule *f.* (*small*)
close *adj.* près; *v.* fermer
closed *adj.* fermé
cloth *n.* tissu *m.*
clothe *v.* habiller, vêtir
clothes *n.pl.* habits *m.pl.*, vêtements *m.pl.*
cloud *n.* nuage *m.*
coast *n.* côte *f.*
coat *n.* manteau *m.*; pelage *m.* (*animal*)
cobbler *n.* cordonnier *m.*, cordonnière *f.*
code *n.* code *m.*
coffee *n.* café *m.*
coffee shop *n.* café *m.*
coffin *n.* cercueil *m.*
coin *n.* pièce de monnaie *f.*
cold *n.* froid *m.*; rhume *m.* (*sick*); *adj.* froid
collect call *n.* appel en PCV *m.*
collection *n.* collection *f.*
college *n.* collège *m.*
collide *v.* entrer en collision
collision *n.* collision *f.*
color *n.* couleur *f.*
column *n.* colonne *f.*
comb *n.* peigne *m.*; *v.* peigner
combination *n.* combinaison *f.*
come *v.* venir; arriver
comfortable *adj.* confortable
comforter *n.* édredon *m.*
comma *n.* virgule *f.*
comment *n.* commentaire *m.*
commission *n.* commision *f.*
committee *n.* comité *m.*
common *adj.* commun
communicate *v.* communiquer
communication *n.* communication *f.*
company *n.* companie *f.*
compare *v.* comparer
comparison *n.* comparaison *f.*
compartment *n.* compartiment *m.*
compass *n.* boussole *f.*
compensate *v.* compenser, dédommager
competition *n.* compétition *f.*, concours *m.*
complain *v.* se plaindre
complaint *n.* plainte *f.*

complete *adj.* complet; *v.* achever
compliment *n.* compliment *m.*; *v.* complimenter
compose *v.* composer
composition *n.* composition *f.*
comprehensive *adj.* complet
computer *n.* ordinateur *m.*
concern *n.* souci *m.*
concert *n.* concert *m.*
concrete *n.* béton; *adj.* concret
condemn *v.* condamner
condition *n.* condition *f.*
condolences *n.pl.* condoléances *f.pl.*
condom *n.* préservatif *m.*
conductor *n.* chef d'orchestre *m.*; chef de train *m.*
confess *v.* confesser
confession *n.* confession *f.*
confidence *n.* confiance *f.*; confidence *f.* (*secret*)
confirm *v.* confirmer
conflict *n.* conflit; *v.* être en conflit
confuse *v.* confondre; embrouiller (*situation*)
congratulate *v.* féliciter
congratulations *n.pl.* félicitations *f.pl.*
connect *v.* relier; passer (*on the phone*); brancher (*install*)
connection *n.* relation *f.*; communication *f.* (*phone*); correspondance *f.* (*train*)
conscious *adj.* conscient
consequence *n.* conséquence *f.*
conserve *v.* conserver
consider *v.* considérer
consonant *n.* consonne *f.*
constipation *n.* constipation *f.*
consul *n.* consul *m.*
consulate *n.* consulat *m.*
contact *n.* contact *m.*; relation *f.* (*person*); *v.* contacter
contact lenses *n.pl.* verres de contact *m.pl.*
contagious *adj.* contagieux
contain *v.* contenir
container *n.* récipient *m.*
contaminate *v.* contaminer
contempt *n.* mépris *m.*
content *n.* contenu *m.*; teneur *f.* (*amount*)
continent *n.* continent *m.*
continue *v.* continuer
contraceptive *n.; adj.* contraceptif *m.*
contract *n.* contract *m.*; *v.* contracter
contrary *n.; adj.* contraire *m.*
control *n.* contrôle *m.*; *v.* contrôler
convent *n.* couvent *m.*
conversation *n.* conversation *f.*
convert *v.* convertir
convertible *n.* décapotable *f.* (*car*)
convince *v.* convaincre
cook *n.* cuisinier *m.*, cuisinière *f.*; *v.* faire la cuisine; cuire
cool *adj.* frais
copy *n.* copie *f.*; exemplaire *m.* (*book*); *v.* copier
cord *n.* corde *f.*
core *n.* noyau *m.*; trognon *m.*, coeur *m.* (*fruit*)
cork *n.* bouchon *m.* (*bottle*)
corner *n.* coin *m.*
corpse *n.* cadavre *m.*
correct *adj.* exact; *v.* corriger
correction *n.* correction *f.*
correspondence *n.* correspondance *f.*
cost *n.* coût *m.*; *v.* coûter
cot *n.* lit de camp *m.*
cotton *n.* cotton *m.*
couch *n.* canapé *m.*, divan *m.*
cough *n.* toux *f.*; *v.* tousser
count *n.* compte *m.*; *v.* compter
counter *n.* comptoir *m.*; guichet *m.* (*bank*)
country *n.* pays *m.*; campagne *f.* (*countryside*); patrie *f.* (*homeland*)
couple *n.* couple *m.*
course *n.* cours *m.*; plat *m.* (*meal*)
court *n.* cour *f.*; tribunal *m.* (*law*); court *m.* (*tennis*)
courtyard *n.* cour *f.*
cousin *n.* cousin *m.*, cousine *f.*
cover *n.* couverture *f.*; couvercle *m.* (*jar*); *v.* couvrir
cow *n.* vache *f.*

cradle *n.* berceau *m.*; *v.* bercer
craft *n.* métier artisanal *m.*
craftsman *n.* artisan *m.*
crash *n.* accident *m.*; fracas *m.* (*noise*); *v.* avoir un accident avec; s'écraser (*plane*)
crawl *v.* ramper
crazy *adj.* fou
cream *n.* crème *f.*
create *v.* créer
credit card *n.* carte de crédit *f.*
crew *n.* équipage *m.*
crib *n.* lit d'enfant *m.*
crime *n.* crime *m.*
criticism *n.* critique *f.*
criticize *v.* critiquer
cross *n.* croix *f.*; *v.* traverser (*street*)
crossword *n.* mots croisés *m.pl.*
crowd *n.* foule *f.*; *v.* affluer
cruise *n.* croisière *f.*; *v.* faire une croisière
crumb *n.* miette *f.*
crumble *v.* émietter
crust *n.* croûte *f.*
crustaceous *n.* crustacé *m.*
crutch *n.* béquille *f.*
cry *n.* cri *m.*; *v.* crier; pleurer (*tear*)
cuff *n.* revers *m.*
culture *n.* culture *f.*
cup *n.* tasse *f.*
cupboard *n.* armoire *f.*, placard *m.*
cure *n.* remède *m.*; *v.* guérir
curious *adj.* curieux
curl *n.* boucle *f.*; *v.* boucler, friser
currency *n.* monnaie *f.*
current *n.* courant *m.*; *adj.* courant
curtain *n.* rideau *m.*
curve *n.* courbe *f.*; *v.* courber
cushion *n.* coussin *m.*
custom *n.* coutume *f.*
customer *n.* client *m.*, cliente *f.*
customs *n.pl.* douane *f.*
cut *n.* coupure *f.*; *v.* couper

D

dad *n.* papa *m.*
daily *adj.* quotidien; *adv.* tous les jours
dairy *n.* laiterie *f.*, crémerie *f.*
damage *n.* dégâts *m.pl.*; *v.* endommager
damp *adj.* humide
dance club *n.* boîte de nuit *f.*
dance *n.* danse *f.*; *v.* danser
danger *n.* danger *m.*
dangerous *adj.* dangereux
dare *v.* défier
dark *adj.* sombre
darkness *n.* obscurité *f.*
date *n.* date *f.*; rendez-vous *m.* (*with somebody*); *v.* dater; sortir avec (*somebody*)
daughter *n.* fille *f.*
daughter-in-law *n.* belle-fille *f.*
dawn *n.* aube *f.*
day *n.* jour *m.*
daycare *n.* garderie *f.*
dead *adj.* mort
deadly *adj.* mortel; meutrier (*gun*)
deaf *adj.* sourd
deafness *n.* surdité *f.*
deal *n.* marché *m.*, affaire *f.*
dealer *n.* marchand *m.*, marchande *f.*
dean *n.* doyen *m.*, doyenne *f.*
dear *adj.* cher
death *n.* mort *f.*
debt *n.* dette *f.*
debut *n.* début *m.*
decade *n.* décennie *f.*
decaffeinated *adj.* décaféiné
deceive *v.* tromper
December *n.* décembre
decision *n.* décision *f.*
deck *n.* pont *m.*; jeu *m.* (*cards*)
declare *v.* déclarer
decline *n.* déclin *m.*; *v.* décliner
decorate *v.* décorer
decoration *n.* décoration *f.*
decrease *n.* diminution *f.*; *v.* diminuer
dedicate *v.* dédier
dedication *n.* dédicace *f.*
deep *adj.* profond
defect *n.* défaut *m.*
defend *v.* défendre
defense *n.* défense *f.*

definition *n.* définition *f.*
deflate *v.* dégonfler
degree *n.* degré *m.*; diplôme *m.* (*université*)
dehydration *n.* déshydratation *f.*
delay *n.* retard *m.*; *v.* retarder
delete *v.* supprimer
delicious *adj.* délicieux
deliver *v.* livrer
delivery *n.* livraison *f.*
demand *n.* exigence *f.*; *v.* exiger
democracy *n.* démocracie *f.*
demonstration *n.*démonstration *f.*, manifestation *f.*
dentist *n.* dentiste *m/f.*
deodorant *n.* déodorant *m.*
departure *n.* départ *m.*
depend *v.* dépendre
deposit *n.* caution *f.* (*apartment*); arrhes *f.pl.* (*part payment*)
depression *n.* dépression *f.*
depth *n.* profondeur *f.*
descend *v.* descendre
descent *n.* descente *f.*
describe *v.* décrire
desert *n.* désert; *v.* déserter
deserve *v.* mériter
desire *n.* désir *m.*; *v.* désirer
desk *n.* réception *f.* (*hotel*); bureau *m.* (*office*); pupitre *m.* (*school*)
dessert *n.* dessert *m.*
destroy *v.* détruire
detach *v.* détacher
detail *n.* détail *m.*; *v.* détailler
detective *n.* détective *m.*
detour *n.* détour *m.*
develop *v.* développer
devil *n.* diable *m.*
dew *n.* rosée *f.*
diabetes *n.* diabète *m.*
diagnosis *n.* diagnostic *m.*
diagonal *adj.* diagonal
dial *v.* composer, faire (*phone number*)
dialect *n.* dialecte *m.*
dialogue *n.* dialogue *m.*
diamond *n.* diamant *m.*
diaper *n.* couche *f.*
diary *n.* journal intime *m.*
dictionary *n.* dictionnaire *m.*
die *n.* dé *m.*; *v.* mourir
diet *n.* régime *m.*
difference *n.* différence *f.*
different *adj.* différent
difficult *adj.* difficile
difficulty *n.* difficulté *f.*
digest *v.* digérer
digestion *n.* digestion *f.*
digital *adj.* digital
digital camera *n.* appareil photo numérique *m.*
dimension *n.* dimension *f.*
dining room *n.* salle à manger *f.*
dinner *n.* dîner *m.*
diplomacy *n.* diplomatie *f.*
direct *adj.* direct
direction *n.* direction *f.*
director *n.* directeur *m.*
dirt *n.* saleté *f.*; terre *f.* (*earth*)
dirty *adj.* sale
disagree *v.* ne pas être d'accord
disagreement *n.* désaccord *m.*
disappear *v.* disparaître
disappointment *n.* déception *f.*
disaster *n.* désastre *m.*
discipline *n.* discipline *f.*
discount *n.* rabais *m.*
discover *v.* découvrir
discreet *adj.* discret
discuss *v.* discuter
discussion *n.* discussion *f.*
disease *n.* maladie *f.*
disgust *n.* dégoût *m.*
dish *n.* plat *m.*
disk *n.* disque *m.*; disquette *f.* (*floppy*)
dislike *n.* aversion *f.*
disobey *v.* désobéir
disposable *adj.* jettable
distance *n.* distance *f.*
distinct *adj.* distinct
distinguish *v.* distinguer
distract *v.* distraire
distribute *v.* distribuer
distribution *n.* distribution *f.*
disturb *v.* déranger

ditch *n.* fossé *m.*
dive *n.* plongeon *m.*; *v.* plonger
diver *n.* plongeur *m.*, plongeuse *f.*
divide *v.* diviser
divorce *n.* divorce *m.*; *v.* divorcer
do *v.* faire
doctor *n.* docteur *m.*, doctoresse *f.*
dog *n.* chien *m.*, chienne *f.*
doll *n.* poupée *f.*
dollar *n.* dollar *m.*
domain *n.* domaine *m.*
donkey *n.* âne *m.*
door *n.* porte *f.*
dormitory *n.* dortoir *m.*
dose *n.* dose *f.*
dot *n.* point *m.*; pois *m.* (*on fabric*)
double *n.; adj.; adv.* double *m.*
doubt *n.* doute *m.*; *v.* douter de
dough *n.* pâte *f.*
down *prep.* en bas de; *adv.* en bas, vers le bas
dozen *n.* douzaine *f.*
draft *n.* courant d'air *m.*
drama *n.* pièce de théâtre *f.* (*play*); drame *m.* (*event*)
draw *v.* tirer; dessiner (*picture*)
drawing *n.* dessin *m.*
dream *n.* rêve *m.*; *v.* rêver
dress *n.* robe *f.*; *v.* habiller
drink *n.* boisson *f.*; verre *m.* (*alcohol*); *v.* boire
drive *v.* conduire
driver *n.* conducteur *m.*, conductrice *f.*, chauffeur *m.*
driver's license *n.* permis de conduire *m.*
drop *n.* goutte *f.*; chute *f.* (*fall*); *v.* tomber
drown *v.* noyer
drug *n.* drogue *f.*; medicament *m.* (*medical*)
drunk *adj.* ivre
dry *adj.* sec; *v.* sécher
dryer *n.* séchoir *m.*
due *n., adj.* dû *m.*
dumb *adj.* bête
during *prep.* pendant
dusk *n.* crepuscule *m.*
dust *n.* poussière *f.*
duty *n.* devoir *m.*
dwarf *n.* nain *m.*
dye *n.* teinture *f.*; *v.* teindre

E

each *adj.* chaque; *pron.* chacun *m.*, chacune *f.*
ear *n.* oreille *f.*
early *adv.* tôt
earn *v.* gagner; rapporter (*interest*)
earnings *n.pl.* salaire *m.*; benefices *m.pl.* (*profits*)
earring *n.* boucle d'oreille *f.*
earth *n.* terre *f.*
easily *adv.* facilement
east *n.* est *m.*
Easter *n.* Pâques *f.pl.*
easy *adj.* facile
eat *v.* manger
economy *n.* économie *f.*
edge *n.* bord *m.*
edition *n.* édition *f.*
education *n.* éducation *f.*; enseignement *m.* (*teaching*)
effect *n.* effet *m.*
effort *n.* effort *m.*
egg *n.* oeuf *m.*
eight *num.* huit
elastic *n.; adj.* élastique *m.*
elbow *n.* coude *m.*
electric *adj.* électrique
electrician *n.* électricien *m.*
electricity *n.* électricité *f.*
elegant *adj.* élégant
elevator *n.* ascenseur *m.*
eleven *num.* onze
else *adv.* d'autre
E-mail *n.* courrier éléctronique *m.*
embarrass *v.* embarrasser
embassy *n.* ambassade *f.*
emergency *n.* urgence *f.*
emigrate *v.* émigrer
employee *n.* employé *m.*, employée *f.*
employer *n.* employeur *m.*
employment *n.* emploi *m.*

empty *adj.* vide; *v.* vider
enclose *v.* clôturer; joindre (*letter*)
enclosure *n.* enceinte *f.*; pièce jointe *f.* (*letter*)
encounter *n.* rencontre *f.*; *v.* rencontrer
encyclopedia *n.* encyclopédie *f.*
end *n.* fin *f.*; *v.* terminer
endless *adj.* sans fin, interminable
enemy *n.* ennemi *m.*, ennemie *f.*
energetic *adj.* énergique
energy *n.* énergie *f.*
engagement *n.* obligation *f.*; fiançailles *f.pl.* (*proposal*)
engine *n.* moteur *m.*
engineer *n.* ingénieur *m.*
England *n.* Angleterre *f.*
English *n.; adj.* Anglais *m.*, Anglaise *f.*
engrave *v.* graver
engraving *n.* gravure *f.*
enjoy *v.* aimer, prendre plaisir à
enlarge *v.* agrandir
enormous *adj.* énorme
enough *adj.; pron.* assez de; *adv.* assez
enter *v.* entrer
entertain *v.* amuser; recevoir (*guests*)
enthusiasm *n.* enthousiasme *m.*
entire *adj.* entier
entrance *n.* entrée *f.*
envelope *n.* enveloppe *f.*
environment *n.* environnement *m.*
epidemic *n.* épidémie *f.*
equal *adj.* égal; *v.* égaler
equality *n.* égalité *f.*
equipment *n.* équipement *m.*
equivalent *n.; adj.* équivalent *m.*
era *n.* ère *f.*, époque *f.*
erase *v.* effacer
eraser *n.* gomme *f.*
error *n.* erreur *f.*
escalator *n.* escalier roulant *m.*, escalator *m.*
escape *v.* échapper
escort *n.* escorte *f.*; *v.* escorter
especially *adv.* surtout
essential *adj.* essentiel
establish *v.* établir
estate *n.* domaine *m.*; biens *m.pl.* (*possessions*)
estimate *n.* estimation *f.*; *v.* estimer
eternal *adj.* éternel
euro *n.* euro *m.*
Europe *n.* Europe *f.*
European *n.; adj.* Européen *m.*, Européenne *f.*
European Community *n.* Communauté européenne *f.*
evacuate *v.* évacuer
evaluate *v.* évaluer
even *adv.* même; *adj.* régulier
evening *n.* soir *m.*; soirée *f.* (*event*)
event *n.* événement *m.*
ever *adv.* jamais; toujours (*at all times*)
every *adj.* chaque
everybody *pron.* tout le monde
everyday *adj.* quotidien
evidence *n.* preuve *f.*
exact *adj.* exact
exaggerate *v.* exagérer
examination *n.* examen *m.*
examine *v.* examiner
example *n.* exemple *m.*
exceed *v.* dépasser
excellent *adj.* excellent
except *prep.* excepté, sauf; *v.* excepter
exception *n.* exception *f.*
excess *n.* excès *m.*
exchange *n.* échange *m.*; change *m.* (*currency*); *v.* échanger
exchange rate *n.* taux de change *m.*
excite *v.* exciter
excitement *n.* excitation *f.*
exclude *v.* exclure
excursion *n.* excursion *f.*
excuse *n.* excuse *f.*; *v.* excuser
execute *v.* exécuter
exercise *n.* exercice *m.*; *v.* exercer
exhaust *n.* pot d'échappement *m.*; *v.* épuiser
exhibit *v.* exposer
exhibition *n.* exposition *f.*
exile *n.* exil *m.*; *v.* exiler
exist *v.* exister

existence *n.* existence *f.*
exit *n.* sortie *f.*; *v.* sortir
expect *v.* attendre
expectation *n.* attente *f.*
expel *v.* expulser
expense *n.* dépense *f.*
expensive *adj.* cher
experience *n.* expérience *f.*
expert *n.; adj.* expert *m.*, experte *f.*
expire *v.* expirer
explain *v.* expliquer
explanation *n.* explication *f.*
explosion *n.* explosion *f.*
express *adj.* exprès, formel
external *adj.* externe
extinguisher *n.* extincteur *m.*
extract *n.* extrait *m.*; *v.* extraire
extraordinary *adj.* extraordinaire
extreme *adj.* extrême
eye *n.* oeil *m.*
eyebrow *n.* sourcil *m.*
eyelash *n.* cil *m.*
eyelid *n.* paupière *f.*

F

fabric *n.* tissu *m.*
face *n.* visage *m.*
fail *v.* échouer
failure *n.* échec *m.*
faint *n.* évanouissement *m.*; *adj.* faible; *v.* s'évanouir
fair *n.* foire *f.*; *adj.* juste; clair (*skin*)
faith *n.* foi *f.*
faithful *adj.* fidèle
fall *n.* automne *m.* (*season*); chute *f.*; *v.* tomber
false *adj.* faux
family *n.* famille *f.*
famous *adj.* fameux
fan *n.* ventilateur *m.*
far *adv.* loin; *adj.* lointain
farm *n.* ferme *f.*
farmer *n.* fermier *m.*, fermière *f.*
fashion *n.* mode *f.*; manière *f.* (*manner*)
fast *adj.* rapide; *adv.* vite
fasten *v.* attacher
fat *n.* graisse *f.*; *adj.* gras, gros
father *n.* père *m.*
father-in-law *n.* beau-père *m.*
faucet *n.* robinet *m.*
fault *n.* défaut *m.*
favor *n.* faveur *f.*
favorite *n.; adj.* favori *m.*, favorite *f.*
fear *n.* peur *f.*; *v.* craindre
feather *n.* plume *f.*
February *n.* février *m.*
fee *n.* prix *m.*; honoraires *m.pl.* (*doctor*)
feed *v.* nourrir
feel *n.* sensation *f.*; *v.* sentir
feeling *n.* sentiment *m.*; sensation *f.* (*physical*)
female *n.; adj.* femelle; *adj.* féminin (*sex*)
feminine *adj.* féminin
fence *n.* barrière *f.*
ferry *n.* bac *m.*; ferry *m.* (*large*)
fever *n.* fièvre *f.*
few *n.; adj.* peu (de)
fiber *n.* fibre *f.*
field *n.* champ *m.*
fight *n.* bagarre *f.*; *v.* se battre (contre, avec)
file *n.* dossier *m.*; *v.* classer
fill *v.* remplir
film *n.* film *m.*
filter *n.* filtre *m.*; *v.* filtrer
filthy *adj.* dégoûtant
final *adj.* final
financial *adj.* financier
find *v.* trouver
fine *n.* amende *f.*
finger *n.* doigt *m.*
fingerprint *n.* empreinte digitale *f.*
finish *v.* finir
fire *n.* feu *m.*; *v.* tirer; renvoyer (*dismiss*)
fireman *n.* pompier *m.*
fireplace *n.* cheminée *f.*
fireworks *n.pl.* feu d'artifice *m.*
firm *adj.* ferme
first *adj.* premier; *adv.* d'abord
fish *n.* poisson *m.*; *v.* pêcher
fisherman *n.* pêcheur *m.*

fist *n.* poing *m.*
fit *adj.* en forme; *v.* aller (*clothes*)
five *num.* cinq
fix *v.* fixer; réparer (*repair*)
flag *n.* drapeau *m.*
flame *n.* flamme *f.*
flash *n.* éclair *m.*; flash *m.* (*photo*); *v.* clignoter (*light*)
flashlight *n.* lampe de poche *f.*
flat *adj.* plat; fixe (*rate*)
flavor *n.* goût *m.*; parfum *m.* (*ice cream*)
flea market *n.* marché aux puces *m.*
flight *n.* vol *m.*
flight attendant *n.* hôtesse de l'air *f.*, steward *m.*
float *v.* flotter
flood *n.* inondation *f.*; *v.* inonder
floor *n.* étage *m.*
florist *n.* fleuriste *m/f.*
flour *n.* farine *f.*
flow *n.* courant *m.*; circulation *f.* (*blood*)
flower *n.* fleur *f.*
flu *n.* grippe *f.*
fluently *adv.* couramment (*language*)
fly *n.* mouche *f.*; *v.* voler
fog *n.* brouillard *m.*
fold *n.* pli *m.*; *v.* plier
folk *n.* gens *m.pl.*; *adj.* folklorique
follow *v.* suivre
food *n.* nourriture *f.*
fool *n.* idiot *m.*, idiote *f.*
foot *n.* pied *m.*
football *n.* ballon de football *m.*; football américain *m.*
for *prep.* pour; pendant, depuis (*time*); *conj.* car
forbid *v.* interdire
force *n.* force *f.*; *v.* forcer
forearm *n.* avant-bras *m.*
forefinger *n.* index *m.*
forehead *n.* front *m.*
foreign *adj.* étranger
foreigner *n.* étranger *m.*, étrangère *f.*
forest *n.* forêt *f.*
forever *adv.* pour toujours
forget *v.* oublier
forgive *v.* pardonner
fork *n.* fourchette *f.*; bifurcation *f.* (*road*)
form *n.* formulaire *m.* (*document*)
formal *adj.* de soirée (*clothes*); cérémonieux
former *adj.* précédent, ancien
formula *n.* formule *f.*
forward *adj.; adv.* en avant
foundation *n.* fondation *f.*
fountain *n.* fontaine *f.*
four *num.* quatre
fragile *adj.* fragile
frame *n.* cadre *m.* (*picture*); monture *f.* (*glasses*)
France *n.* France *f.*
free *adj.* libre; gratuit (*of charge*)
freedom *n.* liberté *f.*
freeze *v.* geler
freezer *n.* congélateur *m.*
French *n.; adj.* Français *m.*, Française *f.*
frequent *adj.* fréquent
fresh *adj.* frais
Friday *n.* vendredi *m.*
friend *n.* ami *m.*, amie *f.*
friendly *adj.* amical, aimable
friendship *n.* amitié *f.*
frog *n.* grenouille *f.*
from *prep.* de; à partir de
front *n.* avant *m.* (*car*); devant *m.* (*building*); *adj.* de devant; avant
fruit *n.* fruit *m.*
fry *v.* frire
frying pan *n.* poêle à frire *f.*
fuel *n.* combustible *m.*; carburant *m.* (*car*)
full *adj.* plein; complet (*hotel, name*); rassasié (*food*)
full time *adj.; adv.* à plein temps
fun *n.* amusement *m.*
funeral *n.* enterrement *m.*
funny *adj.* drôle
fur *n.* fourrure *f.*
furniture *n.* meubles *m.pl.*
fuse *n.* fusible *m.*
future *n.* avenir *m.*; *adj.* futur

G

gallery *n.* galerie *f.*
gallon *n.* gallon *m.*
gamble *v.* jouer
game *n.* jeu *m.*; gibier *m.* (*hunting*)
gap *n.* trou *m.*; intervalle *m.* (*time*)
garage *n.* garage *m.*
garbage *n.* ordures *f.pl.*
garden *n.* jardin *m.*
gardener *n.* jardinier *m.*
garlic *n.* ail *m.*
gas *n.* gaz *m.*; essence *f.* (*gasoline*)
gate *n.* portail *m.*; porte *f.* (*airport*)
gather *v.* rassembler
gay *adj.* gai (*cheerful*); gay (*homosexual*)
geography *n.* géographie *f.*
germ *n.* microbe *m.*
German *n.; adj.* Allemand
Germany *n.* Allemagne *f.*
gesture *n.* geste *m.*
get *v.* obtenir (*obtain*); recevoir (*receive*); devenir (*become*)
gift *n.* cadeau *m.*
girl *n.* fille *f.*
give *v.* donner
glad *adj.* content
glass *n.* verre *m.*
glasses *n.* lunettes *f.pl.*
glove *n.* gant *m.*
glue *n.* colle *f.*; *v.* coller
go *v.* aller; partir (*leave*)
goal *n.* but *m.*
goat *n.* chèvre *f.*
God *n.* Dieu *m.*
goddaughter *n.* filleule *f.*
godfather *n.* parrain *m.*
godmother *n.* marraine *f.*
godson *n.* filleul *m.*
gold *n.* or *m.*
good *n.* bien *m.*; *adj.* bon
Good-bye! *inter.* Au revoir !
goods *n.pl.* marchandises *f.pl.*
government *n.* gouvernement
gown *n.* robe *f.*
grab *v.* attraper
graduate *n.* diplômé; *v.* obtenir son diplôme, graduer
gram *n.* gramme *m.*
grammar *n.* grammaire *f.*
grandchildren *n.pl.* petits-enfants *m.pl.*
granddaughter *n.* petite-fille *f.*
grandfather *n.* grand-père *m.*
grandmother *n.* grand-mère *f.*
grandparents *n.pl.* grands-parents *m.pl.*
grandson *n.* petit-fils *m.*
grant *n.* subvention *f.*; *v.* accorder
grape *n.* raisin *m.*
grass *n.* herbe *f.*
grave *n.* tombe *f.*
gravel *n.* gravier *m.*
gravestone *n.* pierre tombale *f.*
graveyard *n.* cimetière *m.*
gray *adj.* gris
grease *n.* graisse *f.*
great *adj.* grand; formidable
Great Britain *n.* Grande-Bretagne *f.*
great-grandfather *n.* arrière-grand-père *m.*
great-grandmother *n.* arrière-grand-mère *f.*
green *adj.* vert
greet *v.* saluer; accueillir (*welcome*)
grief *n.* chagrin *m.*
grill *n.* gril *m.*
grind *v.* écraser; moudre (*coffee*)
grocer *n.* épicier *m.*
groceries *n.* provisions *f.pl.*
grocery store *n.* épicerie *f.*
ground *n.* sol *m.*
group *n.* groupe *m.*; *v.* grouper
grow *n.* grandir; pousser (*plant*)
grown-up *n.* adulte *m/f.*
growth *n.* croissance *f.*
guarantee *n.* garantie *f.*; *v.* garantir
guard *n.* garde *m.*; garde *f.* (*group*); *v.* garder, surveiller
guess *n.* supposition *f.*; deviner
guest *n.* invité *m.*, invitée *f.*; client *m.*, cliente *f.* (*hotel*)
guide *n.* guide *m.*; *v.* guider
guilt *n.* culpabilité *f.*
guilty *adj.* coupable
gum *n.* gencive *f.*

gun *n.* pistolet *m.*; fusil *m.* (*rifle*)
gutter *n.* gouttière *f.*; caniveau *m.* (*street*)
gynecologist *n.* gynécologue *m/f.*

H

hail *n.* grêle *f.*
hair *n.* cheveux *m.pl.*; poils *m.pl.* (*body*)
haircut *n.* coupe de cheveux *f.*
hairdresser *n.* coiffeur *m.*, coiffeuse *f.*
hairspray *n.* laque *f.*
half *n.* moitié *f.*; *adj.* demi; *adv.* à moitié, à demi
hall *n.* salle *f.*; hall *m.* (*entrance*)
Halloween *n.* veille de la Toussaint *f.*
ham *n.* jambon *m.*
hammer *n.* marteau *m.*
hand *n.* main *f.*; aiguille *f.* (*clock*)
handful *n.* poignée *f.*
handicap *n.* handicap *m.*; *v.* handicaper
handle *n.* poignée *f.*; manier
handshake *n.* poignée de main *f.*
handy *adj.* sous la main (*close*); pratique (*useful*)
hang *v.* accrocher; pendre
hanger *n.* cintre *m.*
hangover *n.* gueule de bois *f.*
happen *v.* arriver; se passer
happiness *n.* bonheur *m.*
happy *adj.* heureux
harass *v.* harceler
harassment *n.* harcèlement *m.*
harbor *n.* port
hard *adj.* dur
harm *n.* mal *m.*; tort *m.* (*wrong*); *v.* faire du mal; nuire (*wrong*)
harness *n.* harnais *m.*
harvest *n.* moisson *f.* (*corn*); récolte *f.* (*fruit*); vendanges *f.pl.* (*grapes*)
hat *n.* chapeau *m.*
hate *n.* haine *f.*; *v.* haïr
have *v.* avoir
hay *n.* foin *m.*
hay fever *n.* rhume des foins *m.*
hazard *n.* risque *m.*
he *pron.* il
head *n.* tête *f.*; chef *m.* (*leader*)
headache *n.* mal de tête *m.*
headlight *n.* phare *m.*
headline *n.* titre *m.*
headquarters *n.* siège *m.*; quartier général *m.* (*military*)
heal *v.* guérir
health *n.* santé *f.*
healthy *adj.* sain; en bonne santé (*person*)
hear *v.* entendre
hearing *n.* ouïe *f.*
heart *n.* cœur *m.*
heat *n.* chaleur *f.*; *v.* chauffer
heater *n.* radiateur *m.*
heaven *n.* paradis *m.*
heavy *adj.* lourd
heel *n.* talon *m.*
height *n.* taille *f.*; hauteur *f.* (*object*); altitude *f.* (*plane*)
helicopter *n.* hélicoptère *m.*
hell *n.* enfer *m.*
Hello! *inter.* Bonjour !
helmet *n.* casque *m.*
help *n.* aide *f.*; *v.* aider; *inter.* Au secours !
hem *n.* ourlet *m.*
herb *n.* herbe *f.*
here *adv.* ici
hesitate *v.* hésiter
Hi! *inter.* Salut !
hide *v.* cacher
high *adj.* haut; élevé (*price*); grand (*speed*)
high school *n.* lycée *m.*
highway *n.* route nationale *f.*
hike *n.* randonnée *f.*; *v.* aller en randonnée
hill *n.* colline *f.*
hip *n.* hanche *f.*
hire *n.* engager
historic *adj.* historique
history *n.* histoire *f.*

hit *n.* coup *m.*; *v.* frapper
hive *n.* ruche *f.*
hold *v.* tenir; contenir (*contain*)
hole *n.* trou *m.*
holiday *n.* jour férié *m.*
holy *adj.* saint
home *n.* maison *f.*; pays natal *m.* (*country*)
homeland *n.* patrie *f.*
homesickness *n.* mal du pays *m.*
homework *n.* devoirs *m.pl.*
honey *n.* miel *m.*
hood *n.* capot *m.* (*car*); capuchon *m.* (*clothes*)
hook *n.* crochet *m.*; hameçon *m.* (*fishing*); *v.* accrocher
hoop *n.* cerceau *m.*
hop *n.* saut *m.*; *v.* sauter
hope *n.* espoir *m.*; *v.* espérer
horn *n.* corne *f.*
hornet *n.* frelon *m.*
horse *n.* cheval *m.*
hose *n.* tuyau *m.*
hospital *n.* hôpital *m.*
hospitality *n.* hospitalité *f.*
host *n.* hôte *m.*
hostess *n.* hôtesse *f.*
hot *adj.* chaud
hotel *n.* hôtel *m.*
hour *n.* heure *f.*
house *n.* maison *f.*; *v.* loger
how *adv.* comment
hug *n.* étreinte *f.*; *v.* serrer dans ses bras
human *adj.* humain
humid *adj.* humide
humor *n.* humour *m.*
hundred *num.* cent
hunger *n.* faim *f.*
hungry *adj.* affamé
hunt *n.* chasse *f.*; *v.* chasser
hunter *n.* chasseur *m.*
hurricane *n.* ouragan *m.*
hurry *n.* hâte *f.*; se dépêcher
hurt *v.* faire mal
husband *n.* mari *m.*
hygiene *n.* hygiène *f.*
hyphen *n.* trait d'union *m.*

I

I *pron.* je
ice *n.* glace *f.*; verglas *m.* (*road*)
ice cream *n.* glace *f.*
ice cube *n.* glaçon *m.*
ice hockey *n.* hockey sur glace *m.*
ice skate *n.* patin à glace *m.*
icy *adj.* glacé; verglassé (*road*)
idea *n.* idée *f.*
ideal *adj.* idéal
identical *adj.* identique
identify *v.* identifier
identity *n.* identité *f.*
identity card *n.* carte d'identité *f.*
idiot *n.; adj.* idiot *m.*, idiote *f.*
if *conj.* si
ignition *n.* allumage *m.*
ignore *v.* ignorer
ill *adj.* malade; mauvais (*bad*)
illegal *adj.* illégal
illness *n.* maladie *f.*
illustration *n.* illustration *f.*
image *n.* image *f.*
imagination *n.* imagination *f.*
imagine *v.* imaginer
imitate *v.* imiter
immediately *adv.* immédiatement
import *n.* importation *f.*; *v.* importer
importance *n.* importance *f.*
important *adj.* important
impossible *adj.* impossible
in *prep.* dans, en
inappropriate *adj.* inopportun
inch *n.* pouce *m.*
incline *n.* pente *f.*; *v.* (s') incliner
include *v.* inclure
income *n.* revenu *m.*
increase *n.* augmentation *f.*; *v.* augmenter
index *n.* index *m.*; catalogue *m.* (*library*); *v.* classer
indicate *v.* indiquer
indifferent *adj.* indifférent
indigestion *n.* indigestion *f.*
industry *n.* industrie *f.*
inedible *adj.* immangeable; non comestible (*plant*)

infect *v.* infecter, contaminer
infection *n.* infection *f.*
information *n.* information *f.*; renseignements *m.pl.*
inhabitant *n.* habitant *m.*, habitante *f.*
initial *n.* initiale *f.*; *adj.* initial
initiate *v.* amorcer
inject *v.* injecter
injection *n.* injection *f.*, piqûre *f.*
injure *v.* blesser
injury *n.* blessure *f.*
ink *n.* encre *f.*
in-laws *n.pl.* beaux-parents *m.pl.*
inn *n.* auberge *f.*
innocent *adj.* innocent
inquire *v.* demander
insect *n.* insecte *m.*
inside *n.; adj.* intérieur *m.*; *adv.* à l'intérieur, dedans; *prep.* à l'intérieur de
insist *v.* insister
insomnia *n.* insomnie *f.*
inspect *v.* inspecter
inspector *n.* inspecteur *m.*
install *v.* installer
installation *n.* installation *f.*
instead of *adv.* au lieu de
instrument *n.* instrument *m.*
insulate *v.* isoler
insulation *n.* isolation *f.*
insult *n.* insulte *f.*; *v.* insulter
insurance *n.* assurance *f.*
insure *v.* assurer
intelligence *n.* intelligence *f.*
interest *n.* intérêt *m.*
interesting *adj.* intéressant
interior *n.; adj.* intérieur
international *adj.* international
Internet *n.* Internet *m.*
interpret *v.* interpréter
intersection *n.* croisement *m.*
intervene *v.* intervenir
intervention *n.* intervention *f.*
interview *n.* interview *m.*; entrevue *f.* (*job*)
intestine *n.* intestin *m.*
into *prep.* dans
intoxicated *adj.* ivre
introduce *v.* introduire
introduction *n.* introduction *f.*
invent *v.* inventer
invention *n.* invention *f.*
investigate *v.* enquêter
invitation *n.* invitation *f.*
invite *v.* inviter
iron *n.* fer *m.*; fer à repasser *m.* (*clothes*); *v.* repasser
ironing board *n.* planche à repasser *f.*
Islam *n.* Islam *m.*
island *n.* île *f.*
isolate *v.* isoler
issue *n.* question *f.*; numéro *m.* (*magazine*)
it *pron.* il, elle; le, la, l'
Italy *n.* Italie *f.*
Italian *n.; adj.* Italien *m.*, Italienne *f.*
itch *n.* démangeaison *f.*
item *n.* article *m.*

J

jack *n.* cric *m.*
jacket *n.* veste *f.*; jaquette *f.* (*book*)
jail *n.* prison *f.*; *v.* emprisonner
jam *n.* confiture *f.*
janitor *n.* concierge *m.*
January *n.* janvier *m.*
jar *n.* pot *m.*; bocal *m.* (*glass*)
jaw *n.* mâchoire *f.*
jealous *adj.* jaloux
jealousy *n.* jalousie *f.*
jeans *n.pl.* jean *m.*
jelly *n.* gelée *f.*
jelly fish *n.* méduse *f.*
jet *n.* jet *m.*
Jew *n.* Juif *m.*, Juive *f.*
jewel *n.* bijou *m.*
jeweler *n.* bijoutier *m.*, bijoutière *f.*
jewelry *n.* bijoux *m.pl.*
Jewish *adj.* juif
job *n.* travail *m.*
jog *v.* faire du jogging
join *v.* unir, joindre

joint *n.* joint *m.*; articulation *f.* (*body*)
joke *n.* plaisanterie *f.*; *v.* plaisanter
journal *n.* journal *m.*
journalist *n.* journaliste *m/f.*
journey *n.* voyage *m.*; trajet *m.* (*distance*)
joy *n.* joie *f.*
judge *n.* juge *m.*; *v.* juger
judgment *n.* jugement *m.*
juice *n.* jus *m.*
juicy *adj.* juteux
July *n.* juillet *m.*
jump *n.* saut *m.*; *v.* sauter
jumper cables *n.pl.* câbles de démarrage *m.pl.*
June *n.* juin *m.*
just *adj.* juste
justice *n.* justice *f.*
juvenile *n.* jeune *m/f.*; *adj.* juvénile; pour enfants (*court*)

K

keep *v.* garder; tenir (*promise*)
kettle *n.* bouilloire *f.*
key *n.* clé *f.*
keyboard *n.* clavier *m.*
keyhole *n.* trou de la serrure *m.*
kid *n.* gamin *m.*, gamine *f.*
kidney *n.* rein *m.*
kill *v.* tuer
killer *n.* tueur *m.*, tueuse *f.*
kilo *n.* kilo *m.*
kilometer *n.* kilomètre *m.*
kind *adj.* gentil *m.*
kindergarten *n.* jardin d'enfants *m.*
kindness *n.* gentillesse *f.*
king *n.* roi *m.*
kingdom *n.* royaume *m.*
kiss *n.* baiser *m.*; *v.* embrasser
kitchen *n.* cuisine *f.*
knee *n.* genou *m.*
knife *n.* couteau *m.*
knit *v.* tricoter
knob *n.* bouton *m.*
knock *v.* frapper
knot *n.* noeud *m.*; *v.* nouer
know *v.* savoir; connaître (*person*)
knowledge *n.* connaissance *f.*
kosher *adj.* kascher

L

label *n.* étiquette *f.*
labor *n.* travail *m.*; main d'œuvre *f.* (*workforce*)
laboratory *n.* laboratoire *m.*
lace *n.* dentelle *f.*; lacet *m.* (*shoe*); *v.* lacer
lack *n.* manque *m.*; *v.* manquer de
ladder *n.* échelle *f.*
lady *n.* dame *f.*
lake *n.* lac *m.*
lamp *n.* lampe *f.*
land *n.* pays *m.*; terre *f.* (*opposed to water*); *v.* atterrir
landlord *n.* propriétaire *m/f.*
landscape *n.* paysage *m.*
lane *n.* voie *f.*
language *n.* langue *f.*
laptop (computer) *n.* (ordinateur) portable *m.*
large *adj.* grand; gros (*person*)
last *adj.* dernier; *adv.* en dernier; *v.* durer
late *adj.* en retard; *adv.* tard
later *adv.* plus tard
laugh *n.* rire *m.*; *v.* rire
Laundromat *n.* laverie automatique *f.*
laundry *n.* linge *m.*; blanchisserie *f.* (*place*)
laundry detergent *n.* produit à lessive *m.*
lavender *n.* lavande *f.*
law *n.* loi *f.*; droit *m.* (*study*)
lawful *adj.* légal
lawn *n.* pelouse *f.*
lawsuit *n.* procès *m.*
lawyer *n.* avocat *m.*, avocate *f.*
laxative *n.* laxatif *m.*
lay *v.* poser, mettre
layer *n.* couche *f.*
lazy *adj.* paresseux

lead *n.* avance *f.*; *v.* mener, conduire
leadership *n.* direction *f.*
leaf *n.* feuille *f.*
league *n.* ligue *f.*
leak *n.* fuite *f.*; *v.* fuire
lean *adj.* maigre
leap year *n.* année bissextile *f.*
learn *v.* apprendre
lease *n.* bail *m.*; *v.* louer à bail
least *adj.* le, la moindre; le moins de
leather *n.* cuir *m.*
leave *v.* laisser; partir; quitter
lecture *n.* conférence *f.*; cours *m.* (*school*)
left *n.; adj.* gauche *f.*; *adv.* à gauche
leg *n.* jambe *f.*
legal *adj.* légal
legend *n.* légende *f.*
legitimate *adj.* légitime
leisure *n.* loisir *m.*, temps libre *m.*
lemon *n.* citron *m.*
lend *v.* prêter
length *n.* longueur *f.*; durée *f.* (*time*)
lens *n.* lentille *f.*; objectif *m.* (*camera*)
Lent *n.* carême *m.*
less *adv.; pron.; prep.* moins; *adj.* moins de
lesson *n.* leçon *f.*
let *v.* laisser
letter *n.* lettre *f.*
liability *n.* responsabilité *f.*
liable *adj.* responsable
liaison *n.* liaison *f.*
liar *n.* menteur *m.*, menteuse *f.*
liberty *n.* liberté *f.*
librarian *n.* bibliothécaire *m/f.*
library *n.* bibliothèque *f.*
license *n.* permis *m.*
license plate *n.* plaque minéralogique *f.*
lie *n.* mensonge *m.*; *v.* mentir; être étendu (*position*)
life *n.* vie *f.*
life jacket *n.* gilet de sauvetage *m.*
lift *v.* soulever
light *n.* lumière *f.*; *adj.* léger; clair (color); *v.* allumer (*fire*); éclairer
lighter *n.* briquet *m.*
lightning *n.* éclair *m.*
like *prep.* comme; *adj.* semblable, pareil; *v.* aimer bien
limb *n.* membre *m.*
limit *n.* limite *f.*; *v.* limiter
limp *v.* boiter
line *n.* ligne *f.*; queue *f.* (*people*)
linen *n.* lin *m* (*fabric*); linge *m.*
link *n.* lien *m.*; *v.* lier
lip *n.* lèvre *f.*
lipstick *n.* rouge à lèvres *m.*
liquid *n.; adj.* liquide *m.*
liquor *n.* alcool *m.*
list *n.* liste *f.*
listen *v.* écouter
liter *n.* litre *m.*
literature *n.* littérature *f.*
litter *n.* détritus *m.pl.*
little *adj.* petit; *adv.* peu
live *adj.* vivant; en public (*performance*); *v.* habiter; vivre
liver *n.* foie *m.*
living room *n.* salle de séjour *f.*
loaf *n.* miche *f.* (*bread*)
loan *n.* prêt *m.*; *v.* prêter
lobby *n.* hall *m.*
local *adj.* local
lock *n.* serrure *f.*; *v.* fermer à clé
locker *n.* casier *m.*
locksmith *n.* serrurier *m.*
log *n.* bûche *f.*; *v.* noter
loneliness *n.* solitude *f.*
long *adj.* long; *adv.* longtemps
look *n.* regard *m.*; aspect *m.*, allure *f.* (*appearance*); *v.* regarder; sembler (*seem*)
lose *v.* perdre
loss *n.* perte *f.*
lost *adj.* perdu
loud *adj.* bruyant; fort (*voice*)
loudspeaker *n.* haut-parleur *m.*
lounge *n.* salon *m.*
love *n.* amour *m.*; *v.* aimer
low *adj.* bas; mauvais (*quality*)

luck *n.* chance *f.*
luggage *n.* bagages *m.pl.*
lunch *n.* déjeuner *m.*
lung *n.* poumon *m.*
luxurious *adj.* luxueux
luxury *n.* luxe *m.*

M

machine *n.* machine *f.*
mad *adj.* fou; furieux (*angry*)
madam *n.* madame *f.*
magazine *n.* magazine *m.*, revue *f.*
magic *n.* magie *f.*; *adj.* magique
magician *n.* magicien *m.*, magicienne *f.*
magnet *n.* aimant *m.*
magnifying glass *n.* loupe *f.*
maid *n.* bonne *f.*
maiden name *n.* nom de jeune fille *m.*
mail *n.* poste *f.*; courrier *m.* (*letters*); *v.* envoyer (par la poste)
mailbox *n.* boîte aux lettres *f.*
main *adj.* principal
majority *n.* majorité
make *v.* faire
makeup *n.* maquillage *m.*
male *n.; adj.* mâle *m.*; *adj.* masculin
mall *n.* centre commercial *m.*
man *n.* homme *m.*
manager *n.* directeur *m.*, directrice *f.*
mandatory *adj.* obligatoire
manner *n.* manière *f.*
manual *n.; adj.* manuel *m.*
many *adj.* beaucoup de; *pron.* beaucoup, un grand nombre
map *n.* carte *f.*; plan *m.* (*street*)
March *n.* mars *m.*
margin *n.* marge *f.*
marine *adj.* marin
mark *n.* marque *f.*; *v.* marquer
market *n.* marché *m.*; *v.* commercialiser
marriage *n.* mariage *m.*
marry *v.* épouser, (se) marier
masculine *adj.* masculin
mask *n.* masque *m.*; *v.* masquer
mason *n.* maçon *m.*
mass *n.* masse *f.*; messe *f.* (*church*)
master *n.* maître *m.*; *v.* maîtriser
match *n.* allumette *f.*; match *m.* (*sport*); *v.* assortir
mate *n.* compagnon *m.*, compagne *f.*
material *n.* matière *f.*; tissu *m.* (*fabric*)
maternity *n.* maternité *f.*
matter *n.* matière *f.*; affaire *f.*
mattress *n.* matelas *m.*
mature *adj.* mûr; *v.* mûrir
maturity *n.* maturité *f.*
maximum *n.; adj.* maximum *m.*
May *n.* mai *m.*
maybe *adv.* peut-être
meal *n.* repas *m.*
mean *adj.* méchant; *v.* signifier, vouloir dire
meaning *n.* sens *m.*, signification *f.*
means *n.pl.* moyen(s) *m.(pl.)*
measure *n.* mesure *f.*; *v.* mesurer
meat *n.* viande *f.*
mechanic *n.* mécanicien *m.*
mechanical *adj.* mécanique
medal *n.* médaille *f.*
medical *adj.* médical
medication *n.* médicaments *m.pl.*
Mediterranean Sea *n.* (mer) Méditerranée *f.*
meet *v.* rencontrer
meeting *n.* rencontre *f.*; réunion *f.* (*session*)
melt *v.* fondre; faire fondre
member *n.* membre *m.*
memorize *v.* apprendre par cœur
memory *n.* mémoire *f.*; souvenir *m.* (*recollection*)
menace *n.* menace *f.*; *v.* menacer
mention *n.* mention *f.*; *v.* mentionner
menu *n.* menu *m.*; carte *f.* (*list of dishes*)
merchandise *n.* marchandises *f.pl.*

Merry Christmas! *inter.* Joyeux Noël !
mess *n.* désordre *m.*
message *n.* message *m.*
messenger *n.* messager *m.*, messagère *f.*
metal *n.* métal *m.*
meter *n.* mètre *m.*
middle *n.* milieu *m.*; *adj.* moyen; du milieu
midnight *n.* minuit *m.*
mild *adj.* doux
mile *n.* mille *m.*
milestone *n.* borne *f.*
military *adj.* militaire
milk *n.* lait *m.*
mill *n.* moulin *m.*
million *n.* million *m.*
mind *n.* esprit *m.*
minimum *adj.* minimum
minister *n.* pasteur *m.*
minor *n.* mineur *m.*, mineure *f.*
minority *n.* minorité *f.*
mint *n.* menthe *f.*
minus *prep.* moins
minute *n.* minute *f.*
mirror *n.* miroir *m.*, glace *f.*
miscellaneous *adj.* divers, varié
miss *n.* mademoiselle *f.*; *v.* manquer
mistake *n.* faute *f.*; *v.* mal comprendre
mister *n.* monsieur *m.*
misunderstanding *n.* malentendu *m.*
mix *v.* mélanger
model *n.* modèle *m.*; mannequin *m.* (*fashion*)
modem *n.* modem *m.*
moderate *adj.* modéré
modern *adj.* moderne
modify *v.* modifier
moist *adj.* humide
moisture *n.* humidité *f.*
mold *n.* moisissure *f.*
moment *n.* moment *m.*, instant *m.*
monastery *n.* monastère *m.*
Monday *n.* lundi *m.*
money *n.* argent *m.*
monk *n.* moine *m.*
monkey *n.* singe *m.*
monster *n.* monstre *m.*
month *n.* mois *m.*
monument *n.* monument *m.*
mood *n.* humeur *f.*
moon *n.* lune *f.*
mop *n.* balai à franges *m.*; *v.* éponger
more *adj.* plus de, encore; *pron.*; *adv.* plus
morning *n.* matin *m.*
mortgage *n.* hypothèque *f.*
mosque *n.* mosquée *f.*
mosquito *n.* moustique *m.*
most *adj.* la plupart de; le plus de; *pron.* la plupart; *adv.* le plus
mother *n.* mère *f.*
mother-in-law *n.* belle-mère *f.*
motion *n.* mouvement *m.*
motivation *n.* motivation *f.*
motive *n.* motif *m.*
motorbike *n.* moto *f.*
mount *n.* mont *m.*
mountain *n.* montagne *f.*
mouse *n.* souris *f.*
mouth *n.* bouche *f.*
move *n.* mouvement *m.*; déménagement *m.* (*house*); *v.* bouger; déménager; émouvoir (*emotion*)
movie *n.* film *m.*
movie theater *n.* cinéma *m.*
much *adj.* beaucoup de; *n.*; *pron.*; *adv.* beaucoup
mud *n.* boue *f.*
mug *n.* grande tasse *f.*; chope *f.* (*beer*)
multiply *v.* multiplier
murder *n.* meurtre *m.*; *v.* assassiner
murderer *n.* meurtrier *m.*, meurtrière *f.*
muscle *n.* muscle *m.*
museum *n.* musée *m.*
mushroom *n.* champignon *m.*
music *n.* musique *f.*
musician *n.* musicien *m.*, musicienne *f.*
must *v.* devoir

mustache *n.* moustache *f.*
mustard *n.* moutarde *f.*
mute *adj.* muet

N

nail *n.* ongle *m.* (*finger*); clou *m.*; *v.* clouer
nail polish *n.* vernis à ongles *m.*
nail polish remover *n.* dissolvant *m.*
naked *adj.* nu
name *n.* nom *m.*; *v.* nommer
nap *n.* somme *m.*; *v.* faire un somme
napkin *n.* serviette *f.*
narrow *adj.* étroit; *v.* se rétrécir (*road*)
nation *n.* nation *f.*
nationality *n.* nationalité *f.*
native *n.* autochtone *m/f.*; *adj.* indigène; natal (*country*)
natural *adj.* naturel
nature *n.* nature *f.*
nausea *n.* nausée *f.*
navel *n.* nombril *n.*
navigate *v.* naviguer
navy *n.* marine *f.*
near *adv.* près; *adj.* proche; *prep.* près de
nearly *adv.* presque
neat *adj.* soigné; bien rangé (*room*)
necessary *adj.* nécessaire
necessity *n.* nécessité *f.*
neck *n.* nuque *f.*
necklace *n.* collier *m.*
need *n.* besoin *m.*; *v.* avoir besoin de
needle *n.* aiguille *f.*
negative *adj.* négatif
neighbor *n.* voisin *m.*, voisine *f.*
neighborhood *n.* quartier *m.*
neither *adj.; pron.* ni l'un ni l'autre
nephew *n.* neveu *m.*
nerve *n.* nerf *m.*
nervous *adj.* nerveux
nest *n.* nid *m.*
net *n.* filet *m.*
network *n.* réseau *m.*
neutral *adj.* neutre
never *adv.* jamais
new *adj.* nouveau; neuf (*brand new*)
news *n.* nouvelle(s) *f.(pl.)*; informations *f.pl.* (*TV*)
newspaper *n.* journal *m.*
newsstand *n.* kiosque à journaux *m.*
New Year *n.* Nouvel An *m.*
New Year's Eve *n.* Saint-Sylvestre *f.*
next *adj.* prochain (*time*); voisin (*seat*); *prep.* à côté
nice *adj.* gentil; joli (*pretty*)
nickname *n.* surnom *m.*
niece *n.* nièce *f.*
night *n.* nuit *f.*; soir *m.* (*evening*)
nightmare *n.* cauchemar *m.*
nine *num.* neuf
no *adv.* non; *adj.* aucun
nobility *n.* noblesse *f.*
nobody *pron.* personne
noise *n.* bruit *m.*
noisy *adj.* bruyant
none *pron.* aucun
noon *n.* midi *m.*
normal *adj.* normal
north *n.* nord *m.*
nose *n.* nez *m.*
nostril *n.* narine *f.*
nosy *adj.* curieux
not *adv.* (ne …) pas
note *n.* note *f.*
notebook *n.* carnet *m.*
nothing *n.; pron.* rien *m.*
notice *v.* remarquer
notify *v.* notifier
noun *n.* nom *m.*
nourishing *adj.* nourrissant
novel *n.* roman *m.*
November *n.* novembre *m.*
now *adv.* maintenant
nowadays *adv.* de nos jours
nowhere *adv.* nulle part
nude *n.; adj.* nu *m.*
number *n.* nombre *m.*; numéro *m.* (*house*)
numerous *adj.* nombreux
nun *n.* religieuse *f.*

nurse *n.* infirmier *m.*, infirmière *f.*; *v.* soigner
nut *n.* noix *f.*; écrou *m.* (*metal*)

O

obese *adj.* obèse
object *n.* objet *m.*
objection *n.* objection *f.*
obscene *adj.* obscène
obscure *adj.* obscur; *v.* obscurcir
observation *n.* observation *f.*
observe *v.* observer
obstacle *n.* obstacle *m.*
obtain *v.* obtenir
obvious *adj.* évident
occasion *n.* occasion *f.*; événement *m.* (*event*)
occasional *adj.* occasionel
occasionally *adv.* de temps en temps
occupation *n.* occupation *f.*; métier *m.* (*job*)
occupy *v.* occuper
occur *v.* se produire
ocean *n.* océan *m.*
October *n.* octobre *m.*
odd *adj.* bizarre
odor *n.* odeur *f.*
of *prep.* de
of course *adv.* bien sûr
offend *v.* offenser, blesser
offensive *adj.* offensant; offensif (*weapon*)
offer *n.* offre *f.*; *v.* offrir
office *n.* bureau *m.*
officer *n.* officier *m.*; agent *m.* (*police*)
official *adj.* officiel
often *adv.* souvent
oil *n.* huile *f.*; pétrole *m.* (*petroleum*); mazout *m.* (*heating*)
oily *adj.* huileux
old *adj.* vieux
old-fashioned *adj.* démodé
on *prep.* sur; *adj.* allumé (*TV*)
once *adv.* une fois
one *num.* un; *pron.* un, une; on (*impersonal*)
onion *n.* oignon *m.*
only *adv.* seulement; *adj.* seul, unique
open *adj.* ouvert; *v.* ouvrir
open-minded *adj.* à l'esprit ouvert
operation *n.* opération *f.*
operator *n.* téléphoniste *m/f.* (*phone*)
opinion *n.* opinion *f.*, avis *m.*
opponent *n.* adversaire *m/f.*
oppose *v.* s'opposer à
opposite *n.* opposé *m.*, contraire *m.*; *adj.* opposé; d'en face; *adv.* en face
optician *n.* opticien *m.*, opticienne *f.*
option *n.* option *f.*, choix *m.*
or *conj.* ou
oral *n.; adj.* oral *m.*
orange *n.; adj.* orange *f.*
orchestra *n.* orchestre *m.*
order *n.* ordre *m.*; commande *f.* (*purchase*); *v.* ordonner; commander
ordinary *adj.* ordinaire
organ *n.* organe *m.*; orgue *m.* (*music*)
organization *n.* organisation *f.*
organize *v.* organiser
origin *n.* origine *f.*
other *adj.* autre
ounce *n.* once *f.*
out *adv.* dehors; sorti (*gone out*)
outdoor *adj.* en plein air
outside *n.; adj.* extérieur *m.*; *adv.* à l'extérieur; *prep.* à l'extérieur de
oven *n.* four *m.*
over *prep.* sur; au-dessus de; *adv.* dessus; *adj.* terminé, fini
overtime *n.* heures supplémentaires *f.pl.*
owe *v.* devoir
own *adj.* propre; *v.* posséder
owner *n.* propriétaire *m/f.*
oxygen *n.* oxygène *m.*

P

pace *n.* pas *m.*; allure *f.* (*speed*)
pacemaker *n.* stimulateur cardiaque *m.*
pack *n.* paquet *m.*; *v.* emballer; faire ses bagages (*suitcase*)
page *n.* page *f.*
pain *n.* douleur *f.*
painful *adj.* douloureux
paint *n.* peinture *f.*; *v.* peindre
painting *n.* peinture *f.*, tableau *m.*
pair *n.* paire *f.*
pajamas *n.pl.* pyjama *m.*
palate *n.* palais *m.*
pale *adj.* pâle
pan *n.* casserole *f.*; poêle *f.* (*frying*)
pants *n.pl.* pantalon *m.*
paper *n.* papier *m.*
paralysis *n.* paralysie *f.*
paralyze *v.* paralyser
parents *n.pl.* parents *m.pl.*
park *n.* parc *m.*; *v.* garer
parking lot *n.* parking *m.*
part *n.* partie *f.*; pièce *f.* (*machine*); rôle *m.* (*theater*)
part-time *adj.; adv.* à mi-temps, à temps partiel
partner *n.* partenaire *m/f.*
party *n.* fête *f.*; parti *m.* (*politics*)
pass *n.* laissez-passer *m.* (*permit*); carte d'abonnement *f.*; col *m.* (*mountain*); *v.* passer; réussir (*exam*)
passenger *n.* passager *m.*, passagère *f.*
passport *n.* passeport *m.*
past *n.; adj.* passé *m.*
pastry *n.* pâtisserie *f.*
path *n.* chemin *m.*
patient *n.; adj.* patient *m.*, patiente *f.*
paw *n.* patte *f.*
pay *n.* paie *f.*, salaire *m.*; *v.* payer
payment *n.* paiement *m.*
peace *n.* paix *f.*
peak *n.* sommet *m.*; pic *m.*
pearl *n.* perle *f.*
pebble *n.* caillou *m.*
pedal *n.* pédale *f.*; *v.* pédaler
pedestrian *n.* piéton *m.*
pen *n.* stylo *m.*
pencil *n.* crayon *m.*
people *n.* gens *m.pl.*; peuple *m.*
pepper *n.* poivre *m.*
percent *n.; adj.; adv.* pour cent *m.*
perfect *adj.* parfait
perfume *n.* parfum *m.*
perhaps *adv.* peut-être
period *n.* période *f.*; époque *f.* (*history*); règles *f.pl.* (*menstruation*)
permit *n.* permis *m.*
person *n.* personne *f.*
pet *n.* animal domestique *m.*
petite *adj.* menu
pharmacy *n.* pharmacie *f.*
phone *n.* téléphone *m.*
phonebook *n.* annuaire *m.*
photo *n.* photo *f.*
photocopy *n.* photocopie *f.*
photograph *v.* photographier
phrase *n.* expression *f.*
physical *adj.* physique
physician *n.* médecin *m.*
picnic *n.* pique-nique *m.*
picture *n.* image *f.*; photo *f.*
pie *n.* tourte *f.*; tarte *f.* (*fruit*)
piece *n.* morceau *m.*
pile *n.* pile *f.*, tas *m.*; *v.* empiler
pill *n.* pilule *f.*
pillow *n.* oreiller *m.*
pillowcase *n.* taie d'oreiller *f.*
pilot *n.* pilote *m.*; *v.* piloter
pin *n.* épingle *f.*; *v.* épingler
pinch *n.* pincée *f.*; *v.* pincer
pine *n.* pin *m.*
pink *adj.* rose
pint *n.* pinte *f.*
pipe *n.* pipe *f.* (*smoking*); tuyau *m.*
place *n.* endroit *m.*, lieu *m.*; place *f.* (*seat*); *v.* placer
plain *n.* plaine *f.*; *adj.* simple; nature (*yogurt*); noir (*coffee*)
plan *n.* plan *m.*
plane *n.* avion *m.*
planet *n.* planète *f.*
plant *n.* plante *f.*

plastic *n.* plastique *m.*
plate *n.* assiette *f.*
play *n.* pièce *f.* (*theater*); *v.* jouer
please *inter.* s'il vous plaît (*pl.; formal*); s'il te plaît (*sing.; informal*)
pleasure *n.* plaisir *m.*
plug *n.* prise *f.* (*electric*); bouchon *m.*; *v.* brancher (*electric*); boucher
plumber *n.* plombier *m.*
plural *n.; adj.* pluriel *m.*
plus *prep.* plus
pocket *n.* poche *f.*
pocketknife *n.* canif *m.*
poetry *n.* poésie *f.*
point *n.* point *m.*; pointe *f.* (*tip*); *v.* indiquer
poison *n.* poison *m.*; *v.* empoisonner
poisonous *adj.* toxique; vénéneux (*plant*); venimeux (*snake*)
pole *n.* poteau *m.*
police *n.pl.* police *f.*
police officer *n.* agent de police *m.*
police station *n.* commissariat de police *m.*
policy *n.* politique *f.*; police *f.* (*insurance*)
polite *adj.* poli
political *adj.* politique
politics *n.pl.* politique *f.*
pond *n.* étang *m.*
pony *n.* poney *m.*
pool *n.* piscine *f.*; billard *m.* (*game*)
poor *adj.* pauvre
pope *n.* pape *m.*
population *n.* population *f.*
pork *n.* porc *m.*
portrait *n.* portrait *m.*
position *n.* position *f.*; *v.* placer
positive *adj.* positif; sûr, certain (*certain*)
possible *adj.* possible
post *n.* poste *m.*
postcard *n.* carte postale *f.*
post office *n.* poste *f.*
pot *n.* casserole *f.*
pottery *n.* poterie *f.*
poultry *n.* volaille *f.*
pound *n.* livre *f.*
pour *v.* verser; pleuvoir à torrents (*rain*)
powder *n.* poudre *f.*
power *n.* pouvoir *m.* (*ability*); courant *m.* (*electric*)
practical *adj.* pratique
pray *v.* prier
prayer *n.* prière *f.*
prefer *v.* préférer
pregnant *adj.* enceinte
prepaid *adj.* payé d'avance
prepare *v.* préparer
prescription *n.* ordonnance *f.*
present *n.* cadeau *m.* (*gift*); *adj.* présent; *v.* présenter
president *n.* président *m.*, présidente *f.*
press *n.* presse *f.*; *v.* presser
pressure *n.* pression *f.*
pretty *adj.* joli; *adv.* assez
prevent *v.* empêcher
previous *adj.* précédent
price *n.* prix *m.*
pride *n.* fierté *f.*
priest *n.* prêtre *m.*
prime minister *n.* premier ministre *m.*
principal *adj.* principal
principle *n.* principe *m.*
prison *n.* prison *f.*
prisoner *n.* prisonnier *m.*, prisonnière *f.*
privacy *n.* intimité *f.*
private *adj.* privé
privilege *n.* privilège *m.*
probably *adv.* probablement
problem *n.* problème *m.*
produce *n.* produits *m.pl.*; *v.* produire
product *n.* produit *m.*
profession *n.* profession *f.*
professor *n.* professeur *m.*
profile *n.* profil *m.*
profit *n.* profit *m.*, bénéfice *m.*; *v.* profiter de
program *n.* programme *m.*
progress *n.* progrès *m.*; *v.* progresser

prohibit *v.* interdire
project *n.* project *m.*; *v.* projeter
promenade *n.* promenade *f.*
promise *n.* promesse *f.*; *v.* promettre
proof *n.* preuve *f.*
property *n.* propriété *f.*
proposal *n.* proposition *f.*; demande en mariage *f.* (*marriage*)
propose *v.* proposer; demander en mariage (*engagement*)
protect *v.* protéger
protection *n.* protection *f.*
protest *n.* protestation *f.*; *v.* protester
Protestant *n.; adj.* protestant *m.*, protestante *f.*
proud *adj.* fier
prove *v.* prouver
proverb *n.* proverbe *m.*
provide *v.* fournir
province *n.* province *f.*
prudent *adj.* prudent
pub *n.* pub *m.*
public *n.; adj.* public *m.*
publicity *n.* publicité *f.*
public transport *n.* transports en commun *m.pl.*
publish *v.* publier
pull *v.* tirer
pulse *n.* pouls *m.*
pump *n.* pompe *f.*; *v.* pomper
purchase *n.* achat *m.*; *v.* acheter
pure *adj.* pur
purple *adj.* violet
purpose *n.* intention *f.*
purse *n.* sac à main *m.*
push *v.* pousser
put *v.* mettre, poser

Q

quality *n.* qualité *f.*
quantity *n.* quantité *f.*
quarantine *n.* quarantaine *f.*
quarter *n.* quart *m.*; trimestre *m.* (*year*)
queasy *adj.* avoir mal au cœur (*feel*)
queen *n.* reine *f.*
question *n.* question *f.*; interroger
quick *adj.* rapide
quiet *adj.* calme, tranquille
quilt *n.* édredon *m.*
quit *v.* quitter; arrêter de (*smoking*)
quite *adv.* assez
quote *n.* citation *f.*; devis *m.* (*estimate*); *v.* citer

R

rabbi *n.* rabbin *m.*
rabbit *n.* lapin *m.*
race *n.* race *f.* (*people*); course *f.*; *v.* faire la course
racism *n.* racisme *m.*
racquet *n.* raquette *f.*
radio *n.* radio *f.*
rage *n.* rage *f.*
railroad *n.* voie ferrée *f.*
rain *n.* pluie *f.*; *v.* pleuvoir
rainbow *n.* arc-en ciel *m.*
raincoat *n.* imperméable *m.*
rainy *adj.* pluvieux
raise *n.* augmentation *f.*; *v.* elever; augmenter
RAM *n.* mémoire vive *f.* (*computer*)
ramp *n.* rampe *f.*; bretelle d'accès *f.* (*highway*)
random *adj.* fait au hasard
range *n.* chaîne *f.* (*mountain*)
rape *n.* viol *m.*; *v.* violer
rare *adj.* rare; saignant (*meat*)
rash *n.* éruption *f.*, rougeur *f.*
rat *n.* rat *m.*
rate *n.* taux *m.*; tarif *m.* (*price*)
raw *adj.* cru
razor *n.* rasoir *m.*
razor blade *n.* lame de rasoir *f.*
react *v.* réagir
reaction *n.* réaction *f.*
read *v.* lire
reader *n.* lecteur *m.*, lectrice *f.*
ready *adj.* prêt

real *adj.* réel, véritable
reality *n.* réalité *f.*
realize *v.* réaliser
rear *n.* arrière; *adj.* arrière, de derrière
reason *n.* raison *f.*
recall *n.* rappel *m.*; *v.* rappeler
receipt *n.* reçu *m.*
receive *v.* recevoir
receiver *n.* récepteur *m.*
recent *adj.* récent
reception *n.* réception *f.*
recipe *n.* recette *f.*
recognize *v.* reconnaître
recommend *v.* recommander
record *n.* disque *m.* (*music*); record *m.* (*sport*); *v.* enregistrer
recover *v.* récupérer; se rétablir (*from illness*)
red *adj.* rouge; roux (*hair*)
reduce *v.* réduire
reduction *n.* réduction *f.*; rabais *m.* (*price*)
refer *v.* adresser à (*medical*); renvoyer à (*note*)
referee *n.* arbitre *m.*
refreshment *n.* rafraîchissement *m.*
refrigerator *n.* réfrigérateur *m.*
refund *n.* remboursement *m.*; *v.* rembourser
regard *n.* respect *m.*; *v.* considérer
regarding *prep.* en ce qui concerne
region *n.* région *f.*
register *n.* registre *m.*; *v.* enregistrer; envoyer en recommandé (*letter*)
regret *n.* regret *m.*; *v.* regretter
regular *adj.* régulier
regulation *n.* règlement *m.*
relationship *n.* relation *f.*
relative *n.* parent *m.*, parente *f.*
relax *v.* (se) détendre
reliable *adj.* fiable
relief *n.* soulagement *m.*
relieve *v.* soulager
religion *n.* religion *f.*
religious *adj.* religieux
rely *v.* compter sur
remain *v.* rester
remark *n.* remarque *f.*; *v.* remarquer
remember *v.* se souvenir, se rappeler
remind *v.* rappeler
remote control *n.* télécommande *f.*
remove *v.* enlever
renew *v.* renouveler
renovate *v.* rénover, restaurer
renown *adj.* renommé
rent *n.* loyer *m.*; *v.* louer
repair *n.* réparation *f.*
repeat *n.* reprise *f.*; *v.* répéter
repellent *n.* insectifuge *m.* (*insect*)
repetition *n.* répétition *f.*
replace *v.* remplacer; remettre (*put back*)
reply *n.* réponse *f.*; *v.* répondre
report *n.* rapport *m.*; *v.* rapporter
represent *v.* représenter
representative *n.* représentant *m.*, représentante *f.*; député *m.* (*politics*)
republic *n.* république *f.*
reputation *n.* réputation *f.*
request *n.* requête *f.*; demande *f.*
require *v.* exiger; demander (*thing*)
requirement *n.* exigence *f.*;
rescue *n.* sauvetage *m.*; *v.* sauver
research *n.* recherche *f.*; *v.* faire des recherches
reservation *n.* réservation *f.*
reserve *v.* réserver
residence *n.* résidence *f.*
resist *v.* résister
resort *n.* station *f.* (*ski*)
respect *n.* respect *m.*; *v.* respecter
respond *v.* répondre
response *n.* réponse *f.*
responsibility *n.* responsabilité *f.*
responsible *adj.* responsable
rest *n.* repos *m.*; *v.* se reposer
restaurant *n.* restaurant *m.*
restore *v.* restaurer
restrict *v.* restreindre
rest room *n.* toilettes *f.pl.*
result *n.* résultat *m.*
retire *v.* prendre sa retraite

return *n.* retour *m.*; *v.* retourner
reverse *n.* marche arrière *f.* (*car*); dos *m.* (*back*)
review *n.* revue *f.*; critique *f.* (*movie*); *v.* passer en revue
reward *n.* récompense *f.*; *v.* récompenser
rhythm *n.* rythme *m.*
rib *n.* côte *f.*
ribbon *n.* ruban *m.*
rice *n.* riz *m.*
rich *adj.* riche
ride *n.* tour *m.*; *v.* faire un tour
right *n.* droite *f.* (*direction*); *adj.* droit; juste (*true*); bon (*best*)
ring *n.* bague *f.* (*finger*); sonnerie *f.* (*bell*)
rinse *v.* rincer
riot *n.* émeute *f.*
ripe *adj.* mûr
rise *v.* monter; se lever
risk *n.* risque *m.*; *v.* risquer
river *n.* rivière *f.*
road *n.* route *f.*
rob *v.* voler
robbery *n.* voleur *m.*, voleuse *f.*
robe *n.* peignoir *m.* (*bath*)
rock *n.* pierre *f.*, caillou *m.*; *v.* bercer (*child*)
rod *n.* baguette *f.*; canne à pêche *f.* (*fishing*)
role *n.* rôle *m.*
roll *n.* rouleau *m.*; petit pain *m.* (*bread*); *v.* rouler
romance *n.* idylle *f.*
roof *n.* toit *m.*
room *n.* pièce *f.*; place *f.* (*space*); salle *f.* (*building*)
roommate *n.* collocataire *m/f.*
rope *n.* corde *f.*
rotten *adj.* pourri
round *adj.* rond
route *n.* itinéraire *m.*
row *n.* rang *m.*
royal *adj.* royal
rubber band *n.* élastique *f.*
rude *adj.* grossier
rug *n.* tapis *m.*
ruin *n.* ruine *f.*; *v.* ruiner
rule *n.* règle *m.*
run *v.* courir; diriger (*business*); tenir (*hotel*)
rush *n.* hâte *f.*; *v.* se dépêcher
rust *n.* rouille *f.*; *v.* rouiller

S

Sabbath *n.* sabbat *m.*
sad *adj.* triste
saddle *n.* selle *f.*
safe *n.* coffre-fort *m.*; *adj.* sûr
safety *n.* sécurité *f.*
safety pin *n.* épingle de nourrice *f.*
sail *n.* voile *f.*
sailboat *n.* voilier *m.*
sailor *n.* marin *m.*
salad *n.* salade *f.*
salary *n.* salaire *m.*
sale *n.* vente *f.*; soldes *f.pl.* (*reduced price*)
saliva *n.* salive *f.*
salt *n.* sel *m.*; *v.* saler
same *adj.* même
sample *n.* échantillon *m.*; *v.* goûter
sand *n.* sable *m.*
sandal *n.* sandale *f.*
sanitary pad *n.* serviette hygiénique *f.*
Santa Claus *n.* père Noël *m.*
satisfy *v.* satisfaire
Saturday *n.* samedi *m.*
savory *adj.* salé
say *v.* dire
scale *n.* échelle *f.*; écaille *f.* (*fish*)
scales *n.pl.* balance *f.*
scar *n.* cicatrice *f.*
scarf *n.* écharpe *f.*; foulard *m.* (*light*)
scenery *n.* paysage *m.*
scent *n.* odeur *f.*; parfum *m.*
schedule *n.* horaire *m.* (*train*); programme *m.*
scholarship *n.* bourse *f.* (*grant*)
school *n.* école *f.*; université *f.* (*university*)
science *n.* science *f.*
scientific *adj.* scientifique

scissors *n.pl.* ciseaux *m.pl.*
scratch *n.* égratignure *f.*; *v.* griffer
scream *n.* cri *m.*; *v.* crier
screen *n.* écran *m.*
screw *n.* vis *f.*
screwdriver *n.* tournevis *m.*
sculpt *v.* sculpter
sculpture *n.* sculpture *f.*
sea *n.* mer *f.*
seam *n.* couture *f.*
search *n.* recherche *f.*; *v.* fouiller
seasickness *n.* mal de mer *m.*
season *n.* saison *f.*; *v.* assaisonner
seat *n.* siège *m.*; place *f.* (*place*)
seat belt *n.* ceinture de sécurité *f.*
seaweed *n.* algue *f.*
second *n.; adj.* second *m.*, seconde *f.*; seconde *f.* (*time*)
secret *n.; adj.* secret *m.*
secretary *n.* secrétaire *m/f.*
security *n.* sécurité *f.*
see *v.* voir
seed *n.* graine *f.*
seem *v.* sembler
seize *v.* saisir
select *v.* choisir
selection *n.* sélection *f.*
self *n.* soi *m.*
self-service *n.; adj.* self-service *m.*
sell *v.* (se) vendre
semester *n.* semestre *m.*
send *v.* envoyer
sender *n.* expéditeur *m.*, expéditrice *f.*
senior citizen *n.* personne âgée *f.*
sentence *n.* phrase *f.*; sentence *f.* (*judgment*)
separate *adj.* séparé; *v.* séparer
separation *n.* séparation *f.*
September *n.* septembre *m.*
series *n.pl.* série *f.*; collection *f.* (*book*)
serious *adj.* sérieux; grave (*injury*)
service *n.* service *m.*
set *n.* poste *m.* (*TV*); *adj.* fixé
settle *v.* régler (*matter*); se fixer
seven *num.* sept
several *pron.; adj.* plusieurs
sew *v.* coudre
sex *n.* sexe *m.*
shade *n.* ombre *f.*; nuance *f.* (*color*)
shake *v.* secouer; trembler
shallow *adj.* superficiel (*person*); peu profond (*pond*)
shame *n.* honte *f.*
shampoo *n.* shampooing *m.*
shape *n.* forme *f.*; *v.* former
share *n.* part *f.*; *v.* partager
shark *n.* requin *m.*
sharp *adj.* tranchant (*blade*); fort (*cheese*); vif (*pain*); précis (*time*)
shave *v.* (se) raser
shaving cream *n.* crème à raser *f.*
she *pron.* elle
sheet *n.* drap *m.*; feuille *f.* (*paper*)
shelf *n.* étagère *f.*; rayon *m.* (*store*)
shell *n.* coquille *f.*; coquillage *m.* (*beach*)
shellfish *n.pl.* fruits de mer *m.pl.*
shelter *n.* abri *m.*
shepherd *n.* berger *m.*
shine *v.* briller
ship *n.* bateau *m.*
shirt *n.* chemise *f.* (*men*); chemisier *m.* (*women*)
shock *n.* choc *m.*; *v.* choquer
shoe *n.* chaussure *f.*
shoelace *n.* lacet *m.*
shoemaker *n.* cordonnier *m.*
shoe polish *n.* cirage *m.*
shoot *v.* tirer
shop *n.* magasin *m.*; *v.* faire des achats
shore *n.* rivage *m.*
short *adj.* court; petit (*person*)
shorten *v.* raccourcir
shot *n.* coup *m.*; piqûre *f.* (*injection*)
shoulder *n.* épaule *f.*
shout *v.* crier
show *n.* spectacle *m.*; exposition *f.* (*exhibit*); *v.* montrer
shower *n.* douche *f.*; averse *f.* (*rain*); *v.* prendre une douche; se doucher
shrink *v.* rétrécir
shut *v.* fermer
shutter *n.* volet *m.*

shuttle *n.* navette *f.*
sick *adj.* malade
side *n.* côté *m.*; bord *m.* (*road*)
sidewalk *n.* trottoir *m.*
sight *n.* vue *f.*
sight-seeing *n.* tourisme *m.*
sign *n.* signe *m.*; panneau *m.* (*road*); *v.* signer
signal *v.* mettre son clignotant (*car*)
signature *n.* signature *f.*
sign language *n.* language des signes *m.*
silence *n.* silence *m.*
silent *adj.* silencieux
silk *n.* soie *f.*
silly *adj.* stupide, bête
silver *n.* argent *m.*
similar *adj.* semblable
simple *adj.* simple
since *prep.; adv.* depuis; *conj.* puisque (*because*); depuis que (*time*)
sincerely *adv.* sincèrement
sing *v.* chanter
singer *n.* chanteur *m.*, chanteuse *f.*
single *adj.* unique; célibataire (*not married*)
sink *n.* évier *m.*; *v.* couler
sip *n.* gorgée *f.*
Sir *n.* Monsieur *m.*
sister *n.* sœur *f.*
sister-in-law *n.* belle-sœur *f.*
sit *v.* s'asseoir
site *n.* site *m.*
six *num.* six
size *n.* taille *f.*; pointure *f.* (*shoes*)
skate *n.* patin *m.*; *v.* patiner
ski *n.* ski *m.*; *v.* skier
skim *v.* écrémer (*milk*)
skin *n.* peau *f.*
skirt *n.* jupe *f.*
sky *n.* ciel *m.*
slang *n.* argot *m.*
sleep *n.* sommeil *m.*; *v.* dormir
sleeping bag *n.* sac de couchage *m.*
sleeping pill *n.* somnifère *m.*
sleeve *n.* manche *f.*
slice *n.* tranche *f.*; *v.* couper en tranches
slide *n.* diapositive *f.* (*photo*); toboggan *m.* (*playground*); *v.* glisser
slipper *n.* pantoufle *f.*
slope *n.* pente *f.*
slow *adj.* lent
small *adj.* petit
smart *adj.* intelligent
smell *n.* odeur *f.*; *v.* sentir
smile *n.; v.* sourire *m.*
smoke *n.* fumée *f.*; *v.* fumer
snack *n.* casse-croûte *m.*
snake *n.* serpent *m.*
sneeze *v.* éternuer
snore *v.* ronfler
snow *n.* neige *f.*; *v.* neiger
snowboard *n.* surf des neiges *m.*
snowflake *n.* flocon de neige *m.*
so *adv.* ainsi; si (*comparison*); tant de (*so much*)
soak *v.* tremper; faire tremper
soap *n.* savon
soccer *n.* football *m.*
sock *n.* chaussette *f.*
sofa *n.* canapé *m.*
sofabed *n.* canapé-lit *m.*
soft *adj.* doux
soil *n.* sol *m.*, terre *f.*
solid *adj.* solide; uni (*color*)
some *pron.* quelques-uns, quelques-unes; *adj.* du, de l', de la, des
somebody *pron.* quelqu'un
something *pron.* quelque chose
sometimes *adv.* quelquefois
son *n.* fils *m.*
song *n.* chanson *f.*, chant *m.*
son-in-law *n.* beau-fils *m.*
soon *adv.* bientôt; tôt (*early*)
sore *adj.* douloureux
sorrow *n.* chagrin *m.*
sorry *adj.* désolé
sound *n.* son *m.*
soup *n.* soupe *f.*
sour *adj.* aigre
south *n.* sud *m.*
souvenir *n.* souvenir *m.*
soy *n.* soja *m.*
spa *n.* station thermale *f.*

space *n.* espace *m.*; place *f.* (*room*)
Spain *n.* Espagne *m.*
Spanish *n.; adj.* Espagnol *m.*, Espagnole *f.*
spare part *n.* pièce de rechange *f.*
speak *v.* parler
special *adj.* spécial
specialty *n.* spécialité *f.*
spectator *n.* spectateur *m.*, spectatrice *f.*
speech *n.* parole *f.* (*ability*); discours *m.* (*talk*)
speed *n.* vitesse *f.*
spell *v.* épeler (*orally*)
spend *v.* dépenser; passer (*time*)
spider *n.* araignée *f.*
spine *n.* colonne vertébrale *f.*
spit *v.* cracher
spoil *v.* abîmer
sponge *n.* éponge *f.*
spontaneous *adj.* spontané
spoon *n.* cuillère *f.*
sport *n.* sport *m.*
spring *n.* printemps *m.* (*season*)
square *n.* carré *m.*; place *f.* (*town*)
stadium *n.* stade *m.*
stage *n.* scène *f.*; stade *m.* (*point*)
stain *n.* tache *f.*
stainless steel *n.* acier inoxydable *m.*
stairs *n.* escalier *m.*
stamp *n.* timbre *m.*
staple *n.* agrafe *f.*; *v.* agrafer
star *n.* étoile *f.*
start *n.* départ *m.*; début *m.*; *v.* commencer
starve *v.* affamer
state *n.* état *m.*
station *n.* gare *f.* (*train*)
statue *n.* statue *f.*
stay *n.* séjour *m.*; *v.* rester
steady *adj.* ferme; régulier (*regular*)
steak *n.* steak *m.*
steal *v.* voler
steam *n.* vapeur *f.*
step *n.* pas *m.*; marche *f.* (*stairs*)
stepbrother *n.* demi-frère *m.*
stepdaughter *n.* belle-fille *f.*
stepfather *n.* beau-père *m.*
stepmother *n.* belle-mère *f.*
stepsister *n.* demi-sœur *f.*
stepson *n.* beau-fils *m.*
still *adj.* immobile; *adv.* encore
sting *n.* piqûre *f.*; *v.* piquer
stink *v.* puer
stitch *n.* point de suture *m.* (*medical*)
stocking *n.* bas *m.*
stomach *n.* estomac *m.*
stone *n.* pierre *f.*
stool *n.* tabouret *m.*
stop *n.* arrêt *m.*; *v.* arrêter
storage *n.* entreposage *m.*
store *n.* magasin *m.*
storm *n.* orage *m.* (*thunder*); tempête *f.* (*snow*)
story *n.* histoire *f.*
stove *n.* cuisinière *f.* (*cooking*); poêle *m.* (*heat*)
straight *adj.* droit; raide (*hair*)
strange *adj.* étrange; inconnu (*not known*)
stranger *n.* inconnu *m.*, inconnue *f.* (*not known*)
straw *n.* paille *f.*
stream *n.* ruisseau *m.*
street *n.* rue *f.*
strength *n.* force *f.*
stress *n.* accent *m.*; stress *m.*
string *n.* ficelle *f.*
stroke *n.* attaque *f.* (*medical*)
strong *adj.* fort *m.*
student *n.* étudiant *m.*, étudiante *f.*
study *v.* étudier
stuff *n.* choses *f.pl.*
stupid *adj.* idiot, stupide
stylish *adj.* chic
subject *n.* sujet *m.*
subtitle *n.* sous-titre *m.*
subtract *v.* soustraire
suburbs *n.pl.* banlieue *f.*
subway *n.* métro *m.*
success *n.* succès *m.*
such *adj.* tel; *adv.* si

suck *v.* sucer
sue *v.* poursuivre en justice
suffer *v.* souffrir
sugar *n.* sucre *m.*
suicide *n.* suicide *m.*
suit *n.* costume *m.* (*men*); tailleur *m.* (*women*)
suitcase *n.* valise *f.*
sum *n.* somme *f.*
summary *n.* résumé *m.*
summer *n.* été *m.*
sun *n.* soleil *m.*
sunblock *n.* écran total *m.*
Sunday *n.* dimanche *m.*
sunflower *n.* tournesol *m.*
sunglasses *n.pl.* lunettes de soleil *f.pl.*
sunny *adj.* ensoleillé
sunrise *n.* lever de soleil *m.*
sunscreen *n.* crème solaire *f.*
sunset *n.* coucher de soleil *m.*
sunstroke *n.* insolation *f.*
supermarket *n.* supermarché *m.*
supper *n.* dîner *m.*; souper *m.*
sure *adj.* certain
surgeon *n.* chirurgien *m.*
surgery *n.* chirurgie *f.*
surroundings *n.pl.* environs *m.pl.*
survive *v.* survivre
suspect *n.; adj.* suspect *m.*; *v.* soupçonner
swallow *v.* avaler
swamp *n.* marais *m.*
swear *v.* jurer
sweat *n.* sueur *f.*; *v.* suer
sweater *n.* pull *m.*
sweep *v.* balayer
sweet *adj.* doux; sucré (*food*)
swell *v.* enfler (*medical*)
swim *v.* nager
swimming pool *n.* piscine *f.*
swimsuit *n.* maillot de bain *m.*
swing *n.* balançoire *f.*; *v.* balancer
Swiss *n.; adj.* Suisse *m/f.*
switch *n.* interrupteur *m.*
Switzerland *n.* Suisse *f.*
symptom *n.* symptôme *m.*
synagogue *n.* synagogue *f.*
syringe *n.* seringue *f.*

T

table *n.* table *f.*
tablecloth *n.* nappe *f.*
tablespoon *n.* cuillère à soupe *f.*
tailor *n.* tailleur *m.*
take *v.* prendre; apporter (*bring*); emmener (*accompany*)
take off *v.* décoller
talk *n.* discussion *f.*; causerie *f.* (*speech*); *v.* parler
tall *adj.* grand (*person*); haut (*thing*)
tampon *n.* tampon *m.*
tan *n.* bronzage *m.*; *v.* bronzer
tap *n.* robinet *m.* (*sink*)
tap water *n.* eau du robinet *f.*
target *n.* cible *f.*
taste *n.* goût *m.*; *v.* goûter; avoir le goût de (*like*)
tasteful *adj.* de bon goût
tasty *adj.* savoureux
tattoo *n.* tatouage *m.*
tax *n.* taxe *f.*; impôts *m.pl.* (*income*); *v.* taxer
taxi *n.* taxi *n.*
tea *n.* thé *m.*
teach *v.* enseigner
teacher *n.* professeur *m.*; instituteur *m.*, institutrice *f.* (*elementary*)
team *n.* équipe *f.*
teapot *n.* théière *f.*
tear *n.* déchirure *f.*; larme *f.*(*cry*); *v.* déchirer
tease *v.* taquiner
teaspoon *n.* cuillère à café *f.*
teenager *n.* adolescent *m.*, adolescente *f.*
teleconferencing *n.* téléconférence *f.*
telephone *n.* téléphone *m.*; *v.* téléphoner (à)
telephone book *n.* annuaire *m.*
telephone number *n.* numéro de téléphone *m.*
television *n.* télévision *f.*
tell *v.* dire; raconter (*story*)
temper *n.* caractère *m.*

temperature *n.* température *f.*
temple *n.* temple *m.*
temporary *adj.* temporaire
ten *num.* dix
tenant *n.* locataire *m/f.*
tennis *n.* tennis *m.*
tent *n.* tente *f.*
tent peg *n.* piquet de tente *m.*
tent pole *n.* montant de tente *m.*
tepid *adj.* tiède
terrace *n.* terrasse *f.*
terrible *adj.* terrible
text *n.* texte *m.*
textbook *n.* manuel *m.*
textile *n.* textile *m.*
than *conj.* que
thank *v.* remercier
thankful *n.* reconnaissant
Thank you! *inter.* Merci !
that *adj.* ce, cet, cette, ces; *pron.* ce; cela, ça; qui, que; *conj.* que
thaw *v.* dégeler
the *art.* le, la, l', les
theater *n.* théâtre *m.*
theft *n.* vol *m.*
then *adv.* ensuite, alors
there *adv.* là
thermometer *n.* thermomètre *m.*
they *pron.* ils, elles
thick *adj.* épais
thickness *n.* épaisseur *f.*
thief *n.* voleur *m.*, voleuse *f.*
thigh *n.* cuisse *f.*
thin *adj.* mince
thing *n.* chose *f.*
think *v.* penser, réfléchir
third *n.* tiers *m.* (*fraction*); *adj.* troisième
thirst *n.* soif *f.*
thirsty *adj.* assoiffé
this *adj.* ce, cet, cette, ces; *pron.* ce; celui-ci, celle-ci, ceci
thought *n.* pensée *f.*
thousand *num.* mille
threat *n.* menace *f.*
threaten *v.* menacer
three *num.* trois
throat *n.* gorge *f.*
through *prep.* à travers; pendant (*time*); *adv.* à travers
throw *v.* lancer, jeter
thumb *n.* pouce *m.*
thunder *n.* tonnerre *m.*
thunderstorm *n.* orage *m.*
Thursday *n.* jeudi *m.*
ticket *n.* billet *m.*; ticket *m.* (*train*)
tickle *v.* chatouiller
tide *n.* marée *f.*
tie *n.* cravate *f.*; match nul *m.* (*sports*); *v.* attacher
time *n.* temps *m.*
tip *n.* bout *m.*; pourboire *m.* (*gratuity*)
tire *n.* pneu *m.*; *v.* fatiguer
tired *adj.* fatigué
tissue *n.* mouchoir *m.*
title *n.* titre *m.*
to *prep.* à
tobacco *n.* tabac *m.*
today *n.; adv.* aujourd'hui *m.*
toe *n.* orteil *m.*
together *adv.* ensemble
toilet *n.* toilettes *f.pl.*
toilet paper *n.* papier hygiènique *m.*
token *n.* jeton *m.*
toll *n.* péage *m.*
tomb *n.* tombe *f.*
tombstone *n.* pierre tombale *f.*
tomorrow *n.; adv.* demain *m.*
tongue *n.* langue *f.*
tonight *n.; adv.* cette nuit *f.*; ce soir (*evening*)
tonsils *n.* amygdales *f.*
too *adv.* trop; aussi (*also*)
tool *n.* outil *m.*
tooth *n.* dent *f.*
toothache *n.* mal de dent *m.*
toothbrush *n.* brosse à dents *f.*
toothpaste *n.* dentifrice *m.*
toothpick *n.* cure-dents *m.*
top *n.* sommet *m.* (*mountain*); haut *m.* (*page*); couvercle *m.* (*lid*)
toss *v.* jeter
total *n.; adj.* total *m.*; *v.* additionner
touch *n.; v.* toucher *m.*
touched *adj.* ému

tough *adj.* dur
tour *n.* tour *m.*
tourism *n.* tourisme *m.*
tourist *n.* touriste *m/f.*
tourist office *n.* syndicat d'initiative *m.*
tournament *n.* tournoi *m.*
tow *v.* remorquer
toward *prep.* vers; envers (*attitude*)
towel *n.* serviette *f.*
tower *n.* tour *f.*
town *n.* ville *f.*
tow truck *n.* dépanneuse *f.*
toy *n.* jouet *m.*
track *n.* piste *f.*; voie *f.* (*train*)
trade *n.* commerce *m.*; *v.* faire du commerce; échanger (*exchange*)
tradition *n.* tradition *f.*
traffic *n.* trafic *m.*
trail *n.* piste *f.*
trailer *n.* caravane *f.*
train *n.* train *m.*; *v.* entraîner (*sports*); former (*apprentice*)
transfer *n.* transfert *m.*
translate *v.* traduire
translation *n.* traduction *f.*
translator *n.* traducteur *m.*, traductrice *f.*
transport *n.* transport *m.*; *v.* transporter
trash *n.* ordures *f.pl.*; camelote *f.* (*no value*)
trash can *n.* poubelle *f.*
travel *n.* voyage *m.*; *v.* voyager
traveler *n.* voyageur *m.*, voyageuse *f.*
traveler's check *n.* chèque de voyage *m.*
tray *n.* plateau *m.*
treasure *n.* trésor *m.*
tree *n.* arbre *m.*
trial *n.* procès *m.*; essai *m.* (*test*)
tribe *n.* tribu *f.*
tribute *n.* hommage *m.*
trouble *n.* problème *m.*
truck *n.* camion *m.*
true *adj.* vrai
trunk *n.* coffre *m.*; tronc *m.* (*tree*)
trust *n.* confiance *f.*; *v.* avoir confiance
truth *n.* vérité *f.*
try *v.* essayer
Tuesday *n.* mardi *m.*
tuition *n.* frais de scolarité *m.pl.*
tumor *n.* tumeur *f.*
tunnel *n.* tunnel *m.*
turn *n.* tour *m.*; tournant *m.* (*road*); *v.* tourner
tweezers *n.pl.* pince à épiler *f.*
twice *adv.* deux fois
twin *n.; adj.* jumeau *m.*, jumelle *f.*
two *num.* deux
typical *adj.* typique

U

ugly *adj.* laid
ulcer *n.* ulcère *m.*
umbrella *n.* parapluie *m.*; parasol *m.* (*sun*)
unable *adj.* incapable
unauthorized *adj.* non autorisé
unaware *adj.* ignorer
unbearable *adj.* insupportable
unbelievable *adj.* incroyable
uncalled-for *adj.* déplacé
uncle *n.* oncle *m.*
uncomfortable *adj.* inconfortable
unconscious *adj.* inconscient
under *prep.* sous; *adv.* au-dessous, en-dessous
underground *adj.* sous-terrain
understand *v.* comprendre
underwear *n.* sous-vêtements *m.pl.*
undo *v.* défaire
undress *v.* se déshabiller
uneasy *adj.* mal à l'aise
uneven *adj.* inégal
unfamiliar *adj.* inconnu, étrange
unfold *v.* déplier
unforgettable *adj.* inoubliable
unhappy *adj.* malheureux
unhealthy *adj.* malsain
uniform *n.; adj.* uniforme *m.*
union *n.* union *f.*
unique *adj.* unique

unit *n.* unité *f.*
United States *n.pl.* États-Unis *m.pl.*
universal *adj.* universel
universe *n.* univers *m.*
university *n.* université *f.*
unknown *adj.* inconnu
unless *conj.* à moins que
unlike *adj.* différent; *prep.* contrairement à
unlikely *adj.* improbable
unlimited *adj.* illimité
unload *v.* décharger
unpack *v.* défaire (sa valise)
unsafe *adj.* peu sûr, dangereux
until *prep.* jusqu'à
unusual *adj.* insolite
up *adv.* en haut; levé (*out of bed*); *prep.* en haut de
upper *adj.* du dessus
upset *v.* déranger; contrarier (*person*)
upside-down *adj.* à l'envers
upstairs *adv.* en-haut
up-to-date *adj.* récent, moderne
urban *adj.* urbain
urge *n.* forte envie *f.*
urgent *adj.* urgent
urinal *n.* urinoir *m.*
urine *n.* urine *f.*
urn *n.* urne *f.*
use *n.* usage *m.*; *v.* utiliser
used *adj.* d'occasion
usual *adj.* habituel
usually *adv.* d'habitude
utensil *n.* ustensile *m.*
U-turn *n.* demi-tour *m.*

V

vacancy *n.* chambre libre *f.*
vacant *adj.* libre
vacation *n.* vacances *f.pl.*
vaccinate *v.* vacciner
vaccine *n.* vaccin *m.*
vacuum cleaner *n.* aspirateur *m.*
valid *adj.* valable
validity *n.* validité *f.*
validate *v.* valider, composter (*train ticket*)
valley *n.* vallée *f.*
valuables *n.* objets de valeur *m.pl.*
value *n.* valeur *f.*
van *n.* camionnette *f.*
vanilla *n.* vanille *f.*
various *adj.* divers
VCR *n.* magnétoscope *m.*
vegetable *n.* légume *m.*
vegetarian *n.; adj.* végétarien *m.*, végétarienne *f.*
vein *n.* veine *f.*
velvet *n.* velours *m.*
venereal disease *n.* maladie vénérienne *f.*
venom *n.* venin *m.*
verb *n.* verbe *m.*
verdict *n.* verdict *m.*
verify *v.* vérifier
versus *prep.* contre
vertebra *n.* vertèbre *f.*
vertigo *n.* vertige *m.*
very *adv.* très
veterinarian *n.* vétérinaire *m.*
victim *n.* victime *m/f.*
video camera *n.* caméra *f.*
view *n.* vue *f.*
villa *n.* villa *f.*
village *n.* village *m.*
vine *n.* vigne *f.*
vinegar *n.* vinaigre *m.*
vineyard *n.* vignoble *m.*
violent *adj.* violent
virgin *n.; adj.* vierge *f.*
visa *n.* visa *m.*
visibility *n.* visibilité *f.*
visit *n.* visite *f.*; *v.* visiter, rendre visite
visitor *n.* visiteur *m.*
vitamin *n.* vitamine *f.*
vocabulary *n.* vocabulaire *m.*
voice *n.* voix *f.*
void *adj.* nul
voltage *n.* voltage *m.*
volunteer *n.* volontaire *m/f.*
vomit *n.* vomi *m.*; *v.* vomir
vote *n.* vote *m.*; *v.* voter
voucher *n.* bon *m.*

vow *n.* vœu *m.*
vowel *n.* voyelle *f.*

W

wage *n.* paye *f.*
waist *n.* taille *f.*
wait *n.* attente *f.*; *v.* attendre
waiter *n.* serveur *m.*
waitress *n.* serveuse *f.*
waiting room *n.* salle d'attente *f.*
wake (up) *v.* (se) réveiller
walk *n.* promenade *f.*; *v.* marcher
wall *n.* mur *m.*
wallet *n.* portefeuille *m.*
want *v.* vouloir
war *n.* guerre *f.*
warm *adj.* chaud; chaleureux (*welcome*)
warn *v.* avertir
warning *n.* avertissement *m.*
warranty *n.* garantie *f.*
wash *v.* (se) laver
washing machine *n.* machine à laver *f.*
wasp *n.* guêpe *f.*
watch *n.* montre *f.*; *v.* regarder
water *n.* eau *f.*; *v.* arroser (*plant*)
waterproof *adj.* imperméable
waterskiing *n.* ski nautique *m.*
watt *n.* watt *m.*
wave *n.* vague *f.*; geste *m.* (*hand*);
wax *n.* cire *f.*
way *n.* chemin *m.*
weak *adj.* faible
weakness *n.* faiblesse *f.*
weapon *n.* arme *f.*
wear *v.* porter
weather *n.* temps *m.*
weather forecast *n.* météo *f.*
website *n.* site Web *m.*
wedding *n.* marriage *m.*
wedding ring *n.* alliance *f.*
Wednesday *n.* mercredi *m.*
week *n.* semaine *f.*
weekday *n.* jour de semaine *m.*
weekend *n.* week-end *m.*
weigh *v.* peser
weight *n.* poids *m.*
weird *adj.* bizarre
welcome *n.* accueil *m.*; *adj.* bienvenu; *v.* accueillir
well *adv.* bien
west *n.* ouest *m.*
wet *adj.* mouillé
what *pron.* que, quoi; ce qui, ce que; *adj.* quel
wheat *n.* blé *m.*
wheel *n.* roue *f.*; volant *m.* (*steering*)
when *adv.; conj.* quand
where *adv.; conj.* où
whether *conj.* si
which *pron.* lequel, laquelle, lesquels, lesquelles; *adj.* quel
while *conj.* pendant que
white *adj.* blanc
who *pron.* qui
whole *adj.* entier, tout
why *conj.* pourquoi
wide *adj.* large
widow *n.* veuve *f.*
widower *n.* veuf *m.*
wife *n.* femme *f.*
wig *n.* perruque *f.*
wild *adj.* sauvage
win *v.* gagner
wind *n.* vent *m.*
window *n.* fenêtre *f.*; vitrine *f.* (*store*)
windshield *n.* pare-brise *m.*
wine *n.* vin *m.*
wing *n.* aile *f.*
winner *n.* gagnant *m.*, gagnante *f.*
winter *n.* hiver *m.*
wipe *v.* essuyer
wish *n.* souhait *m.*; *v.* souhaiter
with *prep.* avec
withdraw *v.* retirer
without *prep.* sans
witness *n.* témoin *m.*
woman *n.* femme *f.*
wonderful *adj.* merveilleux
wood *n.* bois *m.*
wool *n.* laine *f.*
word *n.* mot *m.*
work *n.* travail *m.*; *v.* travailler

world *n.* monde *m.*
worldwide *adj.* universel
worm *n.* ver *m.*
worry *n.* souci *m.*; *v.* (s')inquiéter
worse *n.; adj.* pire *m.*
wound *n.* blessure *f.*; *v.* blesser
wrap *v.* emballer
wreck *v.* démolir
wrinkle *n.* ride *f.*; pli *m.* (*fabric*); *v.* (se) rider; (se) plier
wrist *n.* poignet *m.*
write *v.* écrire
writer *n.* écrivain *m.*
wrong *adj.* faux

XYZ

xenophobia *n.* xénophobie *f.*
X ray *n.* rayon *m.*; radiographie *f.* (*medical*)
yacht *n.* yacht *m.*
yard *n.* jardin *m.*
yawn *n.* bâillement *m.*; *v.* bâiller
year *n.* an *m.*, année *f.*
yell *v.* hurler
yellow *adj.* jaune
yes *adv.* oui
yesterday *n.; adv.* hier *m.*
yield *v.* céder la priorité (*car*)
you *pron.* tu, vous
young *adj.* jeune
youth *n.* jeunesse *f.*
youth hostel *n.* auberge de jeunesse *f.*
zero *num.* zéro
zip code *n.* code postale *m.*
zipper *n.* fermeture éclair *f.*
zone *n.* zone *f.*
zoo *n.* zoo *m.*
zoom *n.* zoom *m.*

PHRASEBOOK CONTENTS

Getting Around

Driving

Eating Out

GETTING STARTED

Everyday words and phrases

Yes.	**Oui.**	*wee*
No.	**Non.**	*non*
Please.	**S'il vous plaît.**	*seel voo play*
Thank you.	**Merci.**	*mair-see*
Thank you very much.	**Merci beaucoup.**	*mair-see boh-koo*
You are welcome.	**Je vous en prie.**	*zher voo zahng pree*
Good.	**Bien.**	*byern*
OK.	**D'accord.**	*dah kohr*
Excuse me.	**Excusez-moi/Pardon.**	*aiks-kew-say-mwah/par-dawng*
I am very sorry.	**Je suis désolé.**	*jer swee day-soh-lay*

Being understood

I do not understand.
Je ne comprends pas.
jer ner kohm-pran pah

I understand.
Je comprends.
jer kohm-pran

Do you understand?
Comprenez-vous ?
kohm-prer-nay-voo

I do not speak French.
Je ne parle pas français.
jer ner pahrl pah fran-say

Do you speak English?
Parlez-vous anglais ?
par-lay-voo an-glay

Can you help me, please?
Pouvez-vous m'aider, s'il vous plaît ?
poo-vay-voo may-day, seel voo play

Could you repeat that?
Pouvez-vous répétez, s'il vous plaît ?
poo-vay voo ray-pay-tay, seel voo play

Please repeat that slowly.
Répétez lentement, s'il vous plaît.
ray-pay-tay lan-ter-man, seel voo play

Please write it down.
Pouvez-vous l'écrire, s'il vous plaît ?
poo-vay voo pay-kreer, seel voo play

Can you translate this for me?
Pouvez-vous me traduire ceci ?
poo-vay-voo me trah-dweer ser-see

Is there someone who speaks English?
Y a-t-il quelqu'un qui parle anglais ?
ee-ah-teel kail-kern kee pahrl an-glay

Please point to the phrase in the book.
Montrez-moi la phrase dans le livre, s'il vous plaît.
mon-tray mwah la frahz dan ler leevr, seel voo play

It does not matter.
Ce n'est rien/Ça ne fait rien.
ser nai ryern/sah ner fay ryern

I do not mind.
Ça ne me dérange pas.
sa ner mer day-ranj pah

This is correct.
C'est ça.
say sah

Greetings and exchanges

Hello!
Bonjour !
bon-joor

Hi!
Salut !
sah-lew

Good morning.
Bonjour.
bon-joor

Good evening.
Bonsoir.
bon-swahr

How are you?
Comment allez-vous ?
koh-man tah-lay voo

I am very well, thank you.
Très bien, merci.
trai byern, mair-see

It is good to see you.
Je suis heureux de vous voir.
jer swee zer-rer der voo vwahr

Nice to meet you.
Enchanté.
an-shan-tay

That is very kind of you.
Vous êtes très aimable.
voo zait trai zai-mahbl

You are very kind.
Vous êtes bien aimable.
voo zait byern ay-mahbl

You are welcome.
Je vous en prie.
jer voo zan pree

Good night.
Bonne nuit.
bohner nwee

Good-bye.
Au revoir.
oh rer-vwahr

See you soon.
A bientôt.
ah byern-toh

My name is ...
Je m'appelle ...
jer mah-pail ...

What is your name?
Comment vous appelez-vous ?
koh-man voo zah-play voo

Here is my son.
Voici mon fils.
vwah-see mon fees

This is … my daughter.
Voici … ma fille.
vwah-see … mah fee

… my husband.
… mon mari.
… mon mah-ree

… my wife.
… ma femme.
… mah fahm

I am on vacation.
Je suis en vacances.
jer swee an vah-kans

I am a student.
Je suis étudiant.
jer swee ay-tew-dyan

I live in New York.
J'habite à New York.
jah-beet ah noo yohrk

I am … American.
Je suis … américain.
jer swee … ah-may-ree-kern

… Canadian.
… canadien.
… kah-nah-dee-ern

… English.
… anglais.
… ang-lay

… Australian.
… australien.
… oh-strah-lyern

Common questions

Where?	**Où ?**	*oo*
Where is…?	**Où est… ?**	*oo ayh*
Where are…?	**Où sont… ?**	*oo son*
When?	**Quand ?**	*kan*
What?	**Quoi/Comment ?**	*kwah/koh-man*
How?	**Comment ?**	*koh-man*
How much?	**Combien ?**	*kohm-byern*
Who?	**Qui ?**	*kee*

Why?	**Pourquoi ?**	*poor-kwah*
Which?	**Lequel ?**	*ler-kail*

Do you have any change?
Avez-vous de la monnaie ?
ahvay voo der lah moh-nay

How long will it take?
Il y en a pour combien de temps ?
eel-yohn-ah poor kohm-byern der tan

How much do I have to pay?
Combien dois-je payer ?
kohm-byern dwaj pay-yay

What do you call this in French?
Comment appelez-vous ça en français ?
koh-man ah-play voo sa an fran-say

What does this mean?
Qu'est-ce que ça veut dire ?
kais-ker sah ver deer

What is the problem?
Quel est le problème ?
kail ai ler proh-blaim

What is this?
Qu'est-ce que c'est ?
kais-ker say

What is wrong?
Qu'est-ce qui ne va pas ?
kais-kee ner vah pah

What time do you close?
A quelle heure fermez-vous ?
ah kail err fair-may voo

Where can I change my clothes?
Où puis-je me changer ?
oo pweej mer shan-jay

Who did this?
Qui a fait ça ?
kee ah fay sah

Whom should I see about this?
A qui puis-je m'adresser ?
ah kee pweej mah-drai-say

Where can I buy a postcard?
Où puis-je acheter une carte postale ?
oo pweej ahsh-tay ewn kahrt pohs-tahl

How can I contact American Express/Visa?
Comment puis-je contacter American Express/Visa ?
koh-man pweej kon-tahk-tay ah-may-ree-kan aik-sprais/vee-zah

Do you know a good restaurant?
Connaissez-vous un bon restaurant ?
koh-nai-say voo ern bon rais-toh-ran

Do you mind if I ...
Est-ce que ça vous dérange si je/j' ...
ais-ker sah voo day-ranj see jer/jh ...

... smoke?
... fume ?
... few-mh

... sit?
... m'assieds ?
... mah-syay

... borrow your map?
... emprunte votre plan ?
... an-prern-th vohtr plan

Sorry to bother you, but could you please ...
Excusez-moi de vous déranger, mais pouvez-vous s'il vous plaît ...
aiks-kew-say-mwah der voo day-ran-jer, may poo-vay voo seel voo play ...

... tell me the address.
... me dire l'adresse.
... mer deer lah-dress

... show me on the map.
... me montrer sur la carte.
... mer mon-tray sewr lah kahrt.

... point the direction.
... m'indiquer la direction.
... mern-dee-kay lah dee-raik-syon.

Asking the time

What time is it?
Quelle heure est-il ?
kail err ay-teel

It is … eleven o'clock.
Il est … onze heures.
eel ai … onz err

… five past ten.
… dix heures cinq.
… deez err sernk

… ten past seven.
… sept heures dix.
… sait err dees

… a quarter past nine.
… neuf heures et quart.
… ner-verr ay kahr

… half past eight sharp.
… huit heures et demie pile.
… weet err ay der-mee peel

… twenty to six.
… six heures moins vingt.
… see-zerr mwan vern

… a quarter to four.
… quatre heures moins le quart.
… kahtr err mwan ler kahr

… noon.
… midi.
… mee-dee

… midnight.
… minuit.
… mee-nwee

… almost five o'clock.
… presque cinq heures.
… praisk sernk err

soon	**bientôt**	*byern-toh*
two hours ago	**il y a deux heures**	*eel ee ah der zerr*
this morning	**ce matin**	*ser mahtern*
this afternoon	**cet après-midi**	*sait ah-prai mee-dee*
this evening/tonight	**ce soir**	*ser swahr*
tonight	**cette nuit**	*sait nwee*
before midnight	**avant minuit**	*ah-van mee-nwee*
around one o'clock	**vers une heure**	*vair ewn err*
after three	**après trois heures**	*ah-prai trwah zerr*
at six thirty	**à six heures et demie**	*ah see-zerr ay der-mee*

at night	**la nuit**	*lah nwee*
in an hour	**dans une heure**	*dan zewn err*
in half an hour	**dans une demi-heure**	*dan zewn der-mee err*
early	**tôt**	*toh*
late	**tard**	*tahr*

Common problems

I have no cash.
Je n'ai pas d'argent liquide.
jer nay pah dahr-jan lee-keed

I dropped a contact lens.
J'ai laissé tomber un verre de contact.
jay lay-say tohm-bay ern vehr der kon-tact

I cannot find my driver's licence.
Je ne trouve pas mon permis de conduire.
jer ner troov pah mon pair-mee der kon-dweer

I have lost my credit cards.
J'ai perdu mes cartes de crédit.
jay pair-dew may kahrt der kray-dee

I want to see a lawyer.
Je veux voir un avocat.
jer ver vwahr ern ah-voh-kah

My car has been stolen.
On m'a volé ma voiture.
on mah voh-lay mah vwah-tewr

My purse has been stolen.
On m'a volé mon sac.
on mah voh-lay mon sahk

My wallet has been stolen.
On m'a volé mon portefeuille.
on mah voh-lay mon pohrt-fery

I would like to contact the American consulate.
Je voudrais contacter le consulat américain.
jer voo-dray kon-tak-tay ler kon-sew-lah ah-mai-ree-kern

AT THE AIRPORT

The main airport in Paris is Charles de Gaulle—known to the French as "Roissy"—though some flights use the other airport at Orly. Regular train and bus services link Orly to Charles de Gaulle, and Paris to both airports. Most major U.S. cities offer direct flights to Paris, and you can find direct flights from New York to Nice and Lyon. For other destinations, you will have to go through Paris, but the flights are frequent.

Buses—called Roissy Bus and Cars Air France—connecting Charles de Gaulle airport to the center of Paris are regular and reasonably priced, although in heavy traffic the journey may take up to an hour (keep this in mind if you decide to take a taxi). Remember to buy your bus ticket inside the airport at a specially marked counter before boarding the bus. Using the *RER* (suburban express train) is a quicker option and is reasonably priced. It departs from Roissy *TGV* station to Gare du Nord and Châtelet, where you can transfer to the subway *(Métro)*.

The airport at Orly also has regular bus services—called Orly Bus and Cars Air France—to the city center, as well as bus links and an automated subway (*Orlyval*) to local RER train stations.

You can visit the airports' website at: www.adp.fr.

Arrival

Here is my passport.
Voici mon passeport.
vwah-see mon pahs-pohr

We have a joint passport.
Nous avons un passeport conjoint.
noo zah-von ern pahs-pohr kon-jwern

I am attending a convention.
Je participe à une convention.
jer pahr-tee-seep ah ewn con-van-syon

I am here on business.
Je suis ici pour affaires.
jer swee ee-see poor ahf-air

I am on vacation.
Je viens en vacances.
jer vyern an vah-kans

I will be staying here for eight weeks.
Je reste huit semaines.
jer raist wee ser-main

We are visiting friends.
Nous sommes chez des amis.
noo sohm shay day-zah-mee

I have nothing to declare.
Je n'ai rien à déclarer.
jer nay ryern ah day-klah-ray

I have the usual allowances.
J'ai les quantités permises.
jay lay kan-tee-tay pair-meez

This is for my own use.
C'est pour mon usage personnel.
sai poor mon ew-sahj pair-soh-nail

Common problems and requests

I have lost my ticket.
J'ai perdu mon billet.
jay pair-dew mon bee-yay

I have lost my traveler's checks.
J'ai perdu mes chèques de voyage.
jay pair-dew may shaik der vohy-ahj

I have lost my bag/purse.
J'ai perdu mon sac.
jay pair-dew mon sahk

I have missed my connection.
J'ai raté ma correspondance.
jay rah-tay mah koh-rais-pon-dans

The people who were supposed to pick me up have not arrived.
Les gens qui devaient venir me chercher ne sont pas arrivés.
lay jan kee der-vay ver-neer mer shair-shay ner son pah zah-ree-vay

I am in a hurry.
Je suis pressé.
jer swee prai-say

I am late.
Je suis en retard.
jer swee an rer-tahr

Where can I find the airline representative?
Où puis-je trouver l'agent de la compagnie aérienne ?
oo pweej troovai lah-jan der lah kon-pah-nee ah-ay-ryain

Where can I exchange some money?
Où puis-je changer de l'argent ?
oo pweej shan-jay der lahr-jan

Where can I cash traveler's checks?
Où puis-je changer des chèques de voyage ?
oo pweej shan-jay day shaik der vwa-yahj

Where is ... the bar?
Où est ... le bar ?
oo ai ... ler bahr

... the lounge?
... la salle d'attente ?
... lah sahl dah-tant

... the transfer desk?
... le guichet de transit ?
... ler gee-shay der tran-seet

... the information desk?
... le bureau de renseignements ?
... ler bew-roh der ran-sain-yer-man

... the rental car office?
... le bureau de location de voiture ?
... ler bew-roh der loh-kah-syon der vwah-tewr

Where is the telephone?
Où se trouve le téléphone ?
oo ser troov ler tai-lai-fohn

Where is the airport information desk?
Où se trouve le comptoir d'information de l'aéroport ?
oo ser troov ler kon-twar dern-for-mah-syon der lah-ay-roh-por

Where can I find an ATM machine?
Où puis-je trouver un distributeur d'argent ?
oo pweej troo-vai ern dees-tree-bew-ter dahr-jan

Where are the restrooms?
Où sont les toilettes ?
oo son lay twah-lait

Is there a bus into town?
Y a-t-il un autobus pour aller en ville ?
ee-ah-teel ern oh-toh-bews poor ah-lay an veel

Is there a shuttle for the hotel...?
Y a-t-il une navette pour l'hôtel... ?
ee-ah-teel ewn nah-vait poor loh-tel...

At what gate can I find the shuttle?
À quelle porte se trouve la navette ?
ah kail pohrt ser troov lah nah-vait

Luggage

Where is the baggage from flight number...?
Où sont les bagages du vol... ?
oo son lay bah-gahj dew vohl...

My luggage has not arrived.
Mes bagages ne sont pas arrivés.
may bah-gahj ner son pah zah-ree-vay

Where is my bag?
Où est mon sac ?
oo ai mon sahk

It is ... a large suitcase.
C'est ... une grande valise.
sait ... ewn grand vah-leez

... a backpack.
... un sac à dos.
... ern sahk ah doh

... a small suitcase.
... une petite valise.
... ewn per-teet vah-leez

These bags are not mine.
Ces sacs ne sont pas à moi.
say sahk ner son pah ah mwah

My suitcase is damaged.
Ma valise est abîmée.
mah vah-leez ay ah-bee-may

Where do I pick up my bags?
Où reprend-on ses bagages ?
oo rer-pran-ton say bah-gahj

Are there any luggage carts?
Y a-t-il des chariots à bagages ?
ee-ah-teel day shah-ryoh ah bah-gahj

Can I have help with my bag?
Y a-t-il un porteur ?
ee-ah-teel ern pohr-terr

Careful, the handle is broken.
Attention, la poignée est cassée.
ah-tan-syon, lah pwah-nyay ai kah-say

This package is fragile.
Ce paquet est fragile.
ser pah-kay ai frah-jeel

I will carry that myself.
Je porterai ça moi-même.
jer pohr-tai-ray sah mwah-maim

Is there a locker?
Y a-t-il une consigne automatique ?
ee-ah-teel ewn kon-seen oh-toh-mah-teek

Is there any charge?
Faut-il payer ?
foh-teel pay-yay

No, do not put that on top.
Non, ne mettez pas ça en haut.
non, ner mai-tay pah sah ohn-oh

Please take these bags to a taxi.
Portez ces valises à un taxi, s'il vous plaît.
pohr-tay say vah-leez ah ern tahk-see, seel voo play

Departure

Can I upgrade to first class?
Puis-je changer mon billet pour une première classe ?
pweej shan-jay mon bee-yay poor ewn prer-myayr klahs

Where do I get the connection flight to Nice?
Où dois-je prendre la correspondance pour Nice ?
oo dwahj prandr lah koh-rais-pon-dans poor nees

Can I check in my bags?
Puis-je enregistrer mes bagages ?
pweej an-rer-jees-tray may bah-gahj

AT THE AIRPORT

Where is the Delta check-in, please?
Où se trouve l'enregistrement pour Delta, s'il vous plaît ?
oo ser troov lan-rer-jees-trer-man poor del-tah, seel voo play

I have lost my boarding pass.
J'ai perdu ma carte d'embarquement.
jay per-dew mah kahrt dan-bahr-ker-man

I am looking for gate number 12.
Je cherche la porte d'embarquement 12.
jer shair-sher lah pohrt dan-bahr-ker-man dooz.

May I have ...
Puis-je avoir ...
pweej ah-wahr ...

... a window seat?
... un siège côté fenêtre ?
... ern seeayj koh-tay fer-naytr

... an aisle seat?
... un siège le long de l'allée ?
... ern seeayj ler lon der lah-lay

Is it a non-smoking flight?
Est-ce que le vol est non-fumeur ?
ais ker ler vohl ay non few-merhr

What you may hear

Le vol ... à destination de ...
ler vohl ... ah dais-tee-nah-syon der ...
Flight number ... to ...

... est annulé.
... ay tah-new-lay
... has been canceled.

... est retardé.
... ay rer-tahr-day
... will be delayed.

Le départ aura lieu à 18 heures.
ler day-pahr oh-rah lee-err ah deez-weet err
The plane will depart at 6:00 P.M.

C'est gratuit.
say grah-twee
There is no charge.

ACCOMMODATIONS

Hotels

French hotels are available at a good value—especially at the lower end of the market. But there are marked regional variations—the southern coast is far more expensive than rural inland areas or other coasts of France.

The best-value hotels in France tend to be *auberges* or country inns. These are often delightful family-run establishments where they take pride in the quality of their food. In large towns and cities, the choice of hotels with character is not as abundant (Paris being the exception), but you can almost always find satisfactory chain hotels. At the luxury end of the market, there are some splendid *châteaux*, as well as beautifully converted mills and farms—all elegantly furnished and often providing food of high quality.

Also remember that in Europe, the first floor is called ground floor (*rez-de-chaussée*), the second floor is called first floor (*premier étage*), the third is called 2nd (*deuxième étage*), and so on.

Star ratings

Hotels in France are officially rated on a star-scale, from simple one-star accommodations to four-star *de luxe*. There are also basic unclassified hotels that are not categorized as *hôtels de tourisme*. The French Tourist Office in New York will provide you with a list of approved hotels. The star ratings are based on facilities—whether there's an elevator, air conditioning, night porter, etc. They tell you roughly what prices to expect but give you no indication of what a place is really like.

Prices

Prices are controlled and should be displayed at the reception and in every bedroom. Rates are quoted for the room, not per person, and are usually the same whether one or two people are using the room. Breakfast is rarely included in the price of the room. Rates include service and tax, except in some deluxe hotels where the service is charged separately. It is quite normal in any hotel to ask to see a room before you agree to take it.

Many hotels offer rates for *pension complète* (all three meals, or full board) and *demi-pension* (breakfast and one meal, or half board). To qualify for *pension complète* you usually have to stay for a minimum of three days and the meals may be different from the other restaurant menus—with less choice.

Meals

The normal French breakfast consists of French bread or croissants and coffee—*café complet.* You can have it in your room, and occasionally you have no choice but to do so.

Although the hotel will expect you to take its breakfast, there is no legal obligation to do so and you will find that the coffee and croissants are a lot cheaper in the local café—and often better too.

In the same way, many hotels will expect you to have an evening meal if you are staying the night, but under French law hoteliers are not allowed to insist that you do so. On the other hand, if it is a hotel that is renowned for the quality of its cuisine, you may not need to venture any farther.

Rooms and beds

In small hotels, double beds (full size) are the norm, though twins are becoming more common. In cheaper hotels, hard bolsters are used instead of pillows, but always check to see if there are pillows in the closet. Occasionally soap might not be provided. Keep in mind that you will not be able to operate American 110 volts electrical items: the voltage is 220 volts. If your computer or electric shaver are compatible, you will still need a plug adaptor. The telephone connection also uses a different jack. These adaptors can be purchased beforehand in the United States.

A number of hotel-restaurants offer rooms that vary from basic to very luxurious. These restaurants-with-rooms are often found at a very good value, but you cannot expect to stay in one unless you are planning to eat there.

Making reservations

Reservations for hotels need to be made well in advance during high season, particularly for Paris and other popular areas. In large cities, at stations and airports, there are offices known as *Accueil de France*, which can reserve accommodations for you in their area or in other main cities. Reservations can be made only up to a week ahead and for individual travelers and families only.

Most hoteliers won't hold rooms after 6 P.M. unless you've called to say you will be late or have paid a deposit.

Bed-and-breakfast

With so many good, quality hotels serving excellent food, it's not surprising that bed-and-breakfasts have traditionally not been a prominent part of the French vacation scene. This is changing, largely because the *Gîtes de France* organization has set up a large-scale plan to market bed-and-breakfasts. They're called *chambres d'hôtes*, and the roadside signs identifying them are now a common sight. This plan promotes country homes offering bed and breakfast and "a very warm family welcome"—ranging from cottages to small châteaux.

Another bed-and-breakfast organization is *Café-Couette* (literally translated as Coffee-Comforter), which offers more than 1,000 homes to stay in. You are treated as a member of the family and you can stay for as long as you like.

Guest membership in the organization entitles you to the reservation service and the guide to all the bed and breakfasts available, graded from 2 to 5 "coffee pots."

Reservations and inquiries

Do you have some rooms available, please?
Avez-vous des chambres libres, s'il vous plaît ?
ah-vay-voo day shanbr leebr, seel voo play

My name is …
Je m'appelle …
jer mah-pail …

I have a reservation.
J'ai réservé une chambre.
jay ray-sair-vay ewn shanbr

I am sorry I am late.
Je suis en retard. Excusez-moi.
jer swee zan rer-tahr. aiks-kew-say mwah

I was delayed at the airport.
J'ai été retenu à l'aéroport.
jay ay-tay rer-ter-new ah lah-ay-roh-por

My flight was late.
Mon vol avait du retard.
mon vohl ah-vay dew rer-tahr

I will be staying until July 4th.
Je reste jusqu'au quatre juillet.
jer raist jews-koh kahtr jwee-yay

I would like to stay for 5 nights.
Je voudrais rester cinq nuits.
jer voo-dray rais-tay sernk nwee

There are five of us.
Nous sommes cinq.
noo sohm sernk

Do you have … a single room?
Avez-vous … une chambre pour une personne ?
ah-vay voo … ewn shanbr poor ewn pair-sohn

… a double room with a bath?
… une chambre pour deux personnes avec bain ?
… ewn shanbr poor der pair-sohn ah-vaik bern

… a room with twin beds and a shower?
… une chambre avec lits jumeaux et douche ?
… ewn shanbr ah-vaik lee jew-moh ay doosh

I need … a double room with a bed for a child.
Je voudrais … une chambre pour deux personnes avec un lit d'enfant.
jer voo-dray … ewn shanbr poor der pair-sohn ah-vaik ern lee dan-fan

… a room with a double bed.
… une chambre avec un grand lit.
… ewn shanbr ah-vaik ern gran lee

Does the price include ... breakfast?
Est-ce que le tarif comprend ... le petit déjeuner ?
ais-ker ler tah-reef kohm-pran ... ler per-tee day-jer-nay

... room and all meals?
... tous les repas ?
... too lay rer-pah

... room and dinner?
... le dîner ?
... ler dee-nay

... taxes and service?
... le service et les taxes ?
... ler sayr-vees ay lay tax

How much is it ... for a child?
C'est combien ... pour un enfant ?
say kohm-byern ... poor ewn an-fan

... per night?
... par nuit ?
... pahr nwee

... per person?
... par personne ?
... pahr pair-sohn

How much is ... full board?
Combien coûte ... la pension complète ?
kohm-byern koot ... lah pan-syon kohm-plai

... half-board?
... la demi-pension ?
... lah der-mee pan-syon

Which floor is my room on?
A quel étage est ma chambre ?
ah kail ay-tahj ai mah shanbr

Can we have breakfast in our room?
Pouvons-nous prendre le petit déjeuner dans la chambre ?
poo-von noo prandr ler per-tee day-jer-nay dan la shanbr

Can we have adjoining rooms?
Pouvons-nous avoir des chambres attenantes ?
poo-von noo ah-vwahr day shanbr a-ter-nant

Are there other children staying at the hotel?
Y a-t-il d'autres enfants à l'hôtel ?
ee-ah-teel dohtr zan-fan ah loh-tail

Are there supervised activities for the children?
Y a-t-il des activités surveillées pour les enfants ?
ee-ah-teel day zahk-tee-vee-tay sewr-vay-yay poor lay zan-fan

Can my son sleep in our room?
Est-ce que mon fils peut coucher dans notre chambre ?
ais-ke mon fees per koo-shay dan nohtr shanbr

Is there … a television?
Y a-t-il … un poste de télévision ?
ee-ah-teel … ern pohst der tay-lay-vee-syon

… a hairdryer?
… un sèche-cheveux ?
… ern saish-sher-ver

… a minibar?
… un minibar ?
… ern mee-nee-bahr

… air conditioning?
… la climatisation ?
… lah klee-mah-tee-zah-syon

… an adaptor for a US plug?
… un adaptateur pour une prise américaine ?
… ern ah-dahp-tah-terr poor ewn preez ah-may-ree-kain

… a room service menu?
… un menu servi dans les chambres ?
… ern mer-new sair-vee dan lay shanbr

… a phone?
… un téléphone ?
… ern tay-lay-fohn

… a casino?
… un casino ?
… ern kah-see-noh

… an elevator?
… un ascenseur ?
… ern ah-san-serr

… a sauna?
… un sauna ?
… ern soh-nah

… a swimming pool?
… une piscine ?
… ewn pee-seen

… a garage?
… un garage ?
… ern gah-rahj

Do you have ... a cot/crib for my baby?
Avez-vous ... un lit d'enfant pour mon bébé ?
ah-vay voo ... an lee dan-fan poor mon bay-bay

... a laundry service?
... un service de blanchisserie ?
... ern sair-vees der blan-shee-ser-ree

... parking?
... un parking ?
... ern pahr-keeng

... a safe for valuables?
... un coffre pour les objets de valeur ?
... ern kohfr poor lay zohb-jay der vah-lerr

... a fax machine?
... un télécopieur ?
... ern tay-lay-koh-pee-err

Is there ... a market in town?
Y a-t-il ... un marché en ville ?
ee-ah-teel ... ern mahr-shay an veel

... a Chinese restaurant?
... un restaurant chinois ?
... ern rais-toh-ran sheen-wah

... a Vietnamese restaurant?
... un restaurant vietnamien ?
... ern rais-toh-ran vyait-nah-myern

Do you have satellite TV?
Recevez-vous les programmes par satellite ?
rer-ser-vay voo lay proh-grahm pahr sah-tay-leet

What time ... does the hotel close?
A quelle heure ... est-ce que l'hôtel ferme ?
ah kail err ... ais-ker loh-tail fairm

... does the restaurant close?
... ferme le restaurant ?
... fairm ler rais-toh-ran

... is breakfast?
... est le petit déjeuner ?
... ai ler per-tee day-jer-nay

... is lunch?
... est le déjeuner ?
... ai ler day-jer-nay

... is dinner?
... est le dîner ?
... ai ler dee-nay

... does the bar open?
... ouvre le bar ?
... oovr ler bahr

Service

Could you please fill the minibar?
Pouvez-vous remplir le minibar, s'il vous plaît ?
poo-vay voo ran-pleer ler mee-nee-bahr, seel voo play

Please send this fax for me.
Pouvez-vous transmettre ce fax, s'il vous plaît ?
poo-vay voo trans-maitr ser fahks, seel voo play

Please turn the heater off.
Pouvez-vous arrêter le chauffage, s'il vous plaît ?
poo-vay voo ahr-rai-tay ler shoh-fahj, seel voo play

Please, wake me at 7 A.M.
Réveillez-moi à sept heures, s'il vous plaît.
ray-vay-yay mwah ah sait err, seel voo play

Can I have ... an ashtray?
Puis-je avoir ... un cendrier ?
pweej ah-vwahr ... ern san-dree-ay

... another blanket?
... une autre couverture ?
... ewn ohtr koo-vair-tewr

... another pillow?
... un autre oreiller ?
... ern ohtr oh-ray-yay

... my key, please?
... ma clé, s'il vous plaît ?
... lah klay, seel voo play

... some coat hangers?
... des cintres ?
... day serntr

... some note paper?
... du papier ?
... dew pah-pyay

... a newspaper?
... un journal ?
... an joor-nahl

Can I have my wallet from the safe?
Puis-je récupérer mon portefeuille dans le coffre ?
pweej ray-kew-pai-ray mon pohrt-fery dan ler kohfr

Can I make a phone call from here?
Puis-je téléphoner d'ici ?
pweej tay-lay-foh-nay dee-see

Can I send this by courier?
Puis-je envoyer ceci par coursier ?
pweej an-vwah-yay ser-see pahr koor-syay

Can I use my credit card?
Puis-je utiliser ma carte de crédit ?
pweej ew-tee-lee-say mah kahrt der kray-dee

How do I use the telephone?
Comment fait-on pour téléphoner ?
koh-man fai-ton poor tay-lay-foh-nay

Can you connect me with the international operator?
Pouvez vous me passer la standardiste internationale ?
poo-vay voo mer pah-say lah stan-dahr-deest an-tair-nah-syo-nahl

Can I have an outside line, please?
Pouvez-vous me donner une ligne extérieure, s'il vous plaît ?
poo-vay voo mer doh-nay ewn leen aiks-tair-yerr, seel voo play

Please charge this to my room.
Mettez cela sur ma note, s'il vous plaît.
mai-tay ser-lah sewr mah noht, seel voo play

Can I dial direct from my room?
Puis-je faire le numéro directement de ma chambre ?
pweej fayr ler new-may-roh dee-raik-ter-man der mah shanbr

Can I use my personal computer here?
Puis-je utiliser mon ordinateur ici ?
pweej ew-tee-lee-say mon or-dee-nah-terr ee-see

I am expecting a fax.
J'attends un fax.
jah-tan ern fahks

Where can I send a fax?
Où peut-on envoyer un fax ?
oo per-ton an-vwah-yay ern fahks

What is the rate?
Quel est le tarif ?
kail ai ler tah-reef

I need a wake-up call at ...
J'ai besoin d'être réveillé à ... heures.
jay ber-zwern daytr ray-vay-yay ah ... err

I need ... some soap.
J'ai besoin ... de savon.
jay ber-zwern ... der sah-von

... some towels.
... de serviettes.
... der sair-vyait

... a razor.
... d'un rasoir.
... dern rah-zwahr

... some toilet paper.
... de papier hygiénique.
... der pah-pyay ee-jyay-neek

I need to ... charge these batteries.
Je dois ... recharger ces piles.
jer dwah ... rer-shahr-jay say peel

... iron these clothes.
... repasser ces vêtements.
... rer-pah-say say vait-man

Has my colleague arrived yet?
Est-ce que mon collègue est arrivé ?
ais-ker mon koh-laig ai tah-ree-vay

Can you recommend a good local restaurant?
Pouvez-vous me recommander un bon restaurant ?
poo-vay voo mer rer-koh-man-day ern bon rais-toh-ran

Problems

Can I speak to the manager?
Puis-je parler au directeur ?
pweej pahr-lay oh dee-raik-terr

Where is the manager?
Où est le directeur ?
oo ai ler dee-raik-terr

I cannot close the window.
La fenêtre ne ferme pas.
lah fer-naitr ner fairm pah

I cannot open the window.
La fenêtre ne s'ouvre pas.
lah fer-naitr ner soovr pah

The air conditioning is not working.
La climatisation ne marche pas.
lah klee-mah-tee-zah-syon ner mahrsh pah

The bathroom is dirty.
La salle de bains est sale.
lah sahl der bern ai sahl

The heater is not working.
Le chauffage ne marche pas.
ler shoh-fahj ner mahrsh pah

The light is not working.
La lumière ne marche pas.
lah lew-myair ner mahrsh pah

The room has not been serviced.
On n'a pas fait le ménage dans la chambre.
on nah pah fay ler may-nahj dan lah shanbr

The room is too noisy.
La chambre est trop bruyante.
lah shanbr ai troh broo yant

The room key does not work.
La clef de la chambre ne marche pas.
lah klay der lah shanbr ner mahrsh pah

There are no towels in the bathroom.
Il n'y a pas de serviettes dans la salle de bains.
eel nyah pah der sair-vyait dan lah sahl der bern

There is no hot water.
Il n'y a pas d'eau chaude.
eel nyah pah doh shohd

There is no plug for the washbasin.
Il n'y a pas de bonde dans le lavabo.
eel nyah pah der bond dan ler lah-vah-boh

My daughter is sick.
Ma fille est malade.
mah fee ai mah-lahd

My son is lost.
Mon fils s'est perdu.
mon fees sai pair-dew

Checking out

At what time do we have to check out?
À quelle heure faut-il libérer la chambre ?
ah kail err foh-teel lee-bai-ray lah shanbr

Could you please keep our luggage until 6 P.M.?
Pourriez-vous garder nos bagages jusqu'à 18 heures, s'il vous plaît ?
poo-ryay voo gahr-day noh bah-gahj jew-skah deez-weet err, seel voo play

Could you call me a taxi please?
Pouvez-vous m'appeler un taxi, s'il vous plaît ?
poo-vay voo mah-per-lay ern tahk-see, seel voo play

Please leave the bags in the lobby.
Laissez les bagages dans le hall, s'il vous plaît.
lay-say lay bah-gahj dan ler ahl, seel voo play

I would like to stay an extra night.
Je voudrais rester une nuit supplémentaire.
jer voo-dray rais-tay ewn nwee sew-play-man-tair

Do I have to change rooms?
Dois-je changer de chambre ?
dwaj shan-jay der shanbr

Can I have the bill please?
Puis-je avoir la note, s'il vous plaît ?
pweej ah-vwahr lah noht, seel voo play

We will be leaving early tomorrow.
Nous partons tôt demain matin.
noo pahr-ton toh der-mern mah-tern

Thank you, we enjoyed our stay.
Merci, nous avons fait un bon séjour.
mair-see, noo zah-von fai ern bon say-joor

Rentals

Vacations in rental properties are very big business in France. There are simple rural cottages, stylish seaside villas, modern high-rise apartments, old farmhouses and barns—even apartments in grand *châteaux*.

If you want a *gîte* or any rental property in high season, you have to reserve well in advance. Seaside accommodations are usually snapped up by December or January, and even remote rural properties are booked up several months in advance. Many tour operators organize packages combining plane tickets and rentals.

Gîtes

Thousands of tourists are now opting for vacations in *gîtes.* These are modestly priced simple country houses or apartments offering a real taste of rural France. There are 30,000 altogether, many of which are renovated farmhouses or country cottages. Some properties are quite remote, others in small villages. Very few are not in rural locations and only a handful are near the sea. Properties are all inspected and graded by the *Gîtes de France* organization. What most *gîtes* can offer is rural charm and character. Each property is privately owned and sometimes the *gîte* may be a self-contained apartment in the owner's house.

Villas and apartments

The most popular area for villa and apartment vacations is the south of France. There you find every type of vacation home, from studios and stylish villas to sparkling new apartment blocks and Provençal-style cottages. In Languedoc-Roussillon, the coast has been developed on a large scale with huge complexes of vacation homes. Other popular coasts for rentals are those of Brittany and the Atlantic.

Renting a house

We have rented this villa.
Nous avons loué cette villa.
noo zah-von loo-ee sait vee-lah

Here is our reservation form.
Voici notre réservation.
vwah-see nohtr ray-sair-vah-syon

Can I contact you at this number?
Puis-je vous joindre à ce numéro ?
pweej voo jwandr ah ser new-may-roh

Could you send a repairman?
Pouvez-vous faire réparer ?
poo-vay voo fair ray-pah-ray

How does this work?
Comment est-ce que ça marche ?
koh-man ais-ker sah mahrsh

What is the voltage here, please?
Quelle est la tension, s'il vous plaît ?
kail ai lah tan-syon, seel voo play

I can't open the shutters.
Les volets ne s'ouvrent pas.
lay voh-lay ner soovr pah

Is the water boiler working?
Est-ce que le chauffe-eau marche ?
ais-ker ler shoh-foh mahrsh

Is there any spare bedding?
Y a-t-il un couchage supplémentaire ?
ee-ah-teel ern koo-shahj sew-plai-man-tair

The stove does not work.
La cuisinière ne marche pas.
lah kwee-see-nyair ner mahrsh pah

The toilet is clogged.
Les WC sont bouchés.
lay vay-say son boo-shay

There is a leak.
Il y a une fuite.
eel-yah ewn fweet

We don't have any water.
Nous n'avons pas d'eau.
noo nah-von pah doh

We need two sets of keys.
Il nous faut deux jeux de clefs.
eel noo foh der jer der klay

When does the cleaning person come?
La femme de ménage vient quel jour ?
lah fahm der may-nahj vyern kail joor

Where is … the fuse box?
Où est … la boîte à fusibles ?
oo ai … lah bwaht ah few-zeebl

… the bathroom?
… la salle de bains ?
… lah sahl der bern

… the outlet for my razor?
… la prise pour le rasoir ?
… lah preez poor ler rah-zwahr

… the key for this door?
… la clef de cette porte ?
… lah klay der sait pohrt

Around the house

kitchen	**cuisine**	*kwee-zeen*
chair	**chaise**	*shaiz*
corkscrew	**tire-bouchon**	*teer-boo-shon*
cup	**tasse**	*tahs*
faucet	**robinet**	*roh-bee-nay*
fork	**fourchette**	*foor-shait*
fridge/ refrigerator	**frigo/ réfrigérateur**	*free-goh/ ray-free-jay-rah-terr*
glass	**verre**	*vair*
knife	**couteau**	*koo-toh*
plate	**assiette**	*ass-yait*
saucepan	**casserole**	*kahs-rohl*
sink	**évier**	*ay-vyay*
spoon	**cuillère**	*kwee-yair*
stove	**cuisinière**	*kwee-see-nyair*
table	**table**	*tahbl*
bathroom	**salle de bains**	*sahl der bern*
bathtub	**baignoire**	*bain-wahr*
mirror	**miroir**	*mee-rwahr*
shower	**douche**	*doosh*
sink (bathroom)	**lavabo**	*lah-vah-boh*
toilet	**toilettes**	*twah-lait*
bedroom	**chambre à coucher**	*shan-brh ah koo-shay*
bed	**lit**	*lee*

brush	**brosse**	*brohs*
sheet	**drap**	*drah*
vacuum cleaner	**aspirateur**	*ahs-pee-rah-terr*

Camping

Camping is extremely popular in France, and the main campgrounds are very well organized. The weather, particularly in the south, is well suited to the outdoor life and the facilities available at some of the campgrounds make camping as comfortable as staying in a simple *gîte*.

Family camping vacations are increasingly popular. The campgrounds are good places for getting to know people, and some put on organized activities to entertain children amused. Such locations will have a restaurant or take-out food service for families who don't want to cook every meal. The overall price for a family works out at roughly the same as that of a *gîte* vacation.

Campground ratings

Campgrounds are classified from one to four stars, depending on the amenities. All are required by law to display their star rating and prices at the entrance. The camping fees are worked out according to the star ratings. At 1- and 2-star campgrounds there normally are separate charges per person, per car, per camper and per campsite. At 3- or 4-star campgrounds there often are fixed charges per site regardless of how many of you there are and what equipment you have. You usually pay to stay from midday to midday, and if you remain on a campsite after noon you normally will be charged for an extra night.

At the simplest campgrounds the only facilities you can expect are covered washing and toilet areas (often inadequate for the number of campers), while at the other end of the market the big 4-star campgrounds might have a pool, tennis courts, shops, laundromat, restaurant, bar, playground and more. In other words, you don't have to move far to enjoy yourself—but you may find you're paying hotel prices.

All rated campgrounds have a minimum space allocated to each campsite, although the restrictions tend to be ignored in high season. It's therefore worth checking out the size of your site before deciding to take it.

Where to go

The most popular areas for camping are Brittany, Normandy, the Atlantic coast, the Dordogne and the southern coast. The South has over 300 officially recognized campgrounds, most of them offering attractive locations and good facilities. The campgrounds on the Mediterranean are notoriously crowded in July and August, so it is important to reserve your campsite in advance; if you don't enjoy being within a stone's throw of your neighbors, the Mediterranean campgrounds are best avoided at that time.

For those who want "to get away from it all," France has ample inland campgrounds, providing privacy and peace. There are places to camp on the grounds of *châteaux*, in the fields of farmhouses, beside rivers, lakes and streams. Some of the cities campgrounds are surprisingly cheap and attractively located, often beside a river. In popular tourist areas, farms offer *camping à la ferme,* which is likely to be on a simple, quiet and non-crowded ground.

Off-ground camping, or *le camping sauvage,* is prohibited in many areas and notably in the south. There are areas of inland France where you can set up a tent—but always ask permission first.

Choosing a campground

The best source for finding a ground is the Michelin guide *Camping Caravaning France.* It is written in French, but the facilities are given in symbols and there are English translations where necessary. It recommends a wide range of campgrounds and gives all the facilities available. The national camping organization, the *Fédération Française de Camping Caravaning,* publishes another useful guide.

For upscale camping, it is worth considering the *Castels et Caravaning* group, which offers accommodation, at forty 4-star campgrounds, many set on the grounds of *châteaux* and historic houses.

If you are traveling independently and wish to make a reservation, you can write directly to the campgrounds, enclosing an International Reply Coupon (available from post offices). But remember that some of the smaller campgrounds don't take advance bookings.

Before going, it's worth buying an International Camping Carnet that shows you have third party insurance coverage. Some upscale campgrounds won't let you in without it. The carnet is available from motoring, camping and caravaning organizations.

Useful camping phrases

Can we camp in your field?
Pouvons-nous camper dans votre champ ?
poo-von noo kan-pay dan vohtr shan

Can we camp nearby?
Pouvons-nous camper près d'ici ?
poo-von noo kan-pay prai dee-see

Can we park our camper here?
Pouvons-nous garer notre caravane ici ?
poo-von noo gah-ray nohtr kah-rah-vahn ee-see

Please can we pitch our tent here?
Pouvons-nous dresser notre tente ici ?
poo-von noo drais-say nohtr tant ee-see

What is the fee per day? per week?
Quel est le tarif par jour ? à la semaine ?
kail ay ler tah-reef pahr joor ? ah lah ser-mayn

Where do I pay?
Où dois-je payer ?
oo dwaj pay-yay

Do I pay when I leave?
Dois-je payer au départ ?
dwaj pay-yay oh day-pahr

Is there a more sheltered site?
Y a-t-il un emplacement plus abrité ?
ee-ah-teel ern an-plahs-man plew zah-bree-tay

Is there a restaurant or a store on site?
Y a-t-il un restaurant ou un magasin sur place ?
ee-ah-teel ern rais-toh-ran oo ern mah-gah-zan sewr plahs

Is there another campground near here?
Y a-t-il un autre terrain de camping près d'ici ?
ee-ah-teel ern ohtr tair-ran der kan-peeng prai dee-see

Is this the drinking water?
Est-ce bien l'eau potable ?
ais byern loh poh-tahbl

The site is very wet and muddy.
L'emplacement est très humide et boueux.
lan-plahs-man ai trai zew-meed ay boo-er

Where can I take a shower?
Où sont les douches ?
oo son lay doosh

Where can we wash our dishes?
Où pouvons-nous faire notre vaisselle ?
oo poo-von noo fair nohtr vai-sail

Is there ... a kiddie pool?
Y a-t-il ... une pataugeoire ?
ee-ah-teel ... ewn pah-toh-jwahr

... a swing set?
... des balançoires ?
... day bah-lan-swahr

... a swimming pool?
... une piscine ?
... ewn pee-seen

Around the campground

air mattress	**matelas pneumatique**	*maht-lah pner-mah-teek*
backpack	**sac à dos**	*sahk ah doh*
bottle opener	**décapsuleur**	*dai-kahp-sew-lerr*
corkscrew	**tire-bouchon**	*teer-boo-shon*
bucket	**seau**	*soh*
camp bed	**lit de camp**	*lee der kan*
camp chair	**chaise pliante**	*shaiz plee-ant*
candle	**bougie**	*boo jee*
can opener	**ouvre-boîte**	*oovr-bwaht*
fire	**feu**	*fer*
flashlight	**lampe électrique**	*lanp ay-laik-treek*
fly sheet	**double toit**	*doobl twah*
folding table	**table pliante**	*tahbl plee-ant*

frying pan, skillet	**poêle (à frire)**	*poh-ail ah freer*
ground	**sol**	*sohl*
ground sheet	**tapis de sol**	*tah-pee der sohl*
mallet	**maillet**	*mah-yay*
matches	**allumettes**	*ah-lew-mait*
pocketknife	**canif**	*kah-neef*
plate	**assiette**	*ah-syait*
rope	**corde**	*kohrd*
shelter	**abri**	*ah-bree*
sleeping bag	**sac de couchage**	*sahk der koo-shahj*
tent	**tente**	*tant*
tent peg	**piquet de tente**	*pee-kay der tant*
tent pole	**montant de tente**	*mon-tan der tant*
thermos flask	**bouteille thermos**	*boo-tery tair-moh*

Hostelling

Although often located at the edge of town or in difficult to reach rural areas, French youth hostels (*auberges de jeunesse*) provide basic adequate and well-priced accommodations for travelers on a budget, often in beautiful surroundings. As well as dormitory beds, rooms for couples are available in more modern hostels. To stay in a youth hostel you must be a member of the International Youth Hostel Federation (IYHF) or Hostelling International (HI). HI membership also covers two rival French youth hostel associations, the *Fédération Unie des Auberges de Jeunesse* and the *Ligue Française pour les Auberges de Jeunesse.*

Are you open during the day?
Etes-vous ouvert pendant la journée ?
ait voo oo-vair pan-dan lah joor-nay

What time do you close?
A quelle heure fermez-vous ?
ah kail err fair-may voo

Can we stay five nights here?
Pouvons-nous rester ici cinq nuits ?
poo-von noo rais-tay ee-see sernk nwee

Can we stay until Sunday?
Pouvons-nous rester jusqu'à dimanche ?
poo-von noo rais-tay jews-kah dee-mansh

Do you serve meals?
Servez-vous des repas ?
sair-vay voo day rer-pah

Can I use the kitchen?
Puis-je me servir de la cuisine ?
pweej mer sair-veer der lah kwee-zeen

Here is my membership card.
Voici ma carte de membre.
vwah-see mah kahrt der manbr

I do not have my card.
Je n'ai pas ma carte sur moi.
jer nay pah mah kahrt sewr mwah

Can I join here?
Puis-je m'inscrire ici ?
pweej mern-skreer ee-see

Thank you, we enjoyed our stay.
Merci, nous avons fait un bon séjour.
mair-see, noo zah-von fai tern bon say-joor

Childcare

Can you warm this milk for me?
Pouvez-vous faire réchauffer ce lait, s'il vous plaît ?
poo-vay voo fair ray-shoh-fay ser lai, seel voo play

Do you have a cot/crib for my baby?
Avez-vous un lit d'enfant pour mon bébé ?
ah-vay voo an lee dan-fan poor mon bay-bay

Do you have a high chair?
Avez-vous une chaise haute ?
ah-vay voo ewn shaiz oht

Is there a baby-sitter?
Y a-t-il une baby-sitter ?
ee-ah-teel ewn bay-bee-see-tair

My daughter/son is 7 years old.
Ma fille/mon fils a sept ans.
mah fee/mon fees ah sait an

She goes to bed at nine o'clock.
Elle se couche à neuf heures.
ail ser koosh ah ner verr

We will be back in two hours.
Nous serons de retour dans deux heures.
noo ser-ron der rer-toor dan der zerr

Where can I ... buy some disposable diapers?
Où puis-je ... trouver des couches à jeter ?
oo pweej ... troo-vay day koosh ah jer-tay

... change the baby?
... changer le bébé ?
... shan-jay ler bay-bay

... feed my baby?
... nourrir mon bébé ?
... noo-reer mon bay-bay

I am very sorry. That was very naughty of him.
Je suis désolé ; il a été très vilain.
jer swee day-soh-lay: eel ah ay-tay trai vee-lern

It will not happen again.
Cela ne se reproduira pas.
ser-lah ner ser rer-proh-dwee-rah pah

GETTING AROUND

Public transportation

France has a very comprehensive rail system covering the whole country. The SNCF (*Société Nationale des Chemins de Fer*), a nationally owned company, runs a fast, efficient, and modern service. The TGV (*Train à Grande Vitesse*) takes just two hours to link Paris and Lyon, which means that from city center to city center it is faster than going by air. Bus services are mainly used to connect rural areas to the rail network. The domestic air service is useful for very long journeys, particularly those not covered by high-speed trains. Public transportation, though, can be prone to disruption by strikes.

Getting around Paris

If you arrive by air at Charles de Gaulle airport, the easiest way to get to the center of Paris is to take the airport buses *(Cars Air France)* to Étoile or to Gare de Lyon and Montparnasse. *Roissybus* will take you to Opéra. A cheaper alternative is to take the shuttle bus to Charles de Gaulle station, then a RER train to the Gare du Nord. If you arrive by train you can get straight on to the subway (*métro*) system.

If you arrive by air at Orly, Air France buses will take you to Montpanasse and Invalides, and *Orlybus* will drive you to Denfert-Rochereau. Several bus lines, an airport bus shuttle and an automated train (*Orlyval*) can also take you to the Métro or RER trains.

The Métro and the RER (*Réseau Express Régional*) suburban lines are quick, efficient and cheap. The system is quite simple as long as you remember that the lines are called by the names of the station at each end (there are two names for each line). When you want to change trains you follow signs saying *Correspondances.* Electronic maps will help you pinpoint the station you want and the fastest route to take. If you are making several journeys, a book of 10 tickets (called a *carnet*) works out cheaper than buying them individually. One ticket takes you as far as you want. *Paris Visite* visitor's passes allow unlimited travel by bus, RER and Métro for

2, 3 or 5 days around Paris and its suburbs. A *Carte Orange* (for which you'll need a passport photo) is valid from Monday to Sunday and allows unlimited travel within specific zones.

Buses are a less convenient form of transport than the Métro, but they will give you the opportunity to see the layout of the city.

Asking for directions

Excuse me, please.
Excusez-moi, s'il vous plaît.
aik-skew-say mwah, seel voo play

Where is … the art gallery?
Où est … la galerie d'art ?
oo ai … lah gah-ler-ree dahr

… the police station?
… le commissariat de police ?
… ler koh-mee-sah-ryah der poh-lees

… the post office?
… le bureau de poste ?
… ler bew-roh der pohst

… the bus station?
… la gare routière ?
… lah gahr roo-tyair

Can you show it to me on the map, please?
Pouvez-vous me le montrer sur le plan, s'il vous plaît ?
poo-vay voo mer ler mon-tray sewr ler plan, seel voo play

I am looking for the Tourist Information Office.
Je cherche l'Office de Tourisme.
jer shairsh loh-fees der too-reesm

I am lost.
Je suis perdu.
jer swee pair-dew

How do I get to the Hôtel de la Gare?
Où se trouve l'hôtel de la Gare ?
oo ser troov loh-tail der lah gahr

I am trying to get to the market.
Je cherche le marché.
jer shairsh ler mahr-shay

I would like to go to the theater.
Je voudrais aller au théâtre.
jer voo-dray ah-lay oh tay-ahtr

Is this the right way to the supermarket?
C'est bien par ici, le supermarché ?
sai byern pahr ee-see, ler sew-pair-mahr-shay

We are looking for a restaurant.
Nous cherchons un restaurant.
noo shair-shon ern rais-toh-ran

Where are the restrooms?
Où sont les toilettes ?
oo son lay twah-lait

Where do I get a bus for the city center?
D'où part le bus pour le centre-ville ?
doo pahr ler bews poor ler santr veel

How long does it take to get to the park?
Il y en a pour combien de temps pour aller au parc ?
eel yan ah poor kohm-byern der tan poor ah-lay oh pahrk

Is it far?
Est-ce loin ?
ais lwern

Can you walk there?
On peut y aller à pied ?
on per ee ah-lay ah pyay

By taxi

Taxis can be picked up at a taxi stand or they will come to your hotel. A tip of a few francs is expected.

I need a taxi … now.
J'aurais besoin d'un taxi … tout de suite.
joh-ray ber-zwern dern tahk-see … too der sweet

… in one hour.
… dans une heure.
… dan zewn err

… at 3 o'clock.
… à 3 heures.
… ah trwah zerr

... tomorrow morning.
... demain matin.
... der-mern mah-tern

Where can I get a taxi?
Où puis-je trouver un taxi ?
oo pweej troo-vay ern tahk-see?

Please show us around town.
Faites-nous faire un tour de la ville, s'il vous plaît.
fait noo fair ern toor der lah veel, seel voo play

Please take me to this address.
Conduisez-moi à cette adresse, s'il vous plaît.
kon-dwee-zay mwah ah sait ah-drais, seel voo play

How much is it per kilometer?
C'est combien le kilomètre ?
sai kohm-byern ler kee-loh-maitr

Can you put the bags in the trunk, please?
Pouvez-vous mettre les valises dans le coffre, s'il vous plaît ?
poo-vay voo maitr lay vah-leez dan ler kohfr, seel voo play

Please wait here for a few minutes.
Attendez ici quelques minutes, s'il vous plaît.
ah-tan-day ee-see kail-ker mee-newt, seel voo play

Please, stop at the corner.
Arrêtez-vous au coin, s'il vous plaît.
ah-rai-tay voo oh kwern, seel voo play

Take me to the airport, please.
Conduisez-moi à l'aéroport, s'il vous plaît.
kon-dwee-zay mwah ah lah-ay-roh-por, seel voo play

The bus station, please.
La gare routière, s'il vous plaît.
lah gahr roo-tyair, seel voo play

I am in a hurry.
Je suis pressé.
jer swee prai-say

Please hurry, I am late.
Depêchez-vous s'il vous plaît, je suis en retard.
day-pai-shay voo seel voo play, jer swee zan rer-tahr

Turn left/right, please.
Tournez à gauche/à droite, s'il vous plaît.
toor-nay ah gohsh/ah drwaht, seel voo play

Wait for me, please.
Attendez-moi, s'il vous plaît.
ah-tan-day mwah, seel voo play

Can you come back in one hour?
Pouvez-vous revenir dans une heure ?
poo-vay voo rer-ver-neer dan zewn err

How much is that, please?
C'est combien, s'il vous plaît ?
sai kohm-byern, seel voo play

Keep the change.
Gardez la monnaie.
gahr-day lah moh-nay

By bus

The most reliable bus services in France follow the SNCF network, and are useful for local journeys and connections to stations. In most cities, they will operate a pay-as-you-enter system and accept travel cards. Privately run services to rural areas that are not reachable by a railway are sometimes infrequent and unreliable. In Paris, métro tickets are used for the buses.

Does this bus go to the castle?
Est-ce que ce bus va au château ?
ais-ker ser bews vah oh shah-toh

How frequent is the service?
Quelle est la fréquence du service ?
kail ai lah fray-kans dew sair-vees

What is the fare to the city center?
C'est combien pour le centre-ville ?
sai kohm-byern poor ler santr veel

When is the last bus?
Quand part le dernier bus ?
kan pahr ler dair-nyay bews

Where do I take the bus for the airport?
D'où part le bus pour l'aéroport ?
doo pahr ler bews poor lah-ay-roh-por

Which bus do I take for the stadium?
Quel bus faut-il prendre pour aller au stade ?
kail bews foh-teel prandr poor ah-lay oh stahd

Please tell me when to get off the bus.
Dites-moi où je dois descendre, s'il vous plaît.
deet mwah oo jer dwah day-sandr, seel voo play

By train

The rail system in France is generally reliable and efficient. The TGV now extends over a wide network, including Lille, Rouen and Nice. The ride in the TGVs (and in the slower long-distance Corail trains) is smooth and comfortable. Prices are reasonable and trains normally arrive on time. Many cities have two or more train stations for trips to different regions.

For night travel, there are two kinds of accommodations: the *wagons-lits* that provide you with a private cabin and a sink, and the *train-couchettes*, or sleeper train, where you share a compartment with other travelers.

Rail Europe, the SNCF's representative in the United States, offers a large selection of economical train passes. You must purchase these before leaving for France. The phone number is 800-4EURAIL, and the website address is www.raileurope.com. The SNCF's website is www.sncf.com.

In France, reservations can be made at main railway stations or by telephone. Advance reservations for the TGV are mandatory but you can make these up to a few minutes before departure at special machines at the station. The SNCF's national number is 08 36 35 35 39.

All tickets bought in France must be validated (*composter*) at the orange machines at the entrance to the platform before you travel and again if you make a break of more than 24 hours in your journey.

When is the next train to Bordeaux?
Quand part le prochain train pour Bordeaux ?
kan pahr ler proh-shern trern poor bohr-doh
Which station is the one for Toulouse, please?
Pour aller à Toulouse, c'est quelle gare, s'il vous plaît ?
Poo rah-lay ah too-looz, say kail gahr, seel voo play

Where can I buy a ticket?
Où puis-je acheter un billet ?
oo pweej ash-tay ern bee-yay

Please give me a round-trip ticket to ...
Je voudrais un aller-retour pour ...
jer voo-dray ern ah-lay-rer-toor poor ...

A one-way ticket to Paris, first class.
Un aller simple pour Paris, en première classe.
ern ah-lay sernpl poor pah-ree, an prer-myair klahs

A smoking compartment, second class.
Compartiment fumeurs, en seconde.
kohm-pahr-tee-man few-merr, an ser-gond

A non-smoking compartment, please.
Un compartiment non-fumeurs, s'il vous plaît.
ern kohm-pahr-tee-man non-few-merr, seel voo play

Second class. A window seat, please.
Deuxième classe. Côté fenêtre, s'il vous plaît.
der-zyaim klahs. koh-tay fer-naitr, seel voo play

I have to leave tomorrow.
Je dois partir demain.
jer dwah pahr-teer der-man

Where are the luggage lockers?
Où est la consigne automatique ?
oo ay lah kon-seen oh-toh-mah-teek

I would like to reserve a seat on the sleeper to Paris.
Je voudrais réserver une couchette dans le train de Paris.
jer voo-dray ray-sair-vay ewn koo-shait dan ler trern der pah-ree

I prefer a lower/middle/upper bunk
Je préfère une couchette inférieure/au milieu/supérieure.
jer pray-fayr ewn koo-shayt ern-fay-ree-erhr/oh mee-lyer/sew-pay-ree-err

Is there a discount for children?
Y a-t-il une réduction pour les enfants ?
ee ah-teel ewn ray-dewk-syon poor lay-zan-fan

What are the times of the trains to Paris?
Quels sont les horaires des trains pour Paris ?
kail son lay zoh-rair day trern poor pah-ree

Where is the departure board?
Où est le tableau d'affichage des départs ?
oo ai ler tah-bloh dah-fee-shaj day day-pahr

Where do I have to change?
Où faut-il changer ?
oo foh-teel shan-jay

Can I take my bicycle?
Puis-je emmener mon vélo ?
pweej an-mer-nay mon vay-loh

Is there a dining car in the train?
Y a-t-il un wagon-restaurant dans le train ?
ee-ah-teel ern vah-gon rais-toh-ran dan ler trern

Do I have time to go shopping?
Ai-je le temps de faire des courses ?
ay-jer ler tan der fair day koors

Which platform do I go to?
C'est sur quel quai ?
sai sewr kail kay

How long do I have before my next train leaves?
Il me reste combien de temps avant le prochain train ?
eel mer raist kohm-byern der tan ah-van ler proh-shern trern

What time does the train leave?
A quelle heure part le train ?
ah kail err pahr ler trern

What time is the last train?
A quelle heure part le dernier train ?
ah kail err pahr ler dair-nyay trern

Is this the Marseilles train?
C'est bien le train pour Marseille ?
sai byern ler trern poor mahr-say

Is this the platform for Grenoble?
C'est bien le quai pour le train de Grenoble ?
sai byern ler kay poor ler trern der grer-nohbl

Is this a direct train?
Est-ce un train direct ?
ais ern trern dee-raikt

Are we at Orléans yet?
Sommes-nous arrivés à Orléans ?
sohm noo ah-ree-vay ah ohr-lay-an

What time do we get to Nantes?
A quelle heure arrivons-nous à Nantes ?
ah kail err ah-ree-von noo ah nant

Do we stop at Le Mans?
Est-ce que le train s'arrête au Mans ?
ais-ker ler trern sah-rait oh man

Are we on time?
On est à l'heure ?
on ais ah lerr

How long will the delay be?
Combien de temps faudra-t-il attendre ?
kohm-byern der tan foh-drah-teel ah-tandr

How long will this take?
Il y en a pour combien de temps?
eel yan ah poor kohm-byern der tan

Can you help me with my bags?
Pouvez-vous m'aider avec mes bagages ?
poo-vay voo may-day ah-vaik may bah-gahj

I would like to leave these bags in a locker.
Je voudrais laisser ces bagages à la consigne.
jer voo-dray lai-say say bah-gahj ah lah kon-seen

I will pick them up this evening.
Je reviendrai les prendre ce soir.
jer rer-vyern-drai lay prandr ser swahr

How much is it per bag/suitcase?
C'est combien par sac/valise ?
sai kohm-byern parh sahk/va-leez

May I open the window?
Puis-je ouvrir la fenêtre ?
pweej oov-reer lah fer-naitr

Is this seat taken?
Est-ce que cette place est libre ?
ais ker sait plahs ai leebr

My wife has my ticket.
C'est ma femme qui a mon billet.
sai mah fahm kee ah mon bee-yay

I have lost my ticket.
J'ai perdu mon billet.
jay pair-dew mon bee-yay

This is a non-smoking compartment.
C'est un compartiment non-fumeurs.
sai tern kohm-pahr-tee-man non-few-merr

This is my seat/my bunk.
C'est ma place/ma couchette.
sai mah plahs/mah koo-shayt

Why have we stopped?
Pourquoi avons-nous stoppé ?
poor-kwah ah-von noo stoh-pay

DRIVING

Renting a car

It is cheaper to organize the rental of a car before you leave home, but you can rent cars at airports and in most cities (a surcharge may be included at the airport). Basic car insurance will be included in the rental fee, but beware of being sold unnecessary coverage that may already be included in your travel insurance, or in your personal car insurance at home.

I would like to rent a car.
Je voudrais louer une voiture.
jer voo-dray loo-ay ewn vwah-tewr

Can I rent a car with an automatic transmission?
Puis-je louer une automatique ?
pweej loo-ay ewn oh-toh-mah-teek

Can I pay for insurance?
Puis-je payer l'assurance ?
pweej pay-yay lah-sew-rans

Do I have to pay a deposit?
Dois-je verser des arrhes ?
dwaj vair-say day zahr

Do I pay in advance?
Dois-je payer d'avance ?
dwaj pay-yay dah-vans

Is tax included?
Est-ce que la taxe est comprise ?
ais-ker lah tahks ai kohm-preez

Is there a charge per kilometer?
Y a-t-il un supplément par kilomètre ?
ee-ah-teel ern sew-play-man pahr kee-loh-maitr

Do you have ... a large car?
Avez-vous ... une grosse voiture ?
ah-vay voo ... ewn grohs vwah-tewr

... a smaller car?
... une voiture plus petite ?
... ewn vwah-tewr plew per-teet

... an automatic?
... une automatique ?
... ewn oh-toh-mah-teek

... a station wagon?
... un break ?
... an braik

... an SUV?
... un quatre-quatre ?
... ern kahtr kahtr

I need it for 2 weeks.
J'en ai besoin pour deux semaines.
john ay ber-zwan poor der ser-main

We will both be driving.
Nous conduirons tous les deux.
noo kohn-dwe-ron too lay der

I need to complete this form.
Je dois remplir ce formulaire.
jer dwah ran-pleer ser fohr-mew-lair

I would like to leave the car at the airport.
Je voudrais laisser la voiture à l'aéroport.
jer voo-dray lai-say lah vwah-tewr ah lah-ay-roh-por

I would like a spare set of keys.
Je voudrais un jeu de clés de rechange.
jer voo-drai ern jer der klay der rer-shanj

Do I have to return the car here?
Faut-il ramener la voiture ici ?
foh-teel rahm-nay lah vwah-tewr ee-see

Please explain these documents.
Expliquez-moi ces documents, s'il vous plaît.
aiks-plee-kay mwah say doh-kew-man, seel voo play

Please show me how to operate the lights.
Montrez-moi comment fonctionnent les phares, s'il vous plaît.
mon-tray mwah koh-man fonk-syonn lay fahr seel voo play

Where is ... reverse gear?
Où est ... la marche arrière ?
oo ai ... lah mahrsh ah-ryair

... the car brochure?
... le manuel de la voiture ?
... ler mah-new-ail der la vwah-tewr

... the car title?
... la carte grise de la voiture ?
... lah kart greez der lah vwah-tewr

... the spare tire?
... la roue de secours ?
... lah roo der ser-koor

How does the steering lock work?
Comment fonctionne l'antivol ?
koh-man fonk-syohn lan-tee-vohl

Getting around by car

Driving in France is quite straightforward and can even be pleasurable. Most of the roads (even minor ones) are fast, straight and not crowded—most of the time, at least.

France has an impressively comprehensive network of highways, although most have only two lanes per roadway. Tolls are charged on almost all of them, and these can mount up to considerable sums. On summer weekends it is important to avoid places notorious for their dense traffic: the highway around Paris and the highway from Paris via Beaune and Lyon to the South.

The roads

There are two main types of ordinary road: a *route nationale* (national road), prefixed with an N, and a *route départementale* ("county" road), prefixed with a D. Many of the N roads have become D roads in the last few years, and although you'll find the new numbers indicated on up-to-date maps, many signposts have not yet been changed and some maps are still out of date. The more important N roads—the country's major arteries before the highways were built—are often straight and fast but can be very hazardous, particularly where they go through towns and villages.

Paying tolls

Normally, as you approach a highway, you will be confronted by a number of gates: head for one with a green light, press a button and take the ticket that emerges. It records where you joined the highway and determines how much you pay when you leave it. There are occasional toll barriers across the main highways—usually as you approach a city—where there may be short stretches that are free or for which you pay a fixed charge. If you have the correct change, you can opt to go through an automatic gate where you toss coins into a chute as you drive through. On some highways, Visa and MasterCard credit cards are accepted.

Service areas

Highway service areas often have impressive catering facilities—a single service area may have everything from a snack bar serving fresh-ground coffee and croissants to a waiter-service restaurant with four-course menus. The best-value meals are the *routier* (truck driver) menus. Holders of the current *Relais Routier Guide* can get a four-course meal with beer, mineral water or a quarter liter of wine for about $15. Service areas are quite frequent, but in between you will often find an *aire de repos*—a rest area with parking, toilets (not always too sanitary) and probably a picnic area with a rustic bench or two.

Route-finding

French highways are notorious for horrendous traffic jams at peak vacation times. But most vacation destinations can be reached using less crowded alternative routes, or *Itinéraires Bis,* indicated by green arrows on white (north to south) and white on green (south to north). The alternative network is marketed under the name *Bison Futé* ("crafty bison"); there are free *Bison Futé* maps available at tollbooths, information centers and some service areas. Watch for the *Bison Futé* signs—a Red Indian who is supposed to know when the palefaces (tourists) will be on the warpath. Watch out also for yellow arrows on blue, labeled *itinéraires de délestage*, showing shorter alternative routes in order to avoid areas of dense traffic at peak periods.

Route-planning maps

The Michelin route-planning map, sheet 911, covers dozens of alternative routes through France using the extensive network of secondary roads (as well as highways and major roads, of course).

They also include information on distances and driving times between towns and the peak vacation times to avoid. Map 915, in booklet form, covers the major routes for the whole of France. An English version of the useful *Bison Futé* brochure is available from the French Tourist Office. You can also go to the *Bison Futé* website, at www.bison-fute.equipement.gouv.fr, which has a section in English.

Touring maps

Once you arrive in a particular area, three good series of maps are available. The yellow-covered Michelin maps, which have a scale of 2 km to 1 cm, have the advantage of linking with the *Michelin Red Guide*, identifying towns and villages that have an entry in the guide and so greatly simplifying the job of finding a good hotel or restaurant when you are on the road. The two other series both have a scale of 2.5 km to 1 cm, covering a bit more ground in a given area of the map.

City maps

Even if you don't plan to do much eating out, the *Michelin Red Guide* to hotels and restaurants is worth buying for its many invaluable city maps. The regional *Michelin Green Guides* (for sight-seeing) also have some city maps. Both types of guide are linked to the Michelin yellow-covered maps by a common system of numbering the main roads into each city. These guides are available in both a French and an international version. Amazon.com and Barnes and Noble carry them.

The rules

Priority to the right: *Priorité à droite* means you have to yield to traffic coming from your right and is the rule on most roads and streets. However, most main roads now have the right of way, indicated by a succession of diamond shaped yellow signs with white borders; the roads that have to yield are indicated by the same diamond sign with a black bar across it.

Traffic circles or Roundabouts: The *priorité* rule on circles (since 1984) means that the cars approaching the circle have to yield to those already on it. Prominent signs on the approaching roads indicate *Vous n'avez pas la priorité* (yield). Even so, you still have to watch out for tiny roundabouts—perhaps going around a village monument—where the cars on the circle have to yield to those those entering it.

Speed limits: Speed limits are slightly higher than in the United States, except when wet. They are now quite strictly enforced. Exceeding the speed limit can result in an on-the-spot cash fine as large as 5,000 francs (about $700).

Open roads: Unless road signs say otherwise, the following general limits apply: 90 km/h (56 mph) on ordinary roads, 110 km/h (68 mph) on dual roadways and toll-free highways, and 130 km/h (80 mph) on toll highways. When wet, and for drivers with less than two years' experience, the limits are lowered to 110 km/h (68 mph) on toll highways and 80 km/h (50 mph) on other roads. There is a minimum speed limit of 80 km/h (50 mph) in the outside lane of highways during daylight.

Towns: The limit in built-up areas is 50 km/h (31 mph); the place-name sign marks the beginning of a town for speed-limit purposes; the end is marked by the name crossed out with a red line.

Other rules: You have to be 18 to drive a car, and 21 (or 25 in some places) to rent one. You cannot drive on a U.S. learner's license, and you must have had your driver's license for at least a year.

Drinking and driving is vigorously policed. The maximum alcohol limit in the blood is 8 g/L. Random breath testing is widespread, and fines can be high: pleading ignorance will get you nowhere. A conviction can result in a prison sentence in France.

Seat belts are mandatory for the driver and front-seat passenger; if seat belts are fitted to the rear seats, passengers in those seats must use them; children under 10 must not travel in the front seat of a car that has a back seat.

Overtaking on the brow of a hill is not permitted. After overtaking on a multi-lane road you must return to the inside lane.

Stopping on open roads is not allowed unless you can drive right off the road.

Fines: There is a system of on-the-spot fines for many motoring offenses. To be accurate, it is not a fine but a deposit system, and the police collect the money only from people who cannot show that they are resident in France. You have to pay in cash and the amounts are steep. Theoretically, you can always attend the subsequent court hearing: if you are not found guilty, your deposit will be returned.

Parking: In some cities, street parking is allowed on one side early in the month and on the other late in the month. An area controlled by parking meters or automatic ticket machines is called a *zone grise* ("gray zone"): you have to pay to park between 9:00 A.M. and 7:00 P.M. In most large cities, you can park in a *zone bleue* ("blue zone") between 9:00 A.M. and 12:30 P.M., and 2:30 P.M. and 7:00 P.M. You have to display a time disc, which allows up to an hour's parking. You can buy discs from police stations; some shops and tourist offices will give you one for free. The *zone bleue* is being phased out in favor of parking meters and automatic ticket machines.

In Paris, you cannot park or even stop on some of the main boulevards called *axes rouges.*

On the road

Breakdowns: Move the car to the shoulder, and either switch on the hazard warning lights or put the red warning triangle about 30 m/100 feet behind the car (100 m/330 feet on a highway). On a highway, call the police from an emergency telephone—there is one every 2 km. On other roads, it will normally be best to find the nearest garage, though you can call the police if necessary (telephone number 17). The local *garagiste* is often a friendly and highly competent mechanic who will charge you modest prices. Main dealers of major brands of cars are listed for each town in the Michelin Red Guide.

Accidents: Inform the police, particularly if someone is injured (telephone 17). Motorists involved in an accident must complete a *constat à l'amiable* (accident statement form) on the spot. If one party refuses to sign, then the case is taken to a local *huissier* (bailiff) who prepares a written report called a *constat d'huissier.* This may take several days and can be expensive. However, if a witness can corroborate your statement and sign the form with you, it will help process the claim.

Filling up: If you ask for the tank to be filled, make sure you don't get charged for more than you have had. It's safer to specify how much you want, in francs if you prefer—e.g. *pour cent cinquante francs.*

Self-service stations are invariably cheaper than those with attendants, and gas costs quite a lot more on highways than on normal roads.

The most useful credit cards are Visa (*Carte Bleue*) and Master Card, but acceptance is far from universal.

Types of fuel: *Pétrole* in French means crude oil or paraffin; Essence graded *super* is what you generally put in the car—though the word *essence* alone will often be taken as a generic term for gas. Octane ratings are shown on pumps: *Super sans plomb 97* (leaded), *Euro Super 95 sans plomb* (unleaded), *Super Plus 98 sans plomb* (unleaded). Your rental car might run on *Diesel*, also called *Gazole* (diesel fuel). Some cars use GPL (liquified petroleum gas LPG).

Road signs

Road sign symbols are more or less international these days, but there are many written signs in France with which you might not be familiar. The main ones are given below. If you are going through a town and there are no signs pointing to the destination you want, follow signs saying *autres directions* (other directions) or *toutes directions* (all directions).

absence de marquage no road markings
accotements non stabilisés/consolidés soft shoulder
agglomération built-up area
aire de service (de repos) service (rest) area
allumez vos phares turn on your headlights
autoroute à péage toll highway
attention aux travaux danger – roadwork
autres directions other directions
bifurcation road fork
bouchon traffic jam
boue mud
cédez le passage give way
centre-ville town center
chantier roadworks
chaussée déformée poor road surface
chute de pierres (possibility of) falling rocks
défense de stationner no parking
déviation detour
éboulement rock slide

entrée interdite no entry
essence gas
éteignez vos phares/feux switch off your headlights
feux traffic lights
fin de end of
gravillons loose gravel
hauteur limitée maximum height
interdit sauf aux livraisons (riverains) no entry except for deliveries (residents)
itinéraire bis alternative route
passage protégé pedestrian crossing, crosswalk
péage toll
poids lourds trucks
priorité à droite priority to the right
préparez votre monnaie get your change ready
prochaine sortie next exit
ralentir slow down
route barrée road closed
sens unique one-way street
serrez à droite keep to the right
sortie exit
stationnement parking
toutes directions all directions
travaux roadworks
un train peut en cacher un autre (*at railroad crossings*) one train can hide another coming the other way
véhicules lents slow vehicles
verglas ice on road
virages switchbacks
voie sans issue no through road

Asking for directions

Where does this road go?
Où mène cette route ?
oo main sait root

Which road do I take to Bordeaux?
Quelle est la route de Bordeaux ?
kail ai lah root der bohr-doh

How do I get onto the highway?
Comment peut-on rejoindre l'autoroute ?
koh-man per-ton rer-jwandr loh-toh-root

How far is it to Nancy?
Il y a combien de kilomètres jusqu'à Nancy ?
eel yah kohm-byern der kee-loh-maitr jewsk-ah nan-see

How long will it take to get there?
Ça prendra combien de temps pour y arriver ?
sah pran-drah kohm-byern der tan poor ee ah-ree-vay

I am looking for the next exit.
Je cherche la prochaine sortie.
jer shairsh lah proh-shain sohr-tee

Is there a gas station near here?
Y a-t-il une station service près d'ici ?
ee-ah-teel ewn stah-syon ser-vees pray dee-see

What is the best route to Lyon?
Quelle est la meilleure route pour aller à Lyon ?
kail ai lah mai-yerr root poor ah-lay ah lee-on

What is the fastest route?
Quelle est la route la plus rapide ?
kail ai lah root lah plew rah-peed

What you may hear

Vous allez … à gauche.
voo zah-lay … ah gohsh
You go … left.

… à droite.
… ah drwaht
… right.

… jusqu'à …
… jewsk-kah …
… as far as …

… vers …
… vair …
… toward …

… juste à côté.
… jewst ah koh-tay
… around the corner.

Continuez tout droit.
kon-tee-nway too drwah
Keep going straight ahead.

Suivez la direction de l'autoroute.
swee-vay lah dee-raik-syon der loh-toh-root
Follow the signs for the highway.

Tournez à gauche.
toor-nay ah gohsh
Turn left.

Tournez à droite.
toor-nay ah drwaht
Turn right.

C'est ... à côté du cinéma.
sai ... ah koh-tay dew see-nay-mah
It is ... next to the cinema.

... à l'étage au-dessus/à l'étage au-dessous.
... ah lay-tahj oh der-sew/ah lay-tahj oh der-soo
... on the next floor (up)/on the next floor (down).

... en face de la gare.
... an fahs der lah gahr
... opposite the railway station.

... là-bas.
... lah bah
... over there.

Il faut régler le péage.
eel foh ray-glay ler pay-ahj
You have to pay the toll.

Prenez la première à droite.
prer-nay lah prer-myair ah drwaht
Take the first road on the right.

Prenez la route d'Albi.
prer-nay lah root dahl-bee
Take the road for Albi.

Prenez la deuxième à gauche.
prer-nay lah der-zyaim ah gohsh
Take the second road on the left.

Traffic and weather conditions

Are there any slow spots/back-ups?
Y a-t-il des bouchons ?
ee-ah-teel day boo-shon

Is the traffic one-way?
Est-ce une route à sens unique ?
ais ewn root ah sans ew-neek

Is the pass open?
Est-ce que le col est ouvert ?
ais ker ler kohl ai too-vair

Is the road to Annecy snowed up?
Est-ce que la route d'Annecy est enneigée ?
ais ker lah root dahn-see ai tan-nai-jay

Is the traffic heavy?
Y a-t-il beaucoup de circulation ?
ee-ah-teel boh-koo der seer-kew-lah-syon

Is there a different way to the stadium?
Y a-t-il une autre route pour aller au stade ?
ee-ah-teel ewn ohtr root poor ah-lay oh stahd

Is there a toll on this highway?
Est-ce que cette autoroute est à péage ?
ais ker sait oh-toh-root ai tah pay-ahj

What is causing this traffic jam?
Pourquoi y a-t-il un embouteillage ?
poor-kwah ee-ah-teel ern an-boo-tery-ahj

What is the speed limit?
Quelle est la limitation de vitesse ?
kail ai lah lee-mee-tah-syon der vee-tais

When is the rush hour?
Quelles sont les heures de pointe ?
kail son lay zerr der pwant

When will the road be clear?
Quand est-ce que la voie sera dégagée ?
kant es ker lah vwah ser-ra day-gah-jay

Do I need snow chains?
Est-ce que j'ai besoin de chaînes ?
ais ker jay ber-zwern der shain

Parking

Can I park here?
Puis-je me garer là ?
pweej mer gah-ray lah

Do I need a parking disc?
Ai-je besoin d'un disque de stationnement ?
aij ber-zwern dern deesk der stah-syonn-man

Do I need coins for the meter?
Faut-il mettre des pièces dans le parcmètre ?
foh-teel maitr day pyais dan ler pahrk-maitr

How long can I stay here?
Combien de temps puis-je stationner ici ?
kohm-byern der tan pweej stah-syonn-ay ee-see

Is it safe to park here?
Peut-on se garer ici sans risque ?
per-ton ser gah-ray ee-see san reesk

What time does the parking lot close?
A quelle heure ferme le parking ?
ah kail err fairm ler pahr-keeng

Where can I get a parking disc?
Où peut-on acheter un disque de stationnement ?
oo per-ton ahsh-tay ern deesk der stah-syonn-man

Is there a parking lot?
Est-ce qu'il y a un parking ?
ais keel-yah ern pahr-keeng

At the gas station

Fill the tank, please.
Le plein, s'il vous plaît.
ler plern, seel voo play

25 liters of unleaded 95.
25 (vingt cinq) litres de sans plomb 95.
vernt-sernk leetr der san plohm kahtr-vern-kernz

25 liters of unleaded 98.
25 litres de sans plomb 98.
vernt-sernk leetr der san plohm kahtr-vern-deez-weet

25 liters of diesel.
25 litres de gazole.
vernt-sernk leetr der gah-zohl

250 francs of super leaded.
250 francs de super 97.
der-san-san-kant fran der sew-perr kahtr-vern-deez-sait

Can you clean the windshield, please?
Pouvez-vous nettoyer le pare-brise, s'il vous plaît ?
poo-vay voo nai-twah-yay ler pahr-breez, seel voo play

Could you check … the oil, please.
Pouvez-vous vérifier … l'huile, s'il vous plaît.
poo-vay voo vay-ree-fyay … lweel, seel voo play

… the water and oil, please.
… les niveaux, s'il vous plaît.
… lay nee-voh, seel voo play

… the tire pressure, please.
… les pneus, s'il vous plaît.
… lay pner, seel voo play

The pressure should be 2.3 at the front and 2.5 at the rear.
C'est 2,3 (deux virgule trois) à l'avant et 2,5 (deux virgule cinq) à l'arrière.
sai der veer-gewl trwah ah lah-van ay der veer-gewl sernk ah lah-ryair

Do you take credit cards?
Acceptez-vous les cartes de crédit ?
ahk-saip-tay voo lay kahrt der kray-dee

Breakdowns and repairs

Can you sell me a can of gasoline, please?
Avez-vous un bidon d'essence, s'il vous plaît ?
ah-vay voo ern bee-don dai-sans, seel voo play

Can you give me … a push?
Pouvez-vous … me pousser ?
poo-vay voo … mer poo-say

… a tow?
… me prendre en remorque ?
… mer prandr an rer-mohrk

Can you send a tow truck?
Pouvez-vous envoyer une dépanneuse ?
poo-vay voo an-vwah-yay ewn day-pah-nerz

Can you take me to the nearest garage?
Pouvez-vous me conduire au garage le plus proche ?
poo-vay voo mer kohn-dweer oh gah-rahj ler plew prohsh

I have run out of gas.
Je n'ai plus d'essence
jer nay plew dai-sans

Is there a telephone nearby?
Y a-t-il un téléphone près d'ici ?
ee-ah-teel ern tay-lay-fohn prai dee-see

Do you have an emergency fan belt?
Avez-vous une courroie de secours ?
ah-vay voo ewn koo-rwah der ser-koor

Do you have jumper cables?
Avez-vous des câbles de démarrage ?
ah-vay voo day kahbl der day-mah-rahj

I have a flat tire.
J'ai un pneu crevé.
jay ern pner krer-vay

I have blown a fuse.
Un fusible a sauté.
ern few-zeebl ah soh-tay

I have locked myself out of the car.
Les clefs sont enfermées à l'intérieur.
lay klay son tan-fair-may ah lan-tay-ryerr

I have locked the ignition key inside the car.
La clef de contact est enfermée à l'intérieur.
lah klay der kohn-tahkt ai tan-fair-may ah lan-tay-ryerr

I have lost my key.
J'ai perdu ma clef.
jay pair-dew mah klay

I need a new fan belt.
Il me faut une courroie de ventilateur neuve.
eel mer foh ewn koo-rwah der van-tee-lah-terr nerv

I think there is a bad connection.
Je crois qu'il y a un mauvais contact.
jer krwah keel yah ern moh-vai kohn-tahkt

Can you repair a flat tire?
Pouvez-vous réparer un pneu crevé ?
poo-vay voo ray-pah-ray ern pner krer-vay

My car … has been towed away.
Ma voiture … a été emmenée à la fourrière.
mah vwah-tewr … ah ay-tay an-mer-nay ah lah foo-ryair

… has broken down.
… est en panne.
… ai tan pahn

... will not start.
... ne démarre pas.
... ner day-mahr pah

My windshield has cracked.
Mon pare-brise est fêlé.
mon pahr-breez ai fai-lay

The air conditioning does not work.
La climatisation ne marche pas.
lah klee-mah-tee-zah-syon ner mahrsh pah

The battery is dead.
La batterie est à plat.
lah bah-ter-ree ay tah plah

The engine has broken down.
Le moteur est en panne.
ler moh-terr ai tan pahn

The engine is overheating.
Le moteur chauffe.
ler moh-terr shohf

The exhaust pipe has fallen off.
J'ai perdu mon pot d'échappement.
jay pair-dew mon poh day-shahp-man

There is a leak in the radiator.
Il y a une fuite au radiateur.
eel yah ewn fweet oh rah-dyah-terr

Can you replace the windshield wiper blades?
Pouvez-vous changer les balais d'essuie-glaces ?
poo-vay voo shan-jay lay bah-lay day-swee-glahs

There is something wrong.
Il y a un problème.
eel yah an proh-blaim

There is something wrong with the car.
La voiture ne marche pas bien.
lah vwah-tewr ner mahrsh pah byern

Is there a mechanic here?
Y a-t-il un mécanicien ?
ee-ah-teel ern may-kah-nee-syern

Can you find out what the trouble is?
Pouvez-vous regarder ce qui ne va pas ?
poo-vay voo rer-gar-day ser kee ner vah pah

Do you have the spare parts?
Avez-vous les pièces de rechange ?
ah-vay voo lay pyais der rer-shanj

Is it serious?
Est-ce grave ?
ais grahv

Can you repair it for the time being?
Pouvez-vous faire une réparation provisoire ?
poo-vay voo fair ewn ray-pah-rah-syon proh-vee-zwar

How long will it take to repair it?
Combien de temps faudra-t-il pour réparer ?
kohm-byern der tan foh-drah-teel poor ray-pah-ray

Accidents and the police

There has been an accident.
Il y a eu un accident.
eel ya ew ern ahk-see-dan

We have to call … an ambulance.
Il faut appeler … une ambulance.
eel foh ah-play … ewn an-bew-lans

… the police.
… la police.
… lah poh-lees

What is your name and address?
Quel est votre nom et votre adresse ?
kail ai vohtr nohm ay vohtr ah-drais

Don't move.
Ne bougez pas.
ner boo-jay pah

He did not stop.
Il ne s'est pas arrêté.
eel ner sai pah ah-rai-tay

He is a witness.
Il est témoin.
eel ai tay-mwan

He overtook on a bend.
Il a doublé dans un virage.
eel ah doo-blay dan zern vee-rahj

He rear-ended my car.
Il m'a embouti à l'arrière.
eel mah an-boo-tee ah lah-ryair

He stopped suddenly.
Il s'est arrêté brusquement.
eel sai tah-rai-tay brewsk-man

He was moving too fast.
Il roulait trop vite.
eel roo-lay troh veet

Here are my insurance documents.
Voici mon assurance.
vwah-see mon nah-sew-rans

Here is my driver's license.
Voici mon permis de conduire.
vwah-see mon pair-mee der kon-dweer

How much is the fine?
Quel est le montant de la contravention ?
kail ai ler mon-tan der lah kon-trah-van-syon

I don't have enough money. Can I pay at the police station?
Je n'ai pas assez d'argent. Puis-je payer au commissariat de police ?
jer nay pah ah-say dahr-jan. pweej pay-yay oh koh-mee-sah-ryah der poh-lees

I am very sorry. I am a visitor.
Je suis désolé. Je suis de passage.
jer swee day-soh-lay. jer swee der pah-sahj

I did not know about the speed limit.
Je ne savais pas que la vitesse était limitée.
jer ner sah-vay pah ker lah vee-tais ay-tay lee-mee-tay

I did not understand the sign.
Je n'ai pas compris le panneau.
jer nay pah kohm-pree ler pah-noh

I did not see the sign.
Je n'ai pas vu le panneau.
jer nay pah vew ler pah-noh

I did not see the bicycle.
Je n'ai pas vu la bicyclette.
jer nay pah vew lah bee-see-klait

I could not stop in time.
Je n'ai pas pu m'arrêter à temps.
jer nay pah pew mah-rai-tay ah tan

I have not had anything to drink.
Je n'ai rien bu.
jer nay ryern bew

I was only driving at 50 km/h.
Je ne roulais qu'à 50 km/h (cinquante kilomètres à l'heure).
jer ner roo-lay kah san-kant kee-loh-maitr ah lerr

I was passing that car.
J'étais en train de dépasser cette voiture.
jay-tay an trern der day-pah-say sait vwah-terr

I was parking.
J'étais en train de me garer.
jay-tay an trern der mer gah-ray

That car was tailgating me.
La voiture me suivait de trop près.
lah vwah-tewr mer swee-vay der troh prai

The brakes failed.
Les freins ont lâché.
lay frern on lah-shay

The licence plate number was ...
Le numéro d'immatriculation était ...
ler new-may-roh dee-mah-tree-kew-lah-syon ay-tay ...

The car skidded.
La voiture a dérapé.
lah vwah-tewr ah day-rah-pay

The car swerved.
La voiture a fait un écart.
lah vwah-tewr ah fai an ay-kahr

The car turned right without signaling.
La voiture a tourné à droite sans prévenir.
lah vwah-tewr ah toor-nay ah drwaht san pray-ver-neer

The road was icy.
La route était verglacée.
lah root ay-tay vair-glah-say

The tire burst.
Le pneu a éclaté.
ler pner ah ay-klah-tay

Car parts

accelerator	**accélérateur**	*ahk-say-lay-rah-terr*
air filter	**filtre à air**	*feeltr ah air*
alternator	**alternateur**	*ahl-tair-nah-terr*
antenna	**antenne**	*an-tain*
antifreeze	**antigel**	*an-tee-jail*
antitheft system	**antivol**	*an-tee-vohl*
automatic	**automatique**	*oh-toh-mah-teek*
axle	**essieu**	*ai-syer*
backup light	**feux de recul**	*fer der rer-kewl*
battery	**batterie**	*bah-ter-ree*
blinker	**clignotant**	*kleen-yoh-tan*
brake fluid	**liquide de frein**	*lee-keed de frern*
brake pads	**plaquettes de frein**	*plah-kait der frern*
brakes	**freins**	*frern*
bulb	**ampoule**	*an-pool*
bumper	**pare-chocs**	*pahr-shohk*
carburetor	**carburateur**	*kahr-bew-rah-terr*
child seat	**siège pour enfant**	*syaij poor an-fan*
choke	**starter**	*stahr-tair*
clutch	**embrayage**	*an-brai-yaj*
cylinder	**cylindre**	*see-lerndr*
disc brake	**freins à disques**	*frern ah deesk*
distributor	**delco**	*dail-koh*
door	**portière**	*pohr-tyair*
dynamo	**dynamo**	*dee-nah-moh*
electrical system	**circuit électrique**	*seer-kwee ay-laik-treek*
engine	**moteur**	*moh-terr*
exhaust system	**échappement**	*ay-shahp-man*
fan belt	**courroie de ventilateur**	*koo-rwah der van-tee-lah-terr*
fog lamps	**feux de brouillard**	*ferr der broo-yahr*
foot pump	**pompe à pied**	*pohmp ah pyay*
fuel gauge	**jauge d'essence**	*johj dai-sans*
fuel pump	**pompe d'alimentation**	*pohmp dah-lee-man-tah-syon*
fuse	**fusible**	*few-seebl*
gasoline	**carburant**	*kahr-bew-rang*
gas tank	**réservoir d'essence**	*ray-zer-war days-sans*

gear box	**boîte de vitesses**	*bwaht der vee-tais*
gearshift	**levier de vitesses**	*lai-vyay der vee-tais*
hammer	**marteau**	*mahr-toh*
hand emergency brake	**frein à main**	*frern ah mern*
hazard lights	**feux de détresse**	*fer der day-trais*
headlights	**phares**	*fahr*
high beams/brights	**feux de route**	*fer der root*
heating system	**chauffage**	*shoh-fahj*
hood	**capot**	*kah-poh*
horn	**klaxon**	*klahk-son*
hose	**tuyau**	*tew-yoh*
hubcap	**enjoliveur**	*anj-oh-lee-verhr*
ignition	**allumage**	*ah-lew-mahj*
ignition key	**clé de contact**	*klay der kon-tahkt*
jack	**cric**	*kreek*
lights	**feux**	*fer*
oil	**huile**	*weel*
oil filter	**filtre à huile**	*feeltr ah weel*
oil pressure	**pression d'huile**	*prai-syon dweel*
pedal	**pédale**	*pay-dahl*
pump	**pompe**	*pohmp*
radiator	**radiateur**	*rah-dyah-terr*
rearview mirror	**rétroviseur**	*ray-troh-vee-serr*
reflectors	**réflecteurs**	*ray-flaik-terr*
roof-rack	**galerie**	*gah-ler-ree*
screwdriver	**tournevis**	*toorn-vees*
seat	**siège**	*syaij*
seat belt	**ceinture de sécurité**	*sern-tewr der say-kew-ree-tay*
shock absorber	**amortisseur**	*ah-mohr-tee-serr*
sidelights	**feux de position**	*fer der poh-zee-syon*
silencer	**silencieux**	*see-lan-syer*
socket set	**prise**	*preez*
spare part	**pièce de rechange**	*pyais der rer-shanj*
spare tire	**roue de secours**	*roo der ser-koor*
spark plug	**bougie**	*boo-jee*
speedometer	**compteur**	*kohmp-terr*
starter	**démarreur**	*day-mah-rerr*
steering	**direction**	*dee-raik-syon*
steering wheel	**volant**	*voh-lan*
stoplight	**stop**	*stohp*
sun roof	**toit ouvrant**	*twa toov-ran*

suspension	**suspension**	*sews-pan-syon*
tire	**pneu**	*pner*
tire pressure	**pression des pneus**	*prai-syon day pner*
tools	**outils**	*oo-tee*
trailer hitch	**barre de remorquage**	*bahr der rer-mohr-kahj*
transmission	**transmission**	*trans-mee-syon*
trunk	**coffre**	*kohfr*
warning light	**voyant lumineux**	*voh-yan lew-mee-ner*
water	**eau**	*oh*
wheel	**roue**	*roo*
windshield	**pare-brise**	*pahr-breez*
wipers	**essuie-glaces**	*ais-wee-glahs*
wrench	**clef anglaise**	*klay an-glayz*

EATING OUT

Good value and good quality

Eating out is a national pastime for the French. Even small towns have at least one ambitious restaurant, and meals are an excellent value. The emphasis is on fresh local produce and even the humblest-looking place may produce food of surprisingly good quality.

Meals and menus

Proper restaurants and hotel dining rooms (other than in the major cities) stick to fairly rigid hours. Lunch (*le déjeuner*) is the main meal of the day. Popular restaurants start filling up soon after noon. Reserve ahead for Sunday lunch. Dinner (*le dîner*) is usually served from around 7:30 P.M. until 10 P.M.

Cafés and brasseries are usually open all day for snacks or more substantial meals, and are useful if you do not have time to linger over a three-course meal. Prices in fashionable places—particularly in Paris—are very high, although you can stay for as long as you like for the price of one drink. At lunchtime, they often offer a *menu du jour* (literally, menu of the day), which is a fixed-price meal. These meals are most of the time a good bargain, for you will get good food at a modest price.

The word "menu" has a more precise meaning in France than in the United States: it means a meal consisting of several courses with a narrow choice of dishes, at a fixed price. Most restaurants offer several such menus at a range of prices, and may or may not also offer a wider choice of individual dishes from *la carte*. Menus invariably offer better value.

The French way

- Meals are not meant to be rushed, so service may seem slow.
- Waiters are not called *garçon*—use *monsieur, madame* or *mademoiselle*.
- The French do not drink coffee or tea during meals, but afterward.

- A simple restaurant will expect you to use the same knife and fork throughout the meal.
- You will automatically be given bread with your meal but not always a side plate or butter.
- Vegetables are often served separately from the meat, salads invariably so.
- Red meat is normally served rare or *saignant;* if you want it practically raw, ask for it *bleu;* if you want it rare, ask for it *saignant,* for medium *à point* and for well done, *bien cuit.*
- Cheese comes before dessert.

Food

Even if France had no other attractions for the visitor, the country would retain the loyalty of many travelers because of its food. The French attitude to food is different from that of the Americans—traditionally lunch is still a leisurely two-hour affair.

Serious students of French food identify different styles of cooking—in particular *haute cuisine,* the rich, expensive fare traditionally associated with top-notch restaurants, and *nouvelle cuisine,* the modern version, using much less cream and butter, and often serving much smaller portions.

Styles of cooking and sauces

Alsacienne (à l') usually with sauerkraut, ham and sausages
Armoricaine (à l') with sauce of tomatoes, herbs, white wine, brandy
Anglaise (à l') plain, boiled
ballotine boned, stuffed and rolled into a bundle
Béarnaise sauce flavored with tarragon and vinegar
Bercy sauce with wine, shallots and bone marrow
Berrichonne (à la) with bacon, cabbage, onions and chestnuts
beurre blanc butter sauce with shallots and dry wine or vinegar
beurre noir browned butter with vinegar
bigarade bitter orange sauce
bonne femme poached in white wine with onions and mushrooms
Bordelaise sauce of red wine and bone marrow
boulangère (à la) braised or baked with onions and potatoes
bourgeoise (à la) with carrots, onions and bacon

Bourguignonne (à la) cooked with burgundy, onions and mushrooms
Bretonne (à la) served with haricot beans, sometimes as a purée
cardinal rich, red fish sauce with mushrooms, truffles (usually for lobster)
chasseur with shallots, mushrooms, tomatoes
chemise (en) wrapped, generally in pastry
confit/e preserved or candied
court-bouillon aromatic poaching liquid
croûte (en) pastry case (in a)
daube meat slowly braised in wine and herbs
diable highly seasoned sauce; also type of cooking pot
Dijonnaise (à la) with mustard sauce
farci/e stuffed
fourré/e filled
galantine cold pressed poultry, meat or fish in jelly
Hollandaise sauce with butter, egg yolk and lemon juice
Lyonnaise (à la) with onions
Normande (à la) with cream and any or all of: calvados, cider, apples
Provençale (à la) with tomatoes, oil and garlic
roulade (de) roll (of)
rouille strongly flavored creamy sauce with fish soups

Cheese

Part of the fun of eating cheese in France is that there are always new varieties to discover and try out. "Try everything once" should be your motto. Be prepared for lots of pleasant surprises and a huge variety of flavors from all over the country, thanks to methods of cheesemaking that are quite diverse and often secret. It is customary in France to eat the cheese course before the dessert. The cheeses will be served with bread but not butter. Wherever you are, be sure to sample the local production.

Principal cheeses

You're likely to come across these major varieties of cheese anywhere in France.

Brie: Soft cheese always made in round disks, varying in size. A good one should be yellow, creamy but not runny. It is made by factories in Brie and other parts of France and often called by the name of the area where it is made, for example Brie de Meaux or Brie de Melun.

Bleu d'Auvergne: Blue mold cheese, originally created by a 19th-century peasant.

Camembert: Small circular soft cheese invented in about 1790 by a farmer's wife, Mme Harel, whose statue you can see in the village of Camembert, near Vimoutiers in Normandy. True connoisseurs eat it runny and smelly.

Livarot: Soft, strong cheese with orange rind, from a small market town in Normandy.

Munster: Large, round, supple cheese with orange rind, matured for three to six weeks, with strong smell and spicy flavor. Made in Alsace.

Pont-l'Evêque: Small, square, pungent cheese, made from whole or skimmed milk.

Port-Salut: Creamy, yellow, whole-milk cheese, first made at the Trappist Monastery of Port du Salut in Brittany.

Reblochon: Soft, smooth cow milk cheese from Savoie, with mild, creamy flavor.

Roquefort: The true Roquefort, made in the little town of the same name in the Massif Central, is manufactured exclusively from ewes' milk. The unique feature of this cheese is that the curds are mixed with a special type of breadcrumbs, causing a green mold to develop. The cheeses are stored in damp, cool caves for 30 or 40 days. Experts say it should then be left to ripen for a year.

Regional cheeses

Bleu de Bresse: Factory-made blue cheese from the Lyonnais in the shape of a small cylinder; creamy and smooth.

Brillat-Savarin: Mild, creamy cheese from Normandy, named after the gastronome.

Cantal: Hard, strong, yellow cheese, with a nutty flavor, made in Auvergne.

Chabichou: Small, cone-shaped goat milk cheese, with strong smell and flavor; from the Poitou area.

Chaource: White, soft and creamy cheese from Burgundy, made in cylinders.

Dauphin: Soft, herb-seasoned cheese from Champagne Ardennes area, said to be named after Louis XIV's son.

Époisses: Soft, whole-milk cheese with spicy smell and flavor made all over Burgundy and central France.

Olivet bleu: Small, rich, fruity cheese with bluish skin, sometimes wrapped in plane tree leaves; it comes from the Loire.

Rollot: Cheese in the form of a disk with yellow rind, spicy smell and flavor.

Saint-Marcellin: Small, round, mild cheese made of cow milk from Savoie.

Tomme: Name for a large number of cheeses, mainly from the Alps. Usually mild.

Ste-Mauré: Soft creamy goat milk cheese from Touraine.

St-Nectaire: Flat, round cheese with mild but aromatic flavor, made on the Dordogne.

Reservations

Should we reserve a table?
Faut-il réserver une table ?
foh-teel ray-sair-vay ewn tahbl

Can I book a table for four at 8 o'clock?
Je voudrais réserver une table pour quatre pour huit heures.
jer voo-dray ray-sair-vay ewn tahbl poor kahtr poor weet err

Can we have a table … for four, please?
Une table … pour quatre, s'il vous plaît.
ewn tahbl poor kahtr, seel voo play

… by the window.
… près de la fenêtre.
… prai der lah fer-naitr

… on the terrace.
… sur la terrasse.
… sewr lah tay-rahs

… non smoking.
… non fumeur.
… non few-merhr

I am a vegetarian.
Je suis végétarien.
jer swee vay-jay-tah-ryern

We have a reservation in the name of …
Nous avons une réservation au nom de …
noo za-von ewn ray-sair-vah-syon oh non der …

Useful questions

Do you have a local speciality?
Avez-vous une spécialité régionale ?
ah-vay voo ewn spay-syah-lee-tay ray-jyon-ahl

Do you have a set menu?
Avez-vous un menu à prix fixe ?
ah-vay voo ern mer-new ah pree feeks

What do you recommend?
Que recommandez-vous ?
ker rer-koh-man-day voo

What is the dish of the day?
Quel est le plat du jour ?
kail ai ler plah dew joor

What is the soup of the day?
Quelle est la soupe du jour ?
kail ai lah soop dew joor

What is this called?
Comment s'appelle ce plat ?
koh-man sah-pail ser plah

What is in this dish?
Qu'y a-t-il dans ce plat ?
kee-ah-teel dan ser plah

Are vegetables included?
Est-ce que les légumes sont inclus ?
ais ker lay lay-gewm son tern-klew

Which local wine do you recommend?
Quel vin de pays recommandez-vous ?
kail vern der payy rer-koh-man-day voo

How is the local wine?
Comment est le vin du pays ?
koh-man ay ler vern der payee

Is this cheese very strong?
Est-ce que ce fromage est très fort ?
ais ker ser froh-mahj ai trai fohr

How much is this?
C'est combien ?
sai kohm-byern

Do you have yogurt?
Avez-vous du yaourt ?
ah-vay voo dew yah-oort

How do I eat this?
Comment mange-t-on cela ?
koh-man manj-ton ser-lah

Ordering your meal

The menu, please.
Le menu, s'il vous plaît.
ler mer-new, seel voo play

Can we start with a soup?
Est-ce que nous pouvons commencer par une soupe, s'il vous plaît ?
ais-ker noo poo-von koh-man-say pahr ewn soop, seel voo play

That is for me.
C'est pour moi.
sai poor mwah

Could we have some bread/butter?
Pouvons-nous avoir du pain/du beurre, s'il vous plaît.
poo-von noo ah-vwar dew pern/dew berr, seel voo play

I will have some salad.
Je prendrai de la salade.
jer pran-drai der lah sah-lahd

I will take that.
Je prendrai ça.
jer pran-drai sah

I will take the set menu.
Je prendrai le menu à prix fixe.
jer pran-drai ler mer-new ah pree feeks

I like my steak ... rare.
J'aime mon steak ... saignant.
jaim mon staik ... sai-nyan

... medium rare.
... à point.
... ah pwan

... very rare.
... bleu.
... bler

... well done.
... bien cuit.
... byern kwee

Can I see the menu again, please?
Repassez-moi le menu, s'il vous plaît.
rer-pah-say mwah ler mer-new, seel voo play

What flavors do you have?
Qu'est-ce que vous avez comme parfums ?
kais-ker voo zah-vay cohm pahr-fern

We will have a drink first.
Nous prendrons un apéritif.
noo pran-dron ern nah-pay-ree-teef

Wine

Wine is an integral part of French life. The vineyards of France produce a significant proportion of the world's wine, and the people of France consume part of that volume themselves. The choice of wines is enormous: everything from *vin ordinaire* in plastic bottles, costing no more than mineral water, to the cream of the crop from Bordeaux and Burgundy—some of the best wines in the world.

Unless you are very familiar with French wines, choosing from the wine list (*la carte des vins*) can be an intimidating experience. Some restaurants produce off-putting lists with pages of wines and prices that are very high.

But if the big-name Bordeaux and Burgundy wines are out of reach, there are often much cheaper alternatives, even in the top restaurants; many wines from the Loire and Rhone valleys or from the south and southwest are now finding their way on to wine lists throughout the country.

The house wine—*la réserve du patron* or *vin de la maison*—is almost always a good bet: if it carries the restaurant's own label, it usually has been carefully selected.

Reading a label

The ways in which wines are described on labels vary widely from region to region. Running across all the variations is a national system of identification employing four classifications.

Appellation (d'Origine) Contrôlée (AC or **AOC)** A guarantee of origin and authenticity, applied to all major wines. An *appellation* may apply to a whole region (for example Bourgogne), a part of a region (for example Côtes de Nuit), a specific village (e.g. Gevrey-Chambertin) or even a particular vineyard (e.g. Grand Cru Clos de Bèze). In general, within a given region, the larger the geographic area described on the label, the cheaper and lesser quality the wine.

Vin Délimité de Qualité Supérieure (VDQS) The second rank of *appellations* for regions producing minor wines. Some are of very good quality, being denied an AC only because they employ non-traditional grapes. As these better wines gain AC status, the VDQS label is being phased out.

Vin de Pays "Country wine" from a specific area, which may be a village or a whole region. Standards vary enormously.

Vin de Table or **Vin Ordinaire** Blended wine, usually sold under a brand name.

Wine vocabulary

Blanc de blancs White wine made from white grapes
Cave Cellar or any wine establishment
Cave coopérative Wine growers' cooperative, often a very good place to taste and buy
Chai Cellar at ground level, sometimes meaning a warehouse
Château A wine-growing estate, with or without a grand house, particularly in the Bordeaux area
Clairet Very light red wine
Claret Traditional English term for red wine from Bordeaux
Clos Prestigious vineyard, often walled, found particularly in Burgundy and Alsace
Côte(s)/côteaux Hillsides, generally producing better wines than lower vineyards
Crémant In Champagne, "less sparkling"; elsewhere, high-quality sparkling wine made by the Champagne method
Cru (Growth) A term used in classifying the wines of different vineyards. In Bordeaux there is an elaborate and confusing system of *crus*, rooted firmly in the 19th century and not an entirely useful guide to quality. In Burgundy and Champagne, *Grand Cru* indicates the most prestigious wines, *Premier Cru* the second rank.

Cuve Close Method of making sparkling wine, generally inferior to the Champagne method
Cuvée du patron House wine
Domaine A wine estate, particularly in Burgundy
Méthode champenoise Sparkling wine made by the Champagne method
Mise (en bouteille) au château/à la propriété/au domaine Bottled on the wine-maker's premises; usually a good thing
Mœlleux Mellow, sweet
Mousseux Sparkling
Négociant Wine merchant
Perlant/perlé Very slightly sparkling
Pétillant Slightly sparkling
Primeur Young wine
Propriétaire-Récoltant Owner-manager
Récolte Crop
Réserve de la maison/du patron House wine in a restaurant
Vendange tardive Late vintage, especially in Alsace; the grapes are picked only when they have reached a certain sweetness.
Vignoble Vineyard
Viticulteur Winegrower

Ordering drinks

The wine list, please.
La carte des vins, s'il vous plaît.
lah kahrt day vern, seel voo play

A bottle of house red wine, please.
Une bouteille de la cuvée du patron, s'il vous plaît.
ewn boo-tery der lah kew-vay dew pah-tron, seel voo play

A glass of dry white wine, please.
Un verre de vin blanc sec, s'il vous plaît.
ern vair der vern blan sayk, seel voo play

Another bottle of red wine, please.
Une autre bouteille de vin rouge, s'il vous plaît.
ewn ohtr boo-tery der vern rooj, seel voo play

Another glass, please.
Un autre verre, s'il vous plaît.
ern ohtr vair, seel voo play

We will take the beaujolais.
Nous prendrons le beaujolais.
noo pran-dron ler boh-joh-lay

Two beers, please.
Deux bières, s'il vous plaît.
der byair, seel voo play

Some tap water, please.
Une carafe d'eau, s'il vous plaît.
ewn kah-rahf doh, seel voo play

A fruit juice, please.
Un jus de fruit, s'il vous plaît.
ern jew der frwee, seel voo play

A soda water, please.
Une eau gazeuse, s'il vous plaît.
ewn noh gah-zerz, seel voo play

Can we have some mineral water?
De l'eau minérale, s'il vous plaît.
der loh mee-nay-rahl, seel voo play

Black coffee, please.
Un café (noir), s'il vous plaît.
ern kah-fay (nwahr), seel voo play

Coffee with milk, please.
Un café-crème, s'il vous plaît.
ern kah-fay kraim, seel voo play

Tea with milk, please.
Un thé au lait, s'il vous plaît.
ern tay oh lay, seel voo play

Paying the bill

The check, please.
L'addition, s'il vous plaît.
lah-dee-syon, seel voo play

Do you accept traveler's checks?
Acceptez-vous les chèques de voyage ?
ahk-saip-tay voo lay shaik der vohy-ahj

I would like to pay with my credit card.
Je voudrais payer avec ma carte de crédit.
jer voo-dray pay-yay ah-vaik mah kahrt der kray-dee

Is there any extra charge?
Y a-t-il un supplément ?
ee-ah-teel ern sew-play-man

Is service included?
Est-ce que le service est compris ?
ais ker ler sair-vees ai kohm-pree

Can I have a receipt?
Puis-je avoir un reçu ?
pweej ah-vwahr ern rer-sew?

Can I have an itemized bill?
Puis-je avoir une note détaillée ?
pweej ah-vwahr ewn not day-tah-yay

I think this is the wrong change.
Je crois qu'il y a une erreur dans la monnaie.
jer krwa keel ee ah ewn er-rerr dan lah moh-nay

This is not correct.
C'est inexact.
sai tee-naig-sahkt

This is not my bill.
Cette addition n'est pas à moi.
sait ahdee-syan nay paz ah mwa

I don't have enough cash.
Je n'ai pas assez de liquide.
jer nay pah ah-say der lee-keed

I do not have enough money.
Je n'ai pas assez d'argent.
jer nay pah ah-say dahr-jan

Complaints and compliments

Waiter! We have been waiting for a long time.
Monsieur/Madame/Mademoiselle ! Nous attendons depuis longtemps.
mer-syer/ma-dam/mad-mwa-zel! noo zah-tan-don der-pwee lon-tan

This is cold.
C'est froid.
sai frwah

This is not what I ordered.
Ce n'est pas ce que j'ai commandé.
ser nai pah ser ker jay koh-man-day

Can I have the recipe?
Puis-je avoir la recette ?
pweej ah-vwahr lah rer-sait

This is excellent.
C'est délicieux.
sai day-lee-syer

The meal was excellent.
Le repas était délicieux.
ler rer-pah ay-tai day-lee-syer

Could I have ... another glass.
Pourriez-vous m'apporter ... un autre verre.
poo-ryay voo mah-pohr-tay ... ern nohtr verhr

... another napkin.
... une autre serviette.
... ewn nohtr ser-vee-ait

The meat is still red.
La viande n'est pas assez cuite.
lah vyand nay pah ah-say kweet

Menu reader

abricot	*ah-bree-koh*	apricot
agneau	*ahn-yoh*	lamb
ail	*ah-ee*	garlic
à la vapeur	*ah-lah vah-perhr*	steamed
ananas	*ah-nah-nah*	pineapple
artichaut	*ahr-tee-shoh*	artichoke
asperge	*ahs-pairj*	asparagus
aubergine	*oh-bair-jeen*	eggplant
aubergines farcies	*oh-bair-jeen fahr-see*	stuffed eggplant
au four	*oh foor*	baked
avocat	*ah-voh-kah*	avocado
banane	*bah-nahn*	banana
basilic	*bah-see-leek*	basil
beignet	*bay-nyay*	doughnut, fritter
betterave	*bait-rahv*	beetroot
beurre	*berr*	butter
bifteck	*beef-taik*	beefsteak
blanquette de veau	*blan-kait der voh*	veal in white sauce
bœuf bourguignon	*berf boor-gee-nyon*	beef stewed in red wine
bœuf braisé	*berf bray-zay*	braised beef
bœuf en daube	*berf an dohb*	beef stew

bouillabaisse	*boo-yah-bais*	spicy fish soup with garlic
bouillon de bœuf	*boo-yon der berf*	beef stock
bouillon de poulet	*boo-yon der poo-lay*	chicken stock
braisé	*bray-zay*	braised
cabillaud	*kah-bee-yoh*	fresh cod
calmar	*kahl-mahr*	squid
canard	*kah-nahr*	duck
canard à l'orange	*kah-nahr ah loh-ranj*	duck with orange
carotte	*kah-roht*	carrot
cassis	*kah-see*	blackcurrant
céleri	*say-ler-ree*	celery
cerfeuil	*sair-fery*	chervil
cerise	*ser-reez*	cherry
champignon	*shan-pee-nyon*	mushroom
champignons à l'ail	*shan-peen-yon ah lah-ee*	mushrooms with garlic
champignons en sauce	*shan-peen-yon an sohs*	mushrooms in sauce
chantilly	*shan-tee-yee*	whipped cream
chicorée	*shee-koh-ray*	chicory, endive
chou	*shoo*	cabbage
choucroute	*shoo-kroot*	sauerkraut
chou-fleur	*shoo-fler*	cauliflower
choux de Bruxelles	*shoo der brew-sail*	Brussels sprouts
ciboulette	*see-boo-lait*	chives
citron	*see-tron*	lemon
civet de lapin	*see-vay der lah-pern*	rabbit stew
compote de pommes	*kohm-poht der pohm*	apple sauce
concombre	*kon-kohmbr*	cucumber
confiture	*kon-fee-tewr*	jam
cornichon	*kohr-nee-shon*	gherkin
côtelette d'agneau	*koht-lait dahn-yoh*	lamb chop
côtelette de porc	*koht-lait der pohr*	pork chop
côtelette de veau	*koht-lait der voh*	veal chop
côtelette grillée	*koht-lait gree-yay*	grilled chop
courge	*koorj*	squash
courgette	*koor-jait*	zucchini
crème anglaise	*kraim an-glayz*	custard
crème caramel	*kraim kah-rah-mail*	caramel custard
crème pâtissière	*kraim pah-tee-see-ayr*	pastry cream

crêpe …	*kraip …*	thin pancake …
… à la confiture	*… ah lah kon-fee-tewr*	… with jam
… au chocolat	*… oh shoh-koh-lah*	… with chocolate
cresson	*krai-son*	watercress
crevette	*krer-vait*	shrimp
croque-monsieur	*krohk-mer-syer*	cheese and ham toasted sandwich
cuisses de grenouilles	*kwees der grer-nooy*	frogs' legs
datte	*daht*	date
dessert	*day-sair*	dessert
dinde	*dernd*	turkey
échalotte	*ay-shah-loht*	shallot
en sauce	*an sohs*	in sauce
entrecôte	*antr-er-koht*	rib-eye steak
épicé	*ay-pee-say*	spicy
épinards	*ay-pee-nahr*	spinach
escalope de veau panée	*ais-kah-lohp der voh pah-nay*	veal scallopini- (wiener schnitzel)
estragon	*ais-trah-gon*	tarragon
faisan	*fay-san*	pheasant
feuille de laurier	*fery der loh-ryay*	bayleaf
fèves	*faiv*	broad beans
filet de bœuf	*fee-lay der berf*	steak fillet
filet de colin	*fee-lay der koh-lern*	hake fillet
fondue savoyarde	*fon-dew sah-voh-yahrd*	cheese fondue
fraise	*fraiz*	strawberry
fraises à la crème fraîche	*fraiz ah lah kraim fraish*	strawberries with cream
framboise	*fran-bwahz*	raspberry
frit	*free*	deep fried
frites	*freet*	French fries
fruits à la chantilly	*frwee ah lah shan-tee-yee*	fruit with whipped cream
fruits de mer	*frwee der mair*	seafood
fumé	*few-may*	smoked
gâteau	*gah-toh*	cake
gâteau aux amandes	*gah-toh oh zah-mand*	almond cake
gâteau de riz	*gah-toh der ree*	rice pudding
gâteau de Savoie	*gah-toh der sah-vwah*	sponge cake

gigot d'agneau	*jee-goh dahn-yoh*	roast leg of lamb
glace	*glahs*	ice cream
grenade	*grer-nahd*	pomegranate
grillé/au feu de bois	*gree-yay/oh fer der bwah*	grilled/cooked inside a wood-burning oven
hachis parmentier	*ahshee pahr-man-tyay*	shepherd's pie
haricots blancs	*ah-ree-koh blan*	white beans
haricots verts	*ah-ree-koh vair*	green beans
homard	*oh-mahr*	lobster
huile	*weel*	oil
huître	*weetr*	oyster
jambon fumé	*jan-bon few-may*	smoked ham
jardinière de légumes	*jahr-dee-nyair der lay-gewm*	diced vegetables
jarret (d'agneau, etc)	*jah-ray (dahn-yoh)*	shank (of lamb etc)
laitue	*lay-tew*	lettuce
langouste	*lan-goost*	crayfish
langue	*lang*	tongue
lapin	*lah-pern*	rabbit
légumes	*lay-gewm*	vegetables
limande	*lee-mand*	lemon sole
maïs	*mah-ees*	corn
maquereau	*mahk-roh*	mackerel
mariné	*mah-ree-nay*	marinated
melon	*mer-lon*	melon
menthe	*mant*	mint
meringue au citron	*may-rerng oh see-tron*	lemon meringue
merlan	*mer-lan*	whiting
mousse au chocolat	*moos oh shoh-koh-lah*	chocolate mousse
moules	*mool*	mussels
moules frites	*mool freet*	mussels and French fries
moules marinière	*mool mah-ree-nyair*	mussels in white wine and garlic
navet	*nah-vay*	turnip
œuf à la coque	*erf ah lah kohk*	soft boiled egg
œufs au bacon	*er oh bah-kon*	eggs with bacon
œufs au jambon	*er oh jan-bon*	eggs with ham
œufs au plat	*er oh plah*	fried eggs
œufs brouillés	*er brwee-yay*	scrambled eggs
oie	*wah*	goose

oignon	*ohn-yon*	onion
olive	*oh-leev*	olive
orange	*oh-ranj*	orange
palourde	*pah-loord*	clam
pamplemousse	*panpl-moos*	grapefruit
panais	*pah-nai*	parsnip
pastèque	*pahs-taik*	watermelon
pâtes	*paht*	pasta
pâtes aux œufs	*paht oh zer*	egg noodles
pêche	*paish*	peach
persil	*pair-seel*	parsley
petit pain	*per-tee pern*	bread roll
petits pois	*per-tee pwah*	peas
poire	*pwahr*	pear
poireau	*pwah-roh*	leek
poisson	*pwah-son*	fish
poisson mariné	*pwah-son mah-ree-nay*	marinated fish
poivron rouge/vert	*pwah-vron rooj/vair*	red/green pepper
pomme	*pohm*	apple
pomme au four	*pohm oh foor*	roast apple
pommes de terre dauphinoises	*pohm der tair doh-fee-nwahz*	sliced potatoes baked with cream and cheese
pommes rôties	*pohm roh-tee*	roast potatoes
porc	*pohr*	pork
potage de haricots rouges	*poh-tahj der ah-ree-koh rooj*	red kidney-bean soup
potage de légumes	*poh-tahj der lay-gewm*	cream of vegetable soup
potage de poireaux	*poh-tahj der pwah-roh*	leek soup
potage de pois	*poh-tahj der pwah*	pea soup
potage de poulet	*poh-tahj der poo-lay*	chicken soup
poulet frit/pané	*poo-lay free/pah-nay*	fried/breaded chicken
poulet rôti	*poo-lay roh-tee*	baked/roasted chicken
prune	*prewn*	plum
purée de pommes de terre	*pew-ray der pohm der tair*	mashed potatoes
radis	*rah-dee*	radish
ragoût de bœuf	*rah-goo der berf*	beef stew
raisin	*rai-zern*	grape
reine-claude	*rain-klohd*	greengage

rillettes	*ree-yait*	potted meat
rognons en sauce	*roh-nyon an sohs*	stewed kidneys
romarin	*roh-mah-rern*	rosemary
rôti	*roh-tee*	roasted
rôti de porc	*roh-tee der pohr*	pork roast
rouget	*roo-jay*	mullet
saint pierre	*sern pee-air*	tilapia
salade	*sah-lahd*	salad
salade composée	*sah-lahd kohm-poh-say*	mixed salad
salade de concombre	*sah-lahd der kon-kohmbr*	cucumber salad
salade de fruits	*sah-lahd der frwee*	fruit salad
salade de maïs	*sah-lahd der mah-ees*	corn salad
salade de pommes de terre	*sah-lahd der pohm der tair*	potato salad
salade de tomates	*sah-lahd der toh-maht*	tomato salad
salade russe	*sah-lahd rews*	Russian salad
sandwich au jambon	*san-dweesh oh jan-bon*	ham sandwich
sardines	*sahr-deen*	sardines
sauce à l'oignon	*sohs ah loh-nyon*	onion sauce
sauce au vin	*sohs oh vern*	wine sauce
sauce tomate	*sohs toh-maht*	tomato sauce
saucisse	*soh-sees*	sausage
sauge	*sohj*	sage
saumon	*soh-mon*	salmon
scampi	*skahm-pee*	scampi
seiche	*saish*	cuttlefish
sole meunière	*sohl mer-nyair*	sole in butter with parsley
steack au poivre	*staik oh pwahvr*	pepper steak
steack frites	*staik freet*	steak and French fries
tarte	*tahrt*	pie
tarte aux pommes	*tahrt oh pohm*	apple pie
thon	*ton*	tuna
thym	*tern*	thyme
tomate	*toh-maht*	tomato
tournedos	*toor-ner-doh*	tenderloin
tripes	*treep*	tripe
truite	*trweet*	trout
truite grillée	*trweet gree-yay*	grilled trout
veau	*voh*	veal

velouté de champignons	*ver-loo-tay der shan-pee-nyon*	cream of mushroom soup
velouté de tomates	*ver-loo-tay der toh-maht*	tomato soup
viande	*vyand*	meat
viande grillée	*vyand gree-yay*	grilled meat
vinaigre	*vee-naigr*	vinegar
yaourt	*yah-oort*	yogurt

Drinks

armagnac	*ahr-mahn-yahk*	armagnac
bière	*byair*	beer
bière brune	*byair brewn*	stout
bière en boîte	*byair an bwaht*	canned beer
canette de bière	*kah-nait der byair*	bottled beer
café	*kah-fay*	black coffee
café au lait	*kah-fay oh lay*	coffee with milk (*breakfast*)
café crème	*kah-fay kraim*	coffee with steamed milk
café glacé	*kah-fay glah-say*	iced coffee
café irlandais	*kah-fay eer-lan-day*	Irish coffee
café soluble	*kah-fay soh-lewbl*	instant coffee
calvados	*kahl-vah-dohs*	apple brandy
camomille	*kah-moh-meel*	chamomile tea
champagne	*shan-pah-nyer*	champagne
cidre	*seedr*	cider
coca-cola	*koh-kah koh-lah*	coke
cognac	*kohn-yahk*	brandy
déca	*day-kah*	decaffeinated coffee
eau minérale	*oh mee-nay-rahl*	mineral water
express	*aiks-prais*	espresso coffee
jus de citron, avec du sucre	*jew der see-tron, ah-vaik dew sewkr*	lemonade, with sugar
jus de pomme	*jew der pohm*	apple juice
jus de raisin	*jew der rai-zern*	grape juice
jus d'orange	*jew doh-ranj*	orange juice
kir	*keer*	blackcurrant liqueur and white wine
kirsch	*keersh*	cherry brandy

liqueur	*lee-kerr*	liqueur
nectar d'abricot	*naik-tahr dah-bree-koh*	apricot juice
nectar de pêche	*naik-tahr der paish*	peach juice
orangeade	*oh-ran-jahd*	orange drink
pastis	*pah-stees*	aniseed spirit
rhum	*rom*	rum
sangria	*sahn-gree-ah*	sangria
Schweppes	*shwaips*	tonic water
soda	*soh-dah*	soda
thé au lait	*tay oh lay*	tea with milk
thé citron	*tay see-tron*	lemon tea
un cognac	*an koh-nyahk*	a brandy
un (verre de) vin blanc	*ern vair der vern blan*	a glass of white wine
un (verre de) vin rouge	*ern vair der vern rooj*	a glass of red wine
vin rosé	*vern roh-zay*	rosé wine
whisky	*wees-kee*	whisky

OUT AND ABOUT

The weather

The climate of France is not generally the main reason why people visit the country—unless they have chosen a skiing holiday. The climate of northern France is prone to rain and unpredictable changes. The center, east and south of France have warmer climates, while the west coast is cooled by its proximity to the Atlantic Ocean.

Isn't it a nice day?
Belle journée, n'est-ce pas ?
bail joor-nay, nais pah

Is it going to get any warmer?
Est-ce qu'il va faire plus chaud ?
ais keel vah fair plew shoh

Is it going to stay like this?
Est-ce que ce temps va durer ?
ais ker ser tan vah dew-ray

Will the weather improve?
Est-ce que le temps va s'arranger ?
ais ker ler tan vah sah-ran-jay

Is there going to be a thunderstorm?
Va-t-il y avoir un orage ?
vah-teel ee ah-vwahr ern oh-rahj

It has stopped snowing.
Il ne neige plus.
eel ner naij plew

There is a cool breeze.
Il y a un vent frais.
eel yah ern van frai

What is the temperature?
Quelle est la température ?
kail ai lah tan-pay-rah-tewr

It is far too hot.
Il fait beaucoup trop chaud.
eel fai boh-koo troh shoh

It is foggy.
Il y a du brouillard.
eel yah dew brwee-yahr

It is going to be sunny.
Il va y avoir du soleil.
eel vah ee ah-vwahr dew soh-leye

It is going to be windy.
Il va y avoir du vent.
eel vah ee ah-vwahr dew van

It is going to rain.
Il va pleuvoir.
eel vah pler-vwahr

It is going to snow.
Il va neiger.
eel vah nai-jay

It is raining again.
Il pleut de nouveau.
eel pler der noo-voh

It is very cold.
Il fait très froid.
eel fai trai frwah

It is very windy.
Il y a beaucoup de vent.
eel yah boh-koo der van

Will the wind die down?
Est-ce que le vent va tomber ?
ais-ker ler van vah tohm-bay

On the beach

Can you recommend a quiet beach?
Pouvez-vous nous recommander une plage tranquille ?
poo-vay voo noo rer-koh-man-day ewn plahj tran-keel

Is it safe to swim here?
Peut-on se baigner ici sans danger ?
per-ton ser bain-yay ee-see san dan-jay

Is the current strong?
Est-ce que le courant est fort ?
ais ker ler koo-ran ai fohr

Is the sea calm?
Est-ce que la mer est calme ?
ais ker lah mair ai kahlm

Is there a lifeguard here?
Y a-t-il un maître nageur ici ?
ee-ah-teel an maitr nah-jerr ee-see

Is this beach private?
Est-ce que la plage est privée ?
ais ker lah plahj ai pree-vay

When is ... high tide?
A quelle heure est ... la marée haute ?
ah kail err ai ... lah mah-ree oht

... low tide?
... la marée basse ?
... lah mah-ree bahs

Can I rent ... a sailboat?
Puis-je louer ... un voilier ?
pweej loo-ay ... ern vwah-lyay

... a rowboat?
... une barque ?
... ewn bahrk

Is it possible to go ... sailing?
Peut-on faire ... de la voile ?
per-ton fair ... der lah vwahl

... surfing?
... du surf ?
... dew serf

... water skiing?
... du ski nautique ?
... dew skee noh-teek

... wind surfing?
... de la planche à voile ?
... der lah plansh ah vwahl

... parasailing?
... du parachute ascensionnel ?
... dew pah-rah-shewt ah-san-syon-nel

... paddle boat?
... du pédalo ?
... dew pay-dah-loh

Sport and recreation

Can we play ... tennis?
Peut-on jouer ... au tennis ?
per-ton joo-ay ... oh tay-nees

... golf?
... au golf ?
... oh gohlf

... volleyball?
... au volley-ball ?
... oh voh-lay-bohl

... soccer?
... au foot ?
... oh foot

Can we go riding?
Peut-on faire du cheval ?
per-ton fayr dew sher-vahl

I would like a map of the hiking trails.
Je voudrais une carte des chemins de randonnées.
jer voo-dray ewn kart day sher-mern der ran-doh-nay

Where can we fish?
Où peut-on faire de la pêche ?
oo per-ton fair der lah paish

Do I need a permit?
Ai-je besoin d'un permis ?
aij ber-zwern dern pair-mee

Can I rent the equipment?
Puis-je louer le matériel ?
pweej loo-ay ler mah-tay-ryail

Is there a heated swimming pool?
Y a-t-il une piscine chauffée ?
ee-ah-teel ewn pee-seen shoh-fay

I would like to take ...
Je voudrais prendre ...
jer voo-dray prandr ...

... tennis lessons.
... des leçons de tennis.
... day leh-son der tennis

... diving lessons.
... des leçons de plongée.
... day leh-son der plang-jay

... ski lessons.
... des leçons de ski.
... day leh-son der skee

I would like to rent ...
Je voudrais louer ...
jer voo-dray loo-ay ...

... ski boots.
... des chaussures de ski.
... day shoh-sew-rer der skee

... cross-country skis.
... des skis de fond.
... day skee der fon

... a bike.
... un vélo.
... ern vay-loh

... a cross-country bike.
... un VTT.
... ern vay-tay-tay

Is there a gym in the hotel?
Y a-t-il une salle de gym dans l'hôtel ?
ee-ah-teel ewn sahl der jeem dan loh-tel

Entertainment

Is there ... a good nightclub?
Y a-t-il ... une bonne boîte de nuit ?
ee-ah-teel ... ewn bohn bwaht der nwee

... a theater?
... un théâtre ?
... ern tay-ahtr

... a casino?
... un casino ?
... ern kah-see-noh

... a movie theater?
... un cinéma ?
... ern see-nay-mah

Are there any films in English?
Y a-t-il des films en anglais ?
ee-ah-teel day feelm an an-glay

How much is it per person?
Ça coûte combien par personne ?
Sah koot kohm-byern pahr pair-sohn

Two tickets, please.
Deux billets, s'il vous plaît.
der bee-yay, seel voo play

How much is it to get in?
C'est combien pour l'entrée ?
sai kohm-byern poor lan-tray

I would like to pay with my credit card.
Je voudrais payer avec ma carte de crédit.
jer voo-dray pay-yay ah-vek mah kahrt der kray-dee

The expiration date is …
La date d'expiration est …
lah dah-ter deks-pee-rah-syon ay …

Is there a discount for children?
Y a-t-il une réduction pour les enfants ?
ee-ah-teel ewn ray-dewk-syon poor lay zan-fan

Could you recommend …
Pouvez-vous me recommander …
poo-vay voo mer rer-koman-day …

… a movie.
… un film.
… ern film

… a concert.
… un concert.
… ern kon-serr

… a night club.
… un cabaret.
… ern kah-bah-ray

Can we take the children to the show?
Pouvons-nous emmener les enfants au spectacle ?
poo-von noo an-mer-nay lay zan-fan oh spek-tah-kler

I am looking for a baby-sitter for tonight.
Je cherche une baby-sitter pour ce soir.
jer shayr-sher ewn bay-bee see-tair poor ser swar

Sightseeing

Where is the Visitor Center?
Où est l'Office du Tourisme ?
oo ay loh-fees dew too-reesm

Are there any ... boat trips on the river?
Y a-t-il ... des promenades en bateau sur la rivière ?
ee-ah-teel ... day prohm-nahd an bah-toh sewr lah reevyair

... guided tours of the castle?
... des visites guidées du château ?
... day vee-seet gee-day dew shah-toh

... guided tours?
... des visites guidées ?
... day vee-seet gee-day

What is the admission fee?
Combien coûte l'entrée ?
kohm-byern koot lan-tray

What is there to see here?
Qu'y a-t-il à voir par ici ?
kyah-teel ah vwahr pahr ee-see

When does it close?
C'est ouvert jusqu'à quelle heure ?
say oo-verr jew-skah kail err

The museum is closed on Tuesdays.
Le musée est fermé le mardi.
ler mew-zay ay fair-may ler mahr-dee

Can we go up to the top?
Peut-on aller jusqu'en haut ?
per-ton ah-lay jewsk an oh

What time does the gallery open?
A quelle heure ouvre la galerie ?
ah kail err oovr lah gah-ler-ree

Can I take photos?
Puis-je prendre des photos ?
pweej prandr day foh-toh

Can I use a flash?
Puis-je utiliser le flash ?
pweej ew-tee-lee-zay ler flahsh

When is the bus tour?
A quelle heure est l'excursion en autocar ?
ah kail err ai laiks-kewr-syon an oh-toh-kahr

How long does the tour take?
Combien de temps dure l'excursion ?
kohm-byern der tan dewr laiks-kewr-syon

What is this building?
Cet édifice, qu'est-ce que c'est ?
sait ay-dee-fees, kais ker sai

When was it built?
Quand a-t-il été construit ?
kan tah-teel ay-tay kon-strwee

Is it open to the public?
Est-il ouvert au public ?
ai-teel oo-vair oh pew-bleek

Can we go in?
Peut-on entrer ?
per-ton an-tray

Do you have a guidebook?
Avez-vous un guide ?
ah-vay voo ern geed

Is there a tour of the cathedral?
Y a-t-il une visite de la cathédrale ?
ee-ah-teel ewn vee-seet der lah kah-tay-drahl

Is there an English-speaking guide?
Y a-t-il un guide qui parle anglais ?
ee-ah-teel ern geed kee pahrl an-glay

Is this the best view?
Est-ce le plus beau panorama ?
ais ler plew boh pah-noh-rah-mah

Souvenirs

Where can I buy … postcards?
Où puis-je acheter … des cartes postales ?
oo pweej ahsh-tay … day kahrt pohs-tahl

… souvenirs?
… des souvenirs ?
… day soo-ver-neer

Do you have … an English guidebook?
Avez-vous … un guide en anglais ?
ah-vay voo … ern geed an an-glay

… any color slides?
… des diapos en couleur ?
… day dyah-poh an koo-lerr

... anything cheaper?
... quelque chose de moins cher ?
... kail-ker shohz der mwan shair

How much does that cost?
C'est combien, s'il vous plaît ?
sai kohm-byern, seel voo play

Going to church

Where is ... the Catholic church?
Où est ... l'église catholique ?
oo ai ... lay-gleez kah-toh-leek

... the Baptist church?
... l'église baptiste ?
... lay-gleez bahp-teest

... the mosque?
... la mosquée ?
... lah mohs-kay

... the Protestant church?
... le temple ?
... ler tanpl

... the synagogue?
... la synagogue ?
... lah see-nah-gohg

What time is the service?
A quelle heure est la messe/le culte ?
ah kail err ai lah mais/ler kewlt

I would like to see ... a priest.
Je voudrais voir ... un prêtre.
jer voo-dray vwahr ... ern praitr

... a minister.
... un pasteur.
... ern pahs-terr

... a rabbi.
... un rabbin.
... ern rah-bern

SHOPPING

General information

Department stores and small supermarkets have little importance outside Paris and other very large city centers; instead, in every town and in most villages, there are small, specialized shops and boutiques, while on the outskirts of larger towns can be found furniture and home-improvement warehouses, as well as enormous supermarkets (*hypermarchés*).

It is the care and flair that the French put into the preparation of food that most visitors find remarkable. Stalls and counters provide a feast for the eyes and a delight to the nose. Every town and sizeable village has regular markets from early morning to midday once or twice a week, which are the best source for fresh fruit and vegetables and often for cheese, meat and fish; prices are often lower than in the stores. The supermarkets are cheap and offer a huge range of high-quality food plus all sorts of other goods. Among the best bargains are table wine, bottled beer, coffee beans, olive oil, and cast-iron cookware.

Most small stores open around 9 A.M. and stay open until 6 or 7 P.M.; they are likely to close for an hour or two at lunchtime. Food shops, particularly bakers, pastry shops and delicatessens, are often open on Sunday morning. Many stores close all day Sunday and Monday. Supermarket business hours are longer—usually 8 A.M. or 10 A.M. to 10 P.M., including Mondays; They are usually closed on Sundays.

Les médicaments (medicines) are sold in *pharmacies,* cosmetics in *parfumeries* or department stores and supermarkets. You can get stamps (*des timbres*) from a general newsstand (*marchand de journaux*), a tobacco shop (*bureau de tabac*), a bookshop (*librairie*), or a post office *(la poste)*.

General phrases and requests

I would like that one.
Je voudrais celui-là.
jer voo-dray ser-lwee-lah

No, the other one.
Non, l'autre.
non, lohtr

Can I have a shopping bag?
Puis-je avoir un sac ?
pweej ah-vwar ern sahk

Can I pay for parcel air insurance?
Puis-je prendre une assurance pour colis avion ?
pweej prandr ewn ah-sew-rans poor koh-lee ah-vyon

Can I see that umbrella?
Puis-je voir ce parapluie ?
pweej vwar ser pah-rah-plwee

Can I use traveler's checks?
Puis-je utiliser des chèques de voyage ?
pweej ew-tee-lee-zay day shaik der voh-yahj

Do you take credit cards?
Prenez-vous les cartes de crédit ?
prer-nay voo lay kahrt der kray-dee

Is there a guarantee?
Y a-t-il une garantie ?
ee-ah-teel ewn gah-ran-tee

Where is the cash register?
Où est la caisse ?
oo ay lah kays

Can you deliver it to my hotel?
Pouvez-vous le livrer à mon hôtel ?
poo-vay voo ler leev-ray ah mon oh-tail

Do you have anything cheaper?
Avez-vous quelque chose de moins cher ?
ah-vay voo kail-ker shohz der mwan shair

How much does that cost?
C'est combien, s'il vous plaît ?
sai kohm-byern, seel voo play

How much is it per kilo?
C'est combien le kilo ?
sai kohm-byern ler kee-loh

How much is it per meter?
C'est combien le mètre ?
sai kohm-byern ler maitr

I am looking for a souvenir.
Je cherche un souvenir.
jer shairsh ern soov-neer

I do not like it.
Ça ne me plaît pas.
sah ner mer plai pah

I like this one.
Celui-ci me plaît.
ser-lwee-see mer plai

I will take this one.
Je vais prendre celui-ci.
jer vai prandr ser-lwee-see

Please forward a receipt to this address.
Envoyez un reçu à cette adresse, s'il vous plaît.
an-vwah-yay ern rer-sew ah sait ah-drais, seel voo play

Could you please pack it for shipment?
Pouvez-vous l'emballer pour l'expédition, s'il vous plaît ?
poo-vay voo lan-bah-lay poor laiks-pay-dee-syon, seel voo play

Please wrap it up for me.
Pourriez-vous me l'emballer, s'il vous plaît ?
poo-ryay voo mer lan-bah-lay, seel voo play

There is no need to wrap it.
Ce n'est pas la peine de l'emballer.
ser nai pah lah pain der lan-bah-lay

Can I exchange this, please?
Puis-je échanger ceci, s'il vous plaît ?
pweej ay-shan-jay ser-see, seel voo play

I prefer to pay cash
Je préfère payer en liquide
jer pray-fayr pay-ay an lee-keed

We need to buy some food.
Nous devons acheter de la nourriture.
noo der-von ahsh-tay der lah noo-ree-tewr

Where can I buy … CDs and DVDs?
Où puis-je acheter des CD et des DVD ?
oo pweej ahsh-tay day say-day ay day day-vay-day

… clothes?
… des vêtements ?
… day vait-man

… tapes for my camcorder?
… des cassettes pour mon caméscope ?
… day kah-sait poor mon kah-may-skohp

Will you send it by air freight?
Pouvez-vous l'expédier par avion ?
poo-vay voo laiks-pay-dyay pahr ah-vyon

Where is ... the children's department?
Où est ... le rayon enfants ?
oo ai ... ler rah-yon an-fan

... the food department?
... le rayon alimentation ?
... ler rah-yon ah-lee-man-tah-syon

I am looking for a present around 150 francs.
Je cherche un cadeau dans les 150 francs.
jer shayr-sher ern kah-doh dan lay san san-kant fran

Do you have this in red?
Avez-vous ce modèle en rouge ?
ah-vay voo ser moh-dail an rooj

Specialty food shops

Boulangeries et pâtisseries: (Bakeries and pastry shops): Most French bread doesn't keep long, so it has to be very fresh every day. The traditional loaf is the long, thin, crusty white *baguette,* sold in various sizes; longer-lasting breads—whole wheat, rye and country loaves—are increasingly available. Breakfast treats include *croissants* and the sweet *brioche* and *pain au chocolat,* flaky pastry with chocolate filling. *Pâtisseries* are for serious cakes, freshly made on the premises. Shops generally have a particular specialty—such as rich chocolate *gâteaux,* fruit tarts, fancy biscuits, or handmade chocolates.

Boucheries et charcuteries (Butchers and delicatessens): High quality and meticulous preparation are the trademarks of a French butcher, so prices may seem high. The selection usually includes a large range of poultry, game, rabbits and hares, and cuts of meat may be different than in the United States. Ground meat (*hâché*) can be prepared in several qualities, including the ultra-lean *tartare,* for eating raw. French delicatessens provide pâtés and terrines, quiches and pizzas, desserts and pies, hams and sausages, and ready-made *hors d'oeuvre* and, sometimes, main dishes such as beef cooked in wine.

Poissonneries (Fish shops): There are far more fish stalls in France than proper fish shops. Even inland, there's a surprisingly good choice, ranging from the tiniest shrimp to tuna fish of massive proportions, invariably very fresh. There is plenty of seafood that you can take home and simply grill—sole, trout, scallops, fresh sardines, for example—and also many less familiar sights that are suitable only for soups and stews. Fish dealers will willingly clean and gut (*vider*) the fish for you. Oysters are an especially good deal. By combining oysters with mussels, prawns, clams and other seafood you can make up your own *plateau de fruits de mer*—an expensive dish in any restaurant but one that you can put together fairly cheaply near the coast.

Crémeries, fromageries et épiceries (Dairy, cheese and grocers' shops): In regions rich in dairy products, specialist *crémeries* (dairies) are common. Milk is commonly UHT—heat-treated and long-lasting, which can be stored in the pantry until you open it and might not be exactly like the one you use at home; non-UHT pasteurized milk is sometimes hard to find. The widest variety of cheese comes from a *fromagerie*. Made from cows', goats' or ewes' milk, it ranges from mild to very strong and smelly; it's worth trying Brie or Camembert made from non-pasteurized milk (*lait cru*), which are quite unlike the average supermarket product at home. Grocers' shops (*épiceries*) are useful, particularly for high-quality tins or jars of vegetables or soups.

Buying groceries

I would like ... a kilo of potatoes.
Je voudrais ... un kilo de pommes de terre.
jer voo-dray ... ern kee-loh der pohm der tair

... a bar of chocolate.
... une tablette de chocolat.
... ewn tah-blait der shoh-koh-lah

... a liter of milk.
... un litre de lait.
... ern leetr der lay

... two steaks.
... deux biftecks.
... der beef-taik

... some sugar.
... du sucre.
... dew sewkr

... a bottle of wine.
... une bouteille de vin.
... ewn boo-teye der vern

... 5 slices of ham.
... cinq tranches de jambon.
... sernk transh der jan-bon

... 100 grams of ground coffee.
... cent grammes de café moulu.
... san grahm der kah-fay moo-lew

... half a dozen eggs.
... six œufs.
... see zer, seel voo play

... half a kilo of butter.
... une livre de beurre.
... ewn leevr der berr, seel voo play

... half a pound of butter
... une plaquette de beurre
... ewn plah-kayt der berr

Groceries

groceries	**provisions**	*proh-vee-syon*
baby food	**aliments pour bébés**	*ah-lee-man poor bay-bay*
bread	**pain**	*pern*
butter	**beurre**	*berr*
cheese	**fromage**	*froh-mahj*
coffee	**café**	*kah-fay*
cookies	**biscuits**	*bees-kwee*
cream	**crème**	*kraim*
egg, eggs	**œuf, œufs**	*erf, er*
flour	**farine**	*fah-reen*
jam	**confiture**	*kon-fee-tewr*
margarine	**margarine**	*mahr-gah-reen*
milk	**lait**	*lay*
mustard	**moutarde**	*moo-tahrd*
oil	**huile**	*weel*
pepper	**poivre**	*pwahvr*
rice	**riz**	*ree*
salt	**sel**	*sail*
soup	**soupe**	*soop*

sugar	**sucre**	*sewkr*
tea	**thé**	*tay*
yogurt	**yaourt**	*yah-oort*

Meat and fish

meat	**viande**	*vyand*
beef	**bœuf**	*berf*
chicken	**poulet**	*poo-lay*
ham	**jambon**	*jan-bon*
kidneys	**rognons**	*rohn-yon*
lamb	**agneau**	*ahn-yoh*
liver	**foie**	*fwah*
pork	**porc**	*pohr*
veal	**veau**	*voh*
fish	**poisson**	*pwah-son*
cod	**cabillaud**	*kah-bee-yoh*
herring	**hareng**	*ah-raing*
mussels	**moules**	*mool*
sole	**sole**	*sohl*

At the newsstand

I would like … some stamps.
Je voudrais … des timbres.
jer voo-dray … day termbr

… some postcards.
… des cartes postales.
… day kahrt pohs-tahl

… a newspaper.
… un journal.
… ern joor-nahl

… some adhesive tape.
… du scotch.
… dew skohtsh

… a pen.
… un stylo.
… ern stee-loh

… a pencil.
… un crayon.
… ern kray-yon

… some envelopes.
… des enveloppes.
… day zan-vai-lohp

… some note paper.
… du papier à lettres.
… dew pah-pyay ah laitr

Do you have … some paperbacks in English?
Avez-vous … des livres de poche en anglais ?
ah-vay voo … day leevr der pohsh an an-glay

… a local map?
… une carte de la région ?
… ewn kahrt der lah ray-jyon

… a city map?
… un plan de la ville ?
… ern plan der lah veel

… a road map?
… une carte routière ?
… ewn kahrt roo-tyair

… colored pencils?
… des crayons de couleur ?
… day kray-yon der koo-lerr

… felt pens?
… des stylos-feutres ?
… day stee-loh fertr

… drawing paper?
… du papier à dessin ?
… dew pah-pyay ah dai-sern

… some American newspapers?
… des journaux américains ?
… day joor-noh zah-may-ree-kern

At the tobacco shop

Do you have … a box of matches?
Avez-vous … une boîte d'allumettes ?
ah-vay voo … ewn bwaht dah-lew-mait

… a cigar?
… un cigare ?
… ern see-gahr

... a pipe?
... une pipe ?
... ewn peep

... a pouch of pipe tobacco?
... un paquet de tabac à pipe ?
... ern pah-kay der tah-bahk ah peep

... some pipe cleaners?
... des cure-pipes ?
... day kewr peep

... a gas lighter?
... un briquet ?
... ern bree-kay

A pack of ... please.
Un paquet de ... s'il vous plaît.
ern pah-kay der ... seel voo play

A pack of ... please, with filter tips.
Un paquet de ... s'il vous plaît, filtre.
ern pah-kay der ... seel voo play, feeltr

A pack of ... please, without filters.
Un paquet de ... s'il vous plaît, sans filtre.
ern pah-kay der ... seel voo play, san feeltr

Do you have any American/English brands?
Qu'est-ce que vous avez comme cigarettes américaines/ anglaises ?
kais-ker voo ah-vay kom see-gah-rait ah-may-ree-kain/an-glaiz

At the drugstore

I need some high-protection suntan lotion.
Je voudrais une crème solaire pour peau délicate.
jer voo-dray ewn kraim soh-lair poor poh day-lee-kaht

Do you sell sunglasses?
Vendez-vous des lunettes de soleil ?
van-day voo day lew-nait der soh-leye

Can you give me something for ... insect bites?
Avez-vous quelque chose pour ... les piqûres d'insectes ?
ah-vay voo kail-ker shohz poor ... lay pee-kewr dern-saikt

... an upset stomach?
... le mal à l'estomac ?
... ler mahl ah lais-toh-mah

... a cold?
... le rhume ?
... ler rewm

... a cough?
... la toux ?
... lah too

... a headache?
... les maux de tête ?
... lay moh der tait

... a sore throat?
... le mal de gorge ?
... ler mahl der gohrj

... hay fever?
... le rhume des foins ?
... ler rewm day fwern

... toothache?
... le mal de dents ?
... ler mahl der dan

... sunburn?
... les coups de soleil ?
... lay koo der soh-lery

... diarrhea?
... la diarrhée ?
... lah dee-ah-ray

Do I need a prescription?
Ai-je besoin d'une ordonnance ?
aij ber-zwern dewn ohr-doh-nans

How many do I take?
Je dois en prendre combien ?
jer dwa an prandr kohm-byern

How often do I take them?
Je les prends tous les combien ?
jer lay pran too lay kohm-byern

Are they safe for children to take?
Est-ce qu'ils conviennent aux enfants ?
ais keel kon-vyain oh zan-fan

Medicines and toiletries

after-shave	**lotion après rasage**	*loh-syon ah-pray rah-zahj*
antihistamine	**antihistaminique**	*an-tee-ees-tah-mee-neek*
antiseptic	**antiseptique**	*an-tee-saip-teek*
aspirin	**aspirine**	*ahs-pee-reen*
bandage	**pansement**	*pans-man*
band-aid	**pansement adhésif**	*pans-man ahd-ay-zeef*
bath salts	**sels de bain**	*sail der bern*
birth control pill	**pilule**	*pee-lewhl*
bubble bath	**bain moussant**	*bern moo-san*
cleansing milk	**lait démaquillant**	*lay day-mah-kee-yan*
condom	**préservatif**	*pray-sair-vah-teef*
cotton wool	**coton hydrophile**	*koh-ton ee-droh-feel*
deodorant	**déodorant**	*day-oh-doh-ran*
disinfectant	**désinfectant**	*day-zern-faik-tan*
eau de Cologne	**eau de Cologne**	*oh der koh-lohn*
eye shadow	**fard à paupières**	*fahr ah poh-pyair*
hair spray	**laque**	*lahk*
hand cream	**crème pour les mains**	*kraim poor lay mern*
insect repellent	**produit contre les moustiques**	*proh-dwee kontr lay moos-teek*
Kleenex	**Kleenex**	*klee-naiks*
laxative	**laxatif**	*lahk-sah-teef*
lipstick	**rouge à lèvres**	*rooj ah laivr*
mascara	**mascara**	*mahs-kah-rah*
mouthwash	**bain de bouche**	*bern der boosh*
nail file	**lime à ongles**	*leem ah ongl*
nail polish	**vernis à ongles**	*vair-nee ah ongl*
nail polish remover	**dissolvant**	*dee-sohl-van*
pain killer	**analgésique**	*ah-nahl-jay-zeek*
perfume	**parfum**	*pahr-fern*
powder	**poudre**	*poodr*
razor blades	**lames de rasoir**	*lahm der rah-zwahr*
sanitary pads	**serviettes hygiéniques**	*sair-vyait ee-jay-neek*
shampoo	**shampooing**	*shan-poo-ern*

shaving cream	**crème à raser**	*kraim ah rah-zay*
skin moisturizer	**crème hydratante**	*kraim eed-rah-tant*
soap	**savon**	*sah-von*
suntan lotion	**crème solaire**	*kraim soh-lair*
talc	**talc**	*tahlk*
tampon	**tampon**	*tan-ponh*
toothpaste	**dentifrice**	*dan-tee-frees*

Shopping for clothes

I am just looking, thank you.
Je ne fais que regarder, merci.
jer ner fai ker rer-gahr-day, mair-see

I like the one in the window.
J'aime bien celui qui est en vitrine.
jaim byern ser-lwee kee ai tan an vee-treen

I like this one.
J'aime bien celui-ci.
jaim byern ser-lwee-see

I like it.
Ça me plaît.
sah mer plai

I do not like it.
Ça ne me plaît pas.
sah ner mer plai pah

I will take it.
Je le prends.
jer ler pran

Can I change it if it does not fit?
Puis-je le rapporter si ça ne me va pas ?
pweej ler rah-pohr-tay see sah ner mer vah pah

Can you please measure me?
Pouvez-vous prendre mes mesures, s'il vous plaît ?
poo-vay voo prandr may mer-sewr, seel voo play

Do you have a larger size?
Avez-vous une plus grande taille ?
ah-vay voo ewn plew grand tahy

Do you have this in other colors?
Avez-vous ceci dans d'autres couleurs ?
ah-vay voo ser-see dan dohtr koo-lerr

I take a large shoe size.
Je chausse grand.
jer shohs gran

I take continental size …
Je chausse du …
jer shohs dew …

I would like this suit.
Je voudrais ce costume.
jer voo-dray ser koh-stewm

I would like one with a zipper.
J'en voudrais un avec une fermeture éclair.
jan voo-dray ern ah-vaik ewn fairm-tewr ay-klair

I would like this hat.
Je voudrais ce chapeau.
jer voo-dray ser shah-poh

I would like a smaller size.
Je voudrais une plus petite taille.
jer voo-dray ewn plew per-teet tahy

Where are the dressing rooms?
Où sont les cabines d'essayage ?
oo son lay kah-been dai-say-yahj

Where can I try it on?
Où puis-je l'essayer ?
oo pweej lai-say-yay

Is it too long/short?
Est-ce trop long/court ?
ais troh lon/koor

Is there a full-length mirror?
Y a-t-il un grand miroir ?
ee-ah-teel ern gran meer-wahr

Is this all you have?
Est-ce tout ce que vous avez ?
ais toos ker voo zah-vay

It does not fit me.
Ce n'est pas à ma taille.
Ser nai pahz ah mah tahy

May I see it in daylight?
Puis-je le regarder à la lumière du jour ?
pweej ler rer-gahr-day ah lah lew-myair dew joor

Does it have to be ironed?
Faut-il le repasser ?
foh-teel ler rer-pah-say

Is it dry-clean only?
Faut-il le nettoyer à sec seulement ?
foh-teel ler nai-twah-yay ah saik serl-man

Is it machine washable?
Est-ce lavable en machine ?
ais lah-vahbl an mah-sheen

What is it made of?
C'est en quel tissu ?
sai tan kail tee-sew

Will it shrink?
Est-ce que ça rétrécit ?
ais ker sah ray-tray-see

Do you have this shirt in a size…?
Avez-vous cette chemise en taille … ?
ah-vay voo sait sher-meez an tahy …

I don't know the French sizes.
Je ne connais pas les tailles françaises.
jer ner ko-nay pah lay tahy fran-sayz

Could you alter this for tomorrow, please?
Pouvez-vous faire les retouches pour demain, s'il vous plaît ?
poo-vay voo fayr lay rer-toosh poor der-man, seel voo play

When will it be ready?
Ce sera prêt dans combien de temps ?
ser ser-rah pray dan kohm-byern der tan

Clothing and shoe size equivalents

Women's Dresses, Skirts, Pants, Suits

US	2	4	6	8	10	12	14	16
France	34	36	38	40	42	44	46	48

Women's Blouses and Sweaters

US	32	34	36	38	40	42	44
France	38	40	42	44	46	48	50

Women's Shoes

US	4, 4½	5, 5½	6, 6 ½	7, 7½	8, 8 ½	9, 9½	10, 10½
France	35	36	37	38	39	40	41

Men's Clothing

US	32	34	36	38	40	42	44	46	48
France	42	44	46	48	50	52	54	56	58

Men's Dress Shirts

US	14	14½	15	15½	16	16½	17	17½	18
France	36	37	38	39/40	41	42	43	44	45

Men's Shoes

US	8, 8½	9, 9½	10, 10½	11, 11½	12, 12½	13, 13½	14, 14½	15, 15½
France	41	42	43	44	45	46	47	48

Children/Youth Shoes

US	5, 5½	6, 6½	7, 7½	8, 8½	9, 9½	10, 10½	11, 11½	12, 12½	13, 13½	1, 1½	2, 2½	3, 3½
France	22	23	24	25	26	27	28	29	30	31	32	33

Clothes and accessories

acrylic	**acrylique**	*ah-kree-leek*
bracelet	**bracelet**	*brahs-lay*
belt	**ceinture**	*sern-tewr*
blouse	**chemisier**	*sher-mee-zyay*
bra	**soutien-gorge**	*soo-tyern gohrj*
brooch	**broche**	*brohsh*
button	**bouton**	*boo-ton*
cardigan	**cardigan**	*kahr-dee-gan*
clothes	**vêtements**	*vait-man*
coat	**manteau**	*man-toh*
corduroy	**velours côtelé**	*ver-loor koht-lay*
denim	**jean**	*djeen*
dress	**robe**	*rohb*
earrings	**boucles d'oreille**	*bookl doh-ray*
fur	**fourrure**	*foo-rewr*
gloves	**gants**	*gan*
hat	**chapeau**	*shah-poh*
jacket	**veste**	*vaist*
jeans	**jean**	*djeen*
lace	**dentelle**	*dan-tail*
leather	**cuir**	*kweer*
linen	**lin**	*lern*
necklace	**collier**	*koh-lyay*
nightgown	**chemise de nuit**	*sher-meez der nwee*
nylon	**nylon**	*nee-lon*
overalls	**salopette**	*sah-loh-pait*
pajamas	**pyjama**	*pee-jah-mah*
pants	**pantalon**	*pan-tah-lon*
pantyhose	**collant**	*koh-lan*
pendant	**pendentif**	*pan-dan-teef*
polyester	**polyester**	*pohl-yais-tair*
pullover	**pull(-over)**	*pewl(-oh-vair)*
purse	**sac à main**	*sahk ah mern*
raincoat	**imper(méable)**	*ern-pair(-may-ahbl)*
rayon	**rayonne**	*ray-ohn*
ring	**bague**	*bahg*
sandals	**sandales**	*san-dahl*
scarf	**écharpe**	*ay-shahrp*
shirt	**chemise**	*sher-meez*
shoes	**chaussures**	*shoh-sewr*
shorts	**short**	*shohrt*
silk	**soie**	*swah*

skirt	**jupe**	*jewp*
slip	**jupon**	*jew-pon*
socks	**chaussettes**	*shoh-sait*
stockings	**bas**	*bah*
suede	**daim**	*derm*
suit (men's)	**complet, costume**	*kohm-plai, koh-stewm*
suit (women's)	**tailleur**	*tah-yerr*
sweater	**chandail**	*shan-dahy*
swimsuit	**maillot de bain**	*mah-yoh der bern*
T-shirt	**T-shirt**	*tee-shairt*
tie	**cravate**	*krah-vaht*
tissue	**mouchoir**	*moo-shwahr*
towel	**serviette**	*sair-vyait*
umbrella	**parapluie**	*pah-rah-plwee*
underpants	**slip**	*sleep*
undershirt	**maillot de corps**	*mah-yoh der kohr*
underwear	**sous-vêtements**	*soo-vai-ter-man*
velvet	**velours**	*ver-loor*
wallet	**porte-monnaie**	*pohrt moh-nai*
watch	**montre**	*montr*
windbreaker	**K-way**	*kah way*
wool	**laine**	*lain*
zipper	**fermeture éclair**	*fairm-tewr ay-klair*

Photography

Can you develop this film, please?
Pouvez-vous développer cette pellicule, s'il vous plaît ?
poo-vay voo dayv-loh-pay sait pay-lee-kewl, seel voo play

I would like this photo enlarged.
Je voudrais un agrandissement de cette photo.
jer voo-dray ern ah-gran-dees-man der sait foh-toh

I would like two reprints of this photo.
Je voudrais deux copies de cette photo.
jer voo-dray der koh-pee der sait foh-toh

When will the photos be ready?
Quand est-ce que les photos seront prêtes ?
kan ais ker lay foh-toh ser-ron prait

I am here to pick up my photos.
Je viens chercher mes photos.
jer vyern shair-shay may foh-toh

I need … a roll of film for this camera.
Je voudrais … une pellicule pour cet appareil-photo.
jer voo-dray … ewn pay-lee-kewl poor sait ah-pah-rery foh-toh

… a tape for this camcorder.
… une cassette pour ce caméscope.
… ewn kah-sait poor ser kah-may-skohp

… a black and white film.
… une pellicule noir et blanc.
… ewn pay-lee-kewl nwahr ay blan

… batteries for the flash.
… des piles pour le flash.
… day peel poor ler flahsh

… a color slide film.
… une pellicule couleur pour diapos.
… ewn pay-lee-kewl koo-lerr poor dyah-poh

… a color print film.
… une pellicule couleur.
… ewn pay-lee-kewl koo-lerr

… a 24-exposure roll.
… une pellicule de 24 poses.
… ewn pay-lee-kewl der vernt-kahtr pohz

… a 200-speed film.
… une pellicule de 200 asa.
… ewn pay-lee-kewl der der san ah-zah

… a disposable camera.
… un appareil jetable.
… ern ah-pah-rery jer-tahbl

Camera repairs

I am having trouble with my camera.
J'ai des problèmes avec mon appareil-photo.
jay day proh-blaim ah-vaik moh nah-pah-rery foh-toh

There is something wrong with my camera.
Mon appareil ne marche pas bien.
moh nah-pah-rery ner mahrsh pah byern

This is broken.
C'est cassé.
sai kah-say

Where can I get my camera repaired?
Où puis-je faire réparer mon appareil ?
oo pweej fair ray-pah-ray moh nah-pah-rery

Do you have a spare part for this?
Avez-vous une pièce de rechange pour ça ?
ah-vay voo ewn pyais der rer-shanj poor sah

The film is jammed.
La pellicule est coincée.
lah pay-lee-kewl ai kwern-say

Camera parts

accessory	**accessoire**	*ahk-sai-swahr*
blue filter	**filtre bleu**	*feeltr bler*
camcorder	**caméscope**	*kah-may-skohp*
cartridge	**cartouche**	*kahr-toosh*
cassette/tape	**cassette**	*kah-sait*
distance	**distance**	*dees-tans*
enlargement	**agrandissement**	*ah-gran-dees-man*
exposure	**pose**	*pohz*
exposure meter	**posemètre**	*pohz-maitr*
flash	**flash**	*flahsh*
focal distance	**distance focale**	*dees-tans foh-kahl*
focus	**mise au point**	*meez oh pwern*
image	**image**	*ee-mahj*
in focus	**net**	*nayt*
lens	**objectif**	*ohb-jaik-teef*
lens cover	**cache**	*kash*
out of focus	**flou**	*floo*
overexposed	**surexposé**	*sewr-aiks-poh-zay*
picture	**photo**	*foh-toh*
projector	**projecteur**	*proh-jaik-terr*
print	**épreuve**	*ay-prerv*
negative	**négatif**	*nay-gah-teef*
red filter	**filtre rouge**	*feeltr rooj*
reel	**bobine**	*boh-been*
shade	**nuance**	*new-ans*
slide	**diapo(sitive)**	*dyah-poh-(zee-teef)*
shutter	**obturateur**	*ohb-tew-rah-terr*
shutter speed	**vitesse d'obturateur**	*vee-tais dohb-tew-rah-terr*

tripod	**tripode**	*tree-pohd*
underexposed	**sous-exposé**	*soo-zaiks-poh-zay*
viewfinder	**viseur**	*vee-zerr*
wide-angle lens	**objectif grand angle**	*ohb-jaik-teef gran tangl*

At the hairdresser's

I would like to make an appointment.
Je voudrais prendre rendez-vous.
jer voo-dray prandr ran-day-voo

I would like a haircut.
Je voudrais une coupe.
jer voo-dray ewn koop

Please cut my hair short.
Coupez court, s'il vous plaît.
koo-pay koor, seel voo play

I want bangs please.
Faites-moi une frange, s'il vous plaît.
fay-ter mwa ewn franj seel voo play

Take a little more off the back.
Dégagez un peu plus à l'arrière.
day-gah-jay ern per plews ah lah-ryair

I just want a trim.
Juste les pointes.
jewst lay pwern-ter

I would like … a conditioner.
Je voudrais … du baume démêlant.
jer voo-dray … dew bohm day-mai-lan

… a perm.
… une permanente.
… ewn pair-mah-nant

… highlights.
… des mèches.
… day maish

… a blow-dry.
… un brushing.
… ern brer-sheeng

… hair spray.
… de la laque.
… der lah lahk

… my hair dyed.
… une teinture.
… ewn tern-tewr

… a shampoo and cut.
… un shampooing et une coupe.
… ern shahm-pweeng ay ewn koop

… a shampoo and set.
… un shampooing et une mise en plis.
… ern shahm pweeng ay ewn mee zan plee

A little shorter … in the neck.
Un peu plus court … dans le cou.
ern per plew koor … dan ler koo

… on the sides.
… sur les côtés.
… sewr lay koh-tay

… in front.
… devant.
… der-van

… on top.
… sur le dessus.
… sewr ler der-sew

Not too short.
Pas trop court.
pah troh koor

That is fine, thank you.
C'est parfait, merci.
sai pahr-fai, mair-see

Not too much off.
Pas trop.
pah troh

The dryer is too hot.
Le séchoir est trop chaud.
ler say-shwahr ai troh shoh

The water is too hot/cold.
L'eau est trop chaude/froide.
loh ai troh shohd/frwahd

Laundry

Is there a Laundromat nearby?
Y a-t-il une laverie automatique près d'ici ?
ee-ah-teel ewn lahv-ree oh-toh-mah-teek prai dee-see

Could you send this to the dry cleaner's, please?
Pouvez-vous donner ça au nettoyage à sec, s'il vous plaît ?
poo-vay voo doh-nay sah oh nai-twah-yahj ah saik, seel voo play

Can you clean this skirt?
Pouvez-vous nettoyer cette jupe ?
poo-vay voo nai-twah-yay sait jewp

Can you wash and press these shirts?
Pouvez-vous laver et repasser ces chemises ?
poo-vay voo lah-vay ay rer-pah-say say sher-meez

Can you wash these clothes?
Pouvez-vous laver ces vêtements ?
poo-vay voo lah-vay say vait-man

This stain is … oil.
C'est une tache … d'huile.
sai tewn tahsh … dweel

… blood.
… de sang.
… der san

… coffee.
… de café.
… der kah-fay

… ink.
… d'encre.
… dankr

This fabric is … delicate.
Ce tissu est … fragile.
ser tee-sew ai … frah-jeel

… damaged.
… abîmé.
… ah-bee-may

… torn.
… déchiré.
… day-shee-ray

Can you do it quickly?
Pouvez-vous le faire rapidement ?
poo-vay voo ler fair rah-peed-man

When should I come back?
Quand dois-je revenir ?
kan dwaj rer-ver-neer

When will my clothes be ready?
Quand puis-je passer prendre mes vêtements ?
kan pweej pah-say prandr may vait-man

How long will it take?
Il y en a pour combien de temps ?
eel yan ah poor kohm-byern der tan

I have lost my dry cleaning ticket.
J'ai perdu mon coupon de nettoyage à sec.
jay pair-dew mon koo-pon der nai-twah-yahj ah saik

General repairs

Can you repair it/them?
Pouvez-vous le/les réparer ?
poo-vay voo ler/lay ray-pah-ray

Would you have a look at this please?
Pourriez-vous y jeter un coup d'œil, s'il vous plaît ?
poo-ryay voo ee jer-tay an koo dery, seel voo play

Here is the guarantee.
Voici la garantie.
vwah-see lah gah-ran-tee

I need new heels on these shoes.
Ces chaussures ont besoin de talons neufs.
say shoh-sewr on ber-zwern der tah-lon nerf

Could you resole these shoes, please?
Pouvez-vous ressemeler ces chaussures, s'il vous plaît ?
poo-vay voo rer-ser-mer-lay say shoh-sewr, seel voo play

I need them in a hurry.
J'en ai besoin aussitôt que possible.
jan nay ber-zwern oh-see-toh ker poh-seebl

I will come back later.
Je reviendrai plus tard.
jer rer-vyern-dray plew tahr

I will come back in an hour.
Je reviens dans une heure.
jer rer-vyern dan zewn err

Please send it to this address.
Expédiez-le à cette adresse, s'il vous plaît.
aiks-pay-dyay ler ah sait ah-drais, seel voo play

At the post office

Stamps are available at post offices (*bureaux de poste* or *PTT*—pronounced *pay tay tay*) and at tobacco shops (*tabacs*). Mailboxes are painted yellow and are usually located near *tabacs*.

Can I have a telegram form, please?
Donnez-moi un formulaire de télégramme, s'il vous plaît.
doh-nay mwah ern fohr-mew-lair der tay-lay-grahm, seel voo play

Can I have six stamps for postcards to the United States, please?
Donnez-moi six timbres pour cartes postales pour les États-Unis, s'il vous plaît.
doh-nay mwah see termbr poor kahrt pohs-tahl poor lay zay-ta-zew-nee, seel voo play

How much is it for a letter to the United States?
C'est combien pour une lettre pour les États-Unis ?
say kohm-byern poor ewn laitr poor lay zay-ta-zew-nee

12 stamps, please.
Douze timbres, s'il vous plaît.
dooz termbr, seel voo play

I need to send … a telegram.
Je voudrais envoyer … un télégramme.
jer voo-dray an-vwah-yay … ern tay-lay-grahm

… this by registered mail
… **ceci en recommandé.**
… *ser-see an rer-koh-man-day*

… this parcel.
… **ce colis.**
… *ser koh-lee*

… this airmail.
… **ceci par avion.**
… *ser-see pahr ah-vyon*

When will it arrive?
Quand arrivera-t-il à destination ?
kan ah-reev-rah teel ah days-tee-nah-syon

Can I use my credit card?
Puis-je utiliser ma carte de crédit ?
pweej ew-tee-lee-say mah kahrt der kray-dee

Using the telephone

When calling the United States from France you must dial 00, then 1, then the area code and finally the person's number. Phone booths operating with coins are being phased out so it is essential to buy a phone card (50 or 120 units), although many phone booths also accept credit cards. Phone cards can be bought at *tabacs*, newsstands and post offices. If using a coin booth, put the money in before dialing the number: they take 50-centimes, 1-franc, 5-franc or 10-franc coins. For longer calls, you may find it more convenient to call from a major post office. You will be allocated a numbered kiosk with an ordinary phone and receive a bill at the end of the call. The drawbacks with this method are that you cannot keep track of what you are spending and that it is more expensive.

Can I use the telephone, please?
Puis-je téléphoner, s'il vous plaît ?
pweej tay-lay-foh-nay, seel voo play

I would like to make a phone call to the United States.
Je voudrais téléphoner aux États-Unis.
jer voo-dray tay-lay-foh-nay oh zay-ta-zew-nee

How much is it to call Paris?
C'est combien pour téléphoner à Paris ?
sai kohm-byern poor tay-lay-foh-nay ah pah-ree

I would like to make a collect call.
Je voudrais téléphoner en PCV.
jer voo-dray tay-lay-foh-nay an pay-say-vay

The number I need is …
Le numéro est le …
ler new-may-roh ai ler …

What is the code for … the United States?
Quel est l'indicatif pour … les États-Unis ?
kail ai lern-dee-kah-teef poor … lay zay-ta-zew-nee

… Great Britain?
… la Grande Bretagne ?
… lah grand-brer-tahn

Please, call me back.
Rappelez-moi, s'il vous plaît.
rah-play mwah, seel voo play

I am sorry. We were cut off.
Je suis désolé. On nous a coupés.
jer swee day-soh-lay. on noo zah koo-pay

What you may hear

J'essaie d'obtenir votre communication.
jai-say dohb-ter-neer vohtr koh-mew-nee-kah-syon
I am trying to connect you.

Je ne peux pas obtenir ce numéro.
jer ner per pah zohb-ter-neer ser new-may-roh
I cannot get through to this number.

Je vous passe Monsieur Brown.
jer voo pahs mer-syer brohn
I am putting you through to Mr. Brown.

La ligne est occupée.
lah leen ai toh-kew-pay
The line is busy.

Le numéro est en dérangement.
ler new-may-roh ai tan day-ranj-man
The number is out of order.

Allez-y, vous êtes en ligne.
ah-lay-zee, voo zait an leen
Please go ahead.

Internet and E-mail

I would like to check my E-mail.
Je voudrais vérifier mon courrier électronique.
jer voo-dray vay-ree-fee-ay mon koo-ree-ay ay-layk-troh-neek

Where can I access the Internet?
Où puis-je accéder à l'Internet ?
oo pweej ahk-say-day ah lern-tair-nait

What is the hourly rate?
Quel est le tarif horaire ?
kail ay ler tah-reef oh-rayrh

What is your E-mail address?
Quelle est votre addresse électronique ?
kail ay vohtr ah-draiss ay-lek-troh-neek

I need to send an E-mail.
Je dois envoyer un courrier électronique.
jer dwa an-vwah-yay ern koo-ree-ay ay-layk-troh-neek

Changing money

Can I change these traveler's checks?
Puis-je changer ces chèques de voyage ?
pweej shan-jay say shaik der voh-yahj

Can I change these bills?
Puis-je changer ces billets ?
pweej shan-jay say bee-yay

Can I contact my bank to arrange for a transfer?
Puis-je contacter ma banque pour organiser un virement ?
pweej kon-tahk-tay mah bank poor ohr-gah-nee-zay ern veer-man

Has my cash arrived?
Est-ce que mes fonds sont arrivés ?
ais-ker may fon son tah-ree-vay

Here is my passport.
Voici mon passeport.
vwah-see mon pahs-pohr

I would like to cash a check with my Visa card.
Je voudrais encaisser un chèque avec ma carte Visa.
jer voo-dray an-kai-say ern shaik ah-vaik mah kahrt vee-zah

I would like to obtain a cash advance with my credit card.
Je voudrais une avance en liquide sur ma carte de crédit.
jer voo-dray ewn ah-vans an lee-keed sewr mah kahrt der kray-dee

This is the name and address of my bank.
Voici le nom et l'adresse de ma banque.
vwah-see ler nohm ay lah-drais der mah bank

What is the exchange rate for the dollar?
Quel est le taux de change pour le dollar ?
kail ai ler toh der shanj poor ler doh-lahr

What is your commission?
Quelle est votre commission ?
kail ai vohtr koh-mee-syon

Where is the closest ATM machine?
Où est le distributeur de billets le plus proche ?
oo ay ler dees-tree-bew-terr der bee-yai ler plew prosh

HEALTH

Health services

Before your trip, check with you health insurance company to see if you are covered outside of the United States. If not, it would be wise to obtain supplementary coverage. You may also want to purchase a medical-assistance policy, which would allow you to be evacuated or repatriated.

The number to call for a medical emergency is 15. The fire brigade is also able to deal with medical emergencies (telephone 18).

What's wrong?

Can I see a doctor?
Puis-je voir un médecin ?
pweej vwahr an mayd-sern

I need a doctor.
Je veux voir un médecin.
jer ver vwahr an mayd-sern

He has been badly injured.
Il a été grièvement blessé.
eel ah ay-tay gree-aiv-man blay-say

He has burnt himself.
Il s'est brûlé.
eel sai brew-lay

He has dislocated his shoulder.
Il s'est démis l'épaule.
eel sai day-mee lay-pohl

He is hurt.
Il s'est fait mal.
eel sai fai mahl

He is unconscious.
Il a perdu connaissance.
eel ah pair-dew koh-nai-sans

She has a temperature.
Elle a de la fièvre.
ail ah der lah fyaivr

She has been bitten.
Elle a été mordue.
ail ah ay-tay mohr-dew

She has sprained her ankle.
Elle s'est tordu la cheville.
ail sai tohr-dew lah sher-vee

My son has cut himself.
Mon fils s'est coupé.
mon fees sai koo-pay

My arm is broken.
Mon bras est cassé.
mon brah ai kah-say

I am badly sunburnt.
J'ai attrapé un mauvais coup de soleil.
jay ah-trah-pay ern moh-vai koo der soh-lery

I am sick.
Je suis malade.
jer swee mah-lahd

I am constipated.
Je suis constipé.
jer swee kon-stee-pay

I am a diabetic.
Je suis diabétique.
jer swee dyah-bay-teek

I am allergic to penicillin.
Je suis allergique à la pénicilline.
jer swee ah-lair-jeek ah lah pay-nee-see-leen

I have … a headache.
J'ai … mal à la tête.
jay … mahl ah lah tait

… a pain here.
… mal là.
… mahl lah

… a rash here.
… des boutons.
… day boo-ton

… sunstroke.
… une insolation.
… ewn ern-soh-lah-syon

... been stung.
... été piqué.
... ay-tay pee-kay

... a sore throat.
... mal à la gorge.
... mahl ah lah gohrj

... an earache.
... mal aux oreilles.
... mahl oh zoh-rery

... a cramp.
... une crampe.
... ewn krahmp

... diarrhea.
... la diarrhée.
... lah dyah-ray

I have ... hurt my arm.
Je me suis ... fait mal au bras.
jer mer swee ... fai mahl oh brah

... hurt my leg.
... fait mal à la jambe.
... fai mahl ah lah janb

... pulled a muscle.
... claqué un muscle.
... klah-kay ern mewskl

... cut myself.
... coupé.
... koo-pay

It is ... inflamed here.
C'est ... enflammé là.
say ... tan-flah-may lah

... painful to walk.
... douloureux de marcher.
... doo-loo-rer der mahr-shay

... painful to breathe.
... douloureux de respirer.
... doo-loo-rer der rers-pee-ray

... painful to swallow.
... douloureux d'avaler.
... doo-loo-rer dah-vah-lay

I feel dizzy.
J'ai des étourdissements.
jay day zay-toor-dees-man

I feel faint.
Je me sens faible.
jer mer san faibl

I feel nauseous.
J'ai la nausée.
jay lah noh-say

I fell.
Je suis tombé.
jer swee ton-bay

I cannot sleep.
Je n'arrive pas à dormir.
jer nah-reev pah ah dohr-meer

I think I have food poisoning.
Je crois que j'ai une intoxication alimentaire.
jer krwah ker jay ewn ern-tohk-see-kah-syon ah-lee-man-tair

My stomach is upset.
J'ai mal à l'estomac.
jay mahl ah lais-toh-mah

I have been sick.
J'ai vomi.
jay voh-mee

My tongue is coated.
J'ai la langue chargée.
jay lah lang shahr-jay

There is a swelling here.
C'est enflé là.
sai tan-flay lah

I need some antibiotics.
J'ai besoin d'antibiotiques.
jay ber-zwan dan-tee-byoh-teek

I suffer from high blood pressure.
Je fais de l'hypertension.
jer fai der lee-pair-tan-syon

I am taking these drugs.
Je prends ces médicaments.
jer pran say may-dee-kah-man

Can you give me a prescription for them?
Pouvez-vous me donner une ordonnance pour ces médicaments ?
poo-vay voo mer doh-nay ewn ohr-doh-nans poor say may-dee-kah-man?

I am on the pill.
Je prends la pilule.
jer pran lah pee-lewl

I am pregnant.
Je suis enceinte.
jer swee zan-cernt

My blood group is ...
Mon groupe sanguin est ...
mon groop san-gwern ai ...

I do not know my blood group.
Je ne sais pas quel est mon groupe sanguin.
jer ner say pah kail ai mon groop san-gwern

At the hospital

Do I have to go to the hospital?
Sera-t-il nécessaire de m'hospitaliser ?
ser-ra-teel nay-say-sair der mohs-pee-tah-lee-zay

Do I need an operation?
Est-ce qu'il faudra m'opérer ?
ais-keel foh-drah moh-pay-ray

How do I get reimbursed?
Comment serai-je remboursé ?
koh-man ser-raij ran-boor-say

Do I have to stay in bed?
Dois-je garder le lit ?
dwaj gahr-day ler lee

When will I be able to travel?
Quand serai-je en état de voyager ?
kan ser-raij an ay-tah der voh-yah-jay

Will I be able to go out tomorrow?
Pourrai-je sortir demain ?
poo-raij sohr-teer der-mern

Parts of the body

ankle	**cheville**	*sher-vee*
arm	**bras**	*brah*
back	**dos**	*doh*
bone	**os**	*ohs*
breast	**sein**	*sern*
cheek	**joue**	*joo*
chest	**poitrine**	*pwah-treen*
ear	**oreille**	*oh-rery*
elbow	**coude**	*kood*
eye	**œil** (pl.: **yeux**)	*ery (yer)*
face	**visage**	*vee-sahj*
finger	**doigt**	*dwah*
foot	**pied**	*pyay*
hand	**main**	*mern*
heart	**cœur**	*kerr*
kidney	**rein**	*rern*
knee	**genou**	*jer-noo*
leg	**jambe**	*janb*
liver	**foie**	*fwah*
lungs	**poumons**	*poo-mon*
mouth	**bouche**	*boosh*
muscle	**muscle**	*mewskl*
neck	**cou**	*koo*
nose	**nez**	*nay*
skin	**peau**	*poh*
stomach	**estomac, ventre**	*ais-toh-mah, vantr*
throat	**gorge**	*gohrj*
wrist	**poignet**	*pwahn-yay*

At the dentist's

I have … a toothache.
J'ai … mal aux dents.
jay … mahl oh dan

… a broken tooth.
… une dent cassée.
… ewn dan kah-say

… lost a crown.
… perdu une couronne.
… pair-dew ewn koo-rohn

I have to see the dentist.
Il faut que je voie le dentiste.
eel foh ker jer vwah ler dan-teest

My false teeth are broken.
Mon dentier est cassé.
mon dan-tyay ai kah-say

My gums are sore.
J'ai mal aux gencives.
jay mahl oh jan-seev

Can you find out what the trouble is?
Savez-vous ce qui ne va pas ?
sah-vay voo ser kee ner vah pah

Please give me an injection.
Faites-moi une piqûre, s'il vous plaît.
Fait mwah ewn pee-kewr, seel voo play

That hurts.
Ça fait mal.
sah fai mahl

The filling has come out.
Le plombage a sauté.
ler plon-baj ah soh-tay

This one hurts.
Celle-ci fait mal.
sail-see fai mahl

Will you have to take it out?
Faudra-t-il l'arracher ?
foh-drah-teel lah-rah-shay

Are you going to fill it?
Allez-vous la plomber ?
ah-lay voo lah plohm-bay

FOR YOUR INFORMATION

Numbers

1	**un**	*ern*
2	**deux**	*der*
3	**trois**	*trwah*
4	**quatre**	*kahtr*
5	**cinq**	*sernk*
6	**six**	*sees*
7	**sept**	*sait*
8	**huit**	*weet*
9	**neuf**	*nerf*
10	**dix**	*dees*
11	**onze**	*onz*
12	**douze**	*dooz*
13	**treize**	*traiz*
14	**quatorze**	*kah-tohrz*
15	**quinze**	*kernz*
16	**seize**	*saiz*
17	**dix-sept**	*deez-sait*
18	**dix-huit**	*deez-weet*
19	**dix-neuf**	*deez-nerf*
20	**vingt**	*vernt*
21	**vingt et un**	*vern tay ern*
22	**vingt-deux**	*vernt-der*
23	**vingt-trois**	*vernt-trwah*
24	**vingt-quatre**	*vernt-kahtr*
25	**vingt-cinq**	*vernt-sernk*
26	**vingt-six**	*vernt-sees*
27	**vingt-sept**	*vernt-sait*
28	**vingt-huit**	*vernt-weet*
29	**vingt-neuf**	*vernt-nerf*
30	**trente**	*trant*
40	**quarante**	*kah-rant*
50	**cinquante**	*sern-kant*
60	**soixante**	*swah-sant*
70	**soixante-dix**	*swah-sant-dees*
80	**quatre-vingts**	*kahtr-vern*
90	**quatre-vingt-dix**	*kahtr-vern-dees*
100	**cent**	*san*
200	**deux cents**	*der san*

300	**trois cents**	*trwah san*
400	**quatre cents**	*kahtr san*
500	**cinq cents**	*sernk san*
600	**six cents**	*see san*
700	**sept cents**	*sait san*
800	**huit cents**	*wee san*
900	**neuf cents**	*nerv san*
1000	**mille**	*meel*
2000	**deux mille**	*der meel*
3000	**trois mille**	*trwah meel*
4000	**quatre mille**	*kahtr meel*
1 000 000	**un million**	*ern mee-lyon*

Ordinals

1st	**premier**	*prer-myay*
2nd	**deuxième**	*der-zyaim,*
	second	*ser-kon*
3rd	**troisième**	*trwah-zyaim*
4th	**quatrième**	*kaht-ryaim*
5th	**cinquième**	*sern-kyaim*
x^{-th}	**énième**	*ain-yaim*

Fractions and percentages

a half	**un demi**	*ern der-mee*
a quarter	**un quart**	*ern kahr*
a third	**un tiers**	*ern tyair*
two thirds	**deux tiers**	*der tyair*
10%	**dix pour cent**	*dee poor san*
double	**le double**	*ler doobl*
half	**la moitié**	*lah mwa-tyay*

Measures

1 mile = 1.609 kilometer (km)
1 kilometer = 0.621 mile = ⅝ mile

1 US gallon = 3.78 liters (L)
1 liter = 0.26 gallon = 1.05 liquid quart

1 inch = 2.54 centimeters (cm)
1 centimeter = 0.39 inch

1 foot = .305 meter (m) = 30.5 centimeters (cm)
1 meter = 39.4 inches

1 pound = 454 grams = 0.45 kg
1 kilogram = 2.2 pounds

Days

Monday	**lundi**	*lern-dee*
Tuesday	**mardi**	*mahr-dee*
Wednesday	**mercredi**	*mair-krer-dee*
Thursday	**jeudi**	*jer-dee*
Friday	**vendredi**	*van-drer-dee*
Saturday	**samedi**	*sahm-dee*
Sunday	**dimanche**	*dee-mansh*

Dates

on Friday	**vendredi**	*van-drer-dee*
next Tuesday	**mardi prochain**	*mahr-dee proh-shern*
last Tuesday	**mardi dernier**	*mahr-dee dair-nyay*
yesterday	**hier**	*yair*
June 1st	**le 1er juin**	*ler prer-myay jwern*
June 2nd	**le 2 juin**	*ler der jwern*
today	**aujourd'hui**	*oh-joor-dwee*
tomorrow	**demain**	*der-mern*
next week	**la semaine prochaine**	*lah ser-main proh-shain*
the following week	**la semaine suivante**	*lah ser-main swee-vant*
in June	**en juin**	*an jwern*
July 14th	**le quatorze juillet**	*ler kah-torz jwee-yay*
last month	**le mois dernier**	*ler mwah dair-nyay*

The seasons

spring	**printemps**	*prern-tan*
summer	**été**	*ay-tay*
fall	**automne**	*oh-tohn*
winter	**hiver**	*ee-vair*

Times of the year

in spring	**au printemps**	*oh prern-tan*
in summer	**en été**	*an nay-tay*
in fall	**en automne**	*an noh-tohn*
in winter	**en hiver**	*an nee-vair*

Months

January	**janvier**	*jan-vyay*
February	**février**	*fayv-ryay*
March	**mars**	*mahrs*
April	**avril**	*ahv-reel*
May	**mai**	*may*
June	**juin**	*jwern*
July	**juillet**	*jwee-yay*
August	**août**	*oot*
September	**septembre**	*saip-tanbr*
October	**octobre**	*ohk-tohbr*
November	**novembre**	*noh-vanbr*
December	**décembre**	*day-sanbr*

Public holidays

New Year's Day
Le Jour de l'An
ler joor der lan

Easter Monday
Le lundi de Pâques
le lern-dee der pahk

Labor Day, May 1
Le premier mai
ler prer-myay may

Armistice Day 1945, May 8
Le 8 mai
le wee mai

The feast of Ascension (40 days after Easter)
L'Ascension
lah-san-syon

Whit Monday (7th Monday after Easter)
Lundi de Pentecôte
lern-dee der pant-koht

Bastille Day, July 14
Le 14 Juillet
ler kah-tohrz jwee-yay

The feast of Assumption August 15
Le 15 août
ler kernz oot

All Saints Day, November 1
La Toussaint
lah too-sern

Armistice Day 1918, November 11
Le 11 novembre
ler onz noh-vanbr

Christmas Day
Noël
noh-ail

Colors

black	**noir**	*nwahr*
blue	**bleu**	*bler*
brown	**brun, marron**	*brern, mah-ron*
cream	**crème**	*kraim*
gold	**doré**	*doh-ray*
gray	**gris**	*gree*
green	**vert**	*vair*
orange	**orange**	*oh-ranj*
pink	**rose**	*rohz*
purple	**violet**	*vyoh-lay*
red	**rouge**	*rooj*
silver	**argenté**	*ahr-jan-tay*
tan	**ocre**	*ohkr*
white	**blanc**	*blan*
yellow	**jaune**	*john*

Common adjectives

bad	**mauvais**	*moh-vay*
beautiful	**beau/magnifique**	*boh/mah-nee-feek*
big, tall	**grand**	*gran*
cheap	**bon marché**	*bon mahr-shay*
cold	**froid**	*frwah*
difficult	**difficile**	*dee-fee-seel*
easy	**facile**	*fah-seel*
expensive	**cher**	*shair*
fast	**rapide**	*rah-peed*
good	**bon/bien**	*bon/byern*
high	**haut**	*oh*
hot	**chaud**	*shoh*
little	**petit**	*per-tee*
long	**long**	*lon*
new	**nouveau/neuf**	*noo-voh/nerf*
old	**vieux**	*vyer*
short	**court**	*koor*
slow	**lent**	*lan*
small	**petit**	*per-tee*
ugly	**laid**	*lay*

Signs and notices (*see also* ***Road signs*** page 146)

agence de voyages	*ahj-ans der voh-yahj*	travel agency
à louer	*ah loo-ay*	for rent
ambulance	*an-bew-lans*	ambulance
arrivées	*ah-ree-vay*	arrivals
ascenseur	*ah-san-serr*	elevator
attention	*ah-tan-syon*	caution
à vendre	*ah vandr*	for sale
avertisseur d'incendie	*ah-vair-tee-serr dern-san-dee*	fire alarm
bagages	*bah-gahj*	baggage
banque	*bank*	bank
bienvenue	*byern-ver-new*	welcome
caisse	*kais*	cashier
chaud	*shoh*	hot
chemin privé	*sher-mern pree-vay*	private road
chien méchant	*shee-ern may-shan*	beware of the dog

compartiment fumeurs	*kohm-pahr-tee-man few-merr*	smoking compartment
dames	*dahm*	ladies
danger	*dan-jay*	danger
danger de mort	*dan-jay der mohr*	danger of death
départs	*day-pahr*	departures
détritus	*day-tree-tews*	litter
déviation	*day-vyah-syon*	detour
douane	*doo-ahn*	customs
eau potable	*oh poh-tahbl*	drinking water
école	*ay-kohl*	school
entrée	*an-tray*	entrance
entrée gratuite	*an-tray grah-tweet*	no admission charge
entrée interdite	*an-tray ern-tair-deet*	no trespassing
entrez sans frapper	*an-tray san frah-pay*	enter without knocking
épuisé	*ay-pwee-zay*	sold out
espace fumeurs	*ais-pahs few-merr*	smoking area
fermé	*fair-may*	closed
fermé l'après-midi	*fair-may lah-prai-mee-dee*	closed in the afternoon
froid	*frwah*	cold
hôpital	*oh-pee-tahl*	hospital
horaires	*oh-rair*	timetable
interdiction de fumer	*ern-tair-deek-syon der few-may*	no smoking
interdiction de marcher sur le gazon	*ern-tair-deek-syon der mahr-shay sewr ler gah-zon*	keep off the grass
interdiction de photographier	*ern-tair-deek-syon der foh-toh-grah-fyay*	no photograph
libre	*leebr*	vacant
liquidation des stocks	*lee-kee-dah-syon day stohk*	closing-down sale
messieurs	*may-syer*	men
ne pas parler au conducteur en cours de route	*ner pah pahr-lay oh kon-dewk-terr an koor der root*	it is forbidden to speak to the driver while the bus is moving
ne pas se pencher au dehors	*ner pah ser pan-shay oh der-ohr*	do not lean out
ne pas toucher	*ner pah too-shay*	do not touch

objets trouvés	*ohb-jay troo-vay*	Lost and Found Office
occupé	*oh-kew-pay*	occupied
offre spéciale	*ohfr spay-syahl*	special offer
ouvert	*oo-vair*	open
parking réservé aux résidents	*pahr-keeng ray-sair-vay oh ray-zee-dan*	parking for residents only
passage interdit	*pah-sahj ern-tair-dee*	no thoroughfare
piste cyclable	*peest seek-lahbl*	bicycle path
poison	*pwah-zon*	poison
police	*poh-lees*	police
police-secours	*poh-lees ser-koor*	emergency services
pour usage externe seulement	*poor ew-zahj aiks-tairn serl-man*	for external use only
poussez	*poo-say*	push
renseignements	*ran-sain-man*	information
réservé	*ray-sair-vay*	reserved
réservé au personnel	*ray-sair-vay oh pair-soh-nail*	employees only
réservé aux ...	*ray-sair-vay oh ...*	allowed only for ...
risque d'incendie	*reesk dern-san-dee*	danger of fire
sapeurs-pompiers	*sah-perr pohm-pyay*	fire department
serrez à droite	*sai-ray ah drwaht*	keep to the right
soldes	*sohld*	sale
sonnette d'alarme	*soh-nait dah-lahrm*	alarm signal
sonnez	*soh-nay*	please ring
sortie	*sohr-tee*	exit
sortie de secours	*sohr-tee der ser-koor*	emergency exit
souvenirs	*soov-neer*	souvenirs
tarifs	*tah-reef*	price list
téléphone	*tay-lay-fohn*	telephone
tirez	*tee-ray*	pull
urgence	*ewr-jans*	emergency
voie sans issue	*vwa san ee-sew*	dead end

EMERGENCIES

Fire department	**Pompiers**	*pohm-pyay*	telephone 18
Ambulance	**Ambulance**	*an-bew-lans*	telephone 15
Police	**Police**	*poh-lees*	telephone 17

Call … an ambulance.
Appelez … une ambulance.
ah-play … ewn an-bew-lans

… the fire department.
… les pompiers.
… lay pohm-pyay

… the police.
… la police.
… lah poh-lees

There is a fire.
Il y a un incendie.
eel-yah ern ern-san-dee

Get a doctor.
Appelez un médecin.
ah-play ern mayd-sern

My son is lost.
Mon fils s'est perdu.
mon fees sai pair-dew

My daughter is ill.
Ma fille est malade.
mah fee ai mah-lahd

Does anyone speak English?
Est-ce qu'il y a quelqu'un qui parle anglais ?
ais-keel ee ah kayl-kern kee pahrl an-glay

Where is the U.S. consulate?
Où se trouve le consulat des États-Unis ?
oo ser troov ler kon-sew-lah day zay-ta-zew-nee

Other Hippocrene French Titles